THE ART OF THE POSSIBLE

THE ART
OF THE
POSSIBLE

Government
and
Foreign Policy
in Canada

UNIVERSITY OF
TORONTO PRESS

George

James Eayrs

11

University of Toronto Press

Diamond ◆ Anniversary 1961

Acknowledgments

This study of how institutions, agencies and servants of government conduct Canada's external affairs is part of a project of the School of International Service of American University, Washington, D.C., which, under a grant from the Rockefeller Foundation, is sponsoring an investigation of the way foreign policy is made in various countries. I am grateful to Dr. Kenneth Thompson of the Foundation for suggesting me as a possible author, and to Dean Ernest S. Griffith of the School for inviting me to take part. I recall with pleasure the lively weekly meetings of the seminar of staff and students at the School directed by Professor Charles O. Lerche, Jr., in which I was as regular a participant as the vagaries of commuting between Toronto and Washington during the Fall and Winter of 1959–60 would permit. I am grateful to the authorities at the University of Toronto for permission to absent myself for two or three days a week for this purpose, and I should like to offer belated thanks to my students of that time for their forbearance while I was living too much "the airport existence."

In writing the book I have been greatly assisted by those who generously allowed me to make use of their own unpublished work: Professor J. R. Mallory of McGill University, who made available chapters of his work in progress on the government of Canada; the Hon. J. W. Pickersgill, who enabled me to consult the first volume of his infinitely valuable *Mackenzie King Record* in proof form; General Maurice Pope, who allowed me to quote passages from the manuscript of his autobiography, which is happily to be published at a later date; Mr. Mitchell Sharp, for allowing me to use his speech, "Reflections of a Former Civil Servant"; Mr. Keith Spicer, who provided me with an unpublished paper on the administration of Canadian foreign aid and placed at my disposal his first-hand knowledge of this subject. I am indebted to my colleague, Professor Paul Fox, for allowing me to make use of the records of his extensive interviews with members of Parliament. I was also fortunate in being able to read the unpublished doctoral thesis of Professor R. Barry Farrell of Northwestern University, on "The Planning and Conduct of Foreign Policy in Canada," representing, so far as I know, the only research done on the subject of my own book. Among the many collections of papers which I have used, none has been more valuable than the papers of the late W. L. Mackenzie King. I am grateful to his literary executors, Dr. W. Kaye Lamb, Mr. F. A. McGregor, the Hon. J. W. Pickersgill, and Mr. Norman Robertson, for permission to quote from this immense source; for permission to quote from certain documents drawn from the period 1924–39 I am indebted as well to Dr. Blair Neatby, who is writing the official biography for these years. I want particularly to pay tribute to the patient and always helpful services of the staff of the Public Archives of Canada, especially Miss Jacqueline Côté (now Mrs. Blair Neatby) and her assistants whose long and careful labours have transformed some two million documents of the King Papers into an incomparable instrument for the study of Canadian politics and society.

I am grateful as well to those who have set aside more important business to read and comment upon my manuscript. Mr. John Holmes, President of the Canadian Institute of International Affairs and formerly Assistant Under Secretary of State for External Affairs, read most of it and offered, out of his great experience, many helpful suggestions. Colonel C. P. Stacey, Director of the Historical Section of the General Staff and now Professor of History at the University of Toronto, read the chapter on "The Military Establishment"; his unrivalled knowledge of this subject, generously shared, prevented a number of errors of fact and judgment large and small. A good friend of many years read the entire manuscript at very short notice, and my gratitude to him is in no way diminished by the fact that, being in government service, he prefers not to be mentioned by name.

The quatrain on page 167 is from *Pagett, M.P.*, by Rudyard Kipling, and is reproduced with the kind permission of Mrs. George Bambridge, the Macmillan Co. of Canada, Methuen and Co., Ltd., and Doubleday & Co., Inc.

My final pleasant duty is to express my thanks to the members of the University of Toronto Press for their helpful co-operation at every stage of the production of my book; and especially to Miss Jean Jamieson, of its Editorial Staff, for so much friendly encouragement and skilful aid.

J.E.

University of Toronto
July 1961

Contents

THE ART OF THE POSSIBLE

To E.K.W.

in gratitude

Chapter One

THE POLITICAL
EXECUTIVE

THE PRIME MINISTER

Politics in Canada have produced governments of extraordinary longevity. They have also produced small and feeble oppositions, to the debility of Parliament and the aggrandizement of the Executive. The Cabinet stands supreme, and within his Cabinet (his, for he makes it and may break it) the Prime Minister enjoys a pre-eminence other parliamentary systems seldom provide.

The greater prestige of his office and the greater power of his person are most obviously accounted for by the lesser lustre of his colleagues in Cabinet, and this in turn by a convention of cabinet-making wherein the political Executive becomes a miniature of the Canadian community. Regions, provinces, races and creeds are represented in the Ministry with as exact fidelity to the original as may be allowed by the sometimes competing considerations of securing tolerable efficiency in administration and having to reward friends and punish foes. No wonder that cabinets of all the talents are rare in Canadian political life: what is more remarkable is that powerful and able ministries occasionally emerge. But the general result is the elevation of the Prime Minister over all the other ministers. Those whose claims to office derive principally from the accidents of geography or the imperatives of party stand on a lower level of competence; while his equals in political sagacity and administrative ability can never forget that it is to the Prime Minister they owe their portfolios and at his pleasure continue to hold them. The usual description of the Prime Minister's relationship to his ministerial colleagues as *primus inter pares* is even less accurate in Canadian than in British parliamentary practice. "He cannot be first among his equals for the very excellent reason that he has no equals."[1]

All this applies with very special force to foreign affairs. The Prime Minister bears inevitably a unique responsibility for his country's external policy even if by taste and temperament he has little interest in it; and circumstances make it likely that he will have too much interest rather than too little. Important officials concerned with the formulation and execution of foreign policy are appointed on his recommendation; ambassadors, generals and deputy ministers are alike beholden to him for their positions. To him are normally addressed important communications from the political heads of foreign governments, and with the technically non-foreign governments of the Commonwealth of Nations consultation proceeds conventionally on a Prime Minister-to-Prime Minister basis. To him are referred important foreign policy communications received in the Departments of External Affairs, National Defence, Trade and Commerce and others. Visiting dignitaries, wishing to exchange impressions of the international scene, will want to confer with the Prime Minister rather than with any of his colleagues. Goodwill tours in foreign lands add further to his range of influential contacts, providing sources of private information long after the journey's end, as do excursions into the increasingly fashionable realm of "summit diplomacy." It is the Prime Minister's task to shape the recommendations of his foreign policy technicians (among whom the Secretary of State for External Affairs may or may not be numbered) to the requirements of domestic politics and to impart to them the correctives deemed necessary for partisan advantage. And in times of crisis, when the nation is roused from its accustomed private preoccupations to apprehensive awareness of external danger, it is the Prime Minister who through press and radio and television must play the father figure, providing reassurance and guidance and hope. Foreign policy is his prerogative; the range and intimacy of his concern are rarely matched by any of his colleagues, even by his foreign secretary.

PRIME MINISTER AND CABINET

The extent to which the Prime Minister allows members of his Cabinet to share in the mysteries of foreign policy is as much a matter of individual temperament and style as it is a matter of constitutional law, perhaps a good deal more. A Prime Minister may resemble in this the Duke of Plazo Toro, leading "his regiment from behind"; another may prefer the vanguard. Some have been possessive, even secretive, in their conduct of foreign affairs; others have taken their colleagues into their confidence and looked to them for counsel. To state with any precision the nature of a Prime Minister's relations with his Cabinet in matters of foreign policy or any other kind of policy is not easy; a strict convention prescribes that Cabinet proceedings are secret and must remain secret.* But from available private papers and certain other evidence (which cannot, however, include Cabinet minutes), some impression may be gained of how various prime ministers have gone about their foreign policy business in relation to their Cabinet colleagues.

Wilfrid Laurier's manner of conducting Cabinet business has been the subject of conflicting opinion. According to his official biographer, "he believed in giving every minister wide latitude and large responsibility. . . . In cabinet councils he never played the dictator."[2] Against this may be set the testimony of Sir Clifford Sifton, a powerful member of his Government: "I was not Sir Wilfrid Laurier's colleague for eight years without finding out that he is, despite his courtesy and gracious charm, a masterful man set on having his own way, and equally resolute that his colleagues shall not have their way unless this is quite agreeable to him."[3] Laurier himself rarely wrote on the matter and when he did, as to a friend during the early years of his administration, not very helpfully: "How little people really know of what is really going on in a Cabinet."[4]

In foreign affairs Laurier was readier than most of his successors to allow the participation of his Cabinet colleagues. Such a disposition owed much to his serenity of spirit and a temperament to which secretiveness and paranoia were wholly alien. It was also a consequence of strong and often conflicting views held by his colleagues about the major issues: reciprocity (which brought about Sifton's resignation in 1910), imperial preference, the Boer War, the contribution to Empire defence, oriental immigration. In addition, lack of diplomatic representatives abroad meant that negotiations were frequently entrusted to ministers of departments principally concerned (see below, chapter VII). Such functional division of labour in external affairs naturally imparted a collegial character to consideration of foreign policy matters. It also tended to delay their settlement. "It has been impossible to get anything out of your Ministers," the British ambassador at Washington complained to the Governor General in 1910:

I had taken up the Behring Sea Seal Treaty with the U.S. and they were very compliant, apparently disposed to meet all Canada's objections. But since I reported this, now some three weeks ago, not a word in reply can be got, even though I have written both to Laurier and to your Administrator. Perhaps this is due to the scattering of Ministers, and to the habit

*As an illustration of the severity of this convention one may note that a resigning Minister is not allowed to disclose the differences with his colleagues that have led to his resignation without the authorization of the Prime Minister as the custodian of Cabinet secrets.

of embodying all decisions in a Minute of the Privy Council. That is a plan which is really quite unfitted for negotiations with another power. It makes every step in progress depend on the possibility of getting Ministers together for a Council. . . .[5]

All this did not mean, of course, that the Prime Minister might not embark on negotiations without the knowledge or consent of his Cabinet; as R. L. Borden put it in 1909, when Leader of the Opposition, "matters of a confidential character, some of which possibly could not be disclosed even to the Cabinet as a whole, should come in the first instance to the Prime Minister."[6] Thus, Laurier's attempt in 1910 to enlist the support of the Vatican to overcome clerical opposition to his naval policy remained a secret between himself and his confidential envoy, the Chief Justice of Canada; and Borden kept his own counsel while corresponding with Winston Churchill in 1912–14 on the nature of the emergency created by the German naval programme. But in these early years of the century the usual practice was to place foreign policy matters before the Cabinet as they arose.

Few problems of external policy, naval policy apart, troubled the Government of R. L. Borden between 1911 and the outbreak of war, and even war left Canada relatively free from foreign policy decisions until 1917 when the creation of the Imperial War Cabinet provided machinery for the Dominions to obtain what was ambiguously described in a famous constitutional document as "an adequate voice in foreign policy and in foreign relations." It was at the meetings of the Imperial War Cabinet that Sir Robert Borden (as he had then become) first expressed a Canadian viewpoint on such questions as peace terms, the post-war settlement, and grand strategy. It might be thought that the Prime Minister's participation at such exalted gatherings left little scope for the judgment of colleagues in foreign and imperial decision-making. But so far from trying to exploit his privileged position, Borden was anxious that other members of his Government accompany him to the United Kingdom, and his important interventions in the Imperial War Cabinet were usually preceded by consultation with them. Indeed, it was at Borden's insistence that N. W. Rowell, the leading Liberal in the coalition Union Government and whose interests in international affairs were no less than his own, attended meetings of the Imperial War Cabinet in 1918. Such solicitude might owe something to the difficulties of running a coalition administration (the head of which is more than ordinarily beholden to ministers not of his own party), but it was also entirely in keeping with Borden's manner of leadership. Borden possessed many of the characteristics of his distinguished predecessor. Like

Laurier he was prepared and on occasion anxious to delegate responsibility; his diary expresses irritation when colleagues pestered unduly.* He allowed two members of his Cabinet to remain in London throughout most of the war (Sir George Perley as Acting High Commissioner and A. E. Kemp as Overseas Minister of Militia), whereas Mackenzie King was later sternly determined to prevent the High Commissioner from sharing in the making of policy and strongly disapproved of overseas ministers. Alone of the Dominion prime ministers at the Paris Peace Conference, Borden brought no fewer than three members of his Cabinet (Sir George Foster, A. L. Sifton and C. J. Doherty) and all were assigned major responsibilities. Borden's methods of reaching decisions in foreign policy are well illustrated by the following extracts from telegrams exchanged between Borden in Paris and the Acting Prime Minister, Sir Thomas White, in Ottawa, concerning the despatch of Canadian troops to Siberia at the end of the war:

White to Borden (November 22, 1918): Many members of Council strongly opposed to our sending troops now ready to Siberia and continuing expedition. Mewburn [Minister of Militia and Defence] has delayed ship sailing on Monday. . . .

Borden to White (November 24, 1918): Telegram received. In my judgment we shall stand in an unfortunate situation unless we proceed with Siberia expedition. We made definite arrangements with British Government on which they have relied. They could reasonably hold us responsible for great inevitable delay in making other arrangements. Canada's present position and prestige would be singularly impaired by deliberate withdrawal from definite arrangements under these conditions. . . . However I leave the matter to judgment of Council with the strong feeling that withdrawal from our deliberate engagement will have extremely unfortunate effect. Foster, Sifton, Doherty concur.

White to Borden (November 25, 1918): Very strong feeling in Council against continuance Siberian Expedition, Ballantyne, Crerar, Calder and Reid most strongly opposed. Crerar has written me letter of protest. So far as I can judge public opinion will not support further action on any large scale if at all. . . . My own view after hearing many discussions in Council is that Canada should, now that the war is over and no necessity exists for the re-establishment of the Eastern front, discontinue further participation and expense. . . .

Borden to White (November 28, 1918): Your telegram . . . respecting Siberian expedition. If feeling both in Cabinet and among public is so strongly opposed we leave question to your own determination. . . .

*"Rowell began to bombard me with letters about various subjects . . ." (June 9, 1918); "Rowell still bombarding me with letters . . ." (June 15, 1918); "Rowell left this morning and shortly after a shower of letters . . ." (July 27, 1918); "Telegrams from White thick as autumn leaves in Vallambrosa . . ." (Nov. 27, 1918).

White to Borden (November 28, 1918): We have decided to proceed with Siberian expedition as originally planned. . . . You may regard the matter as closed. . . .[7]

Arthur Meighen, who succeeded Borden as Prime Minister in the Union Government in July 1920, displayed during the year and a half before the defeat of his administration a style of leadership very different from his predecessor's. "His intellectual arrogance," an unfriendly critic has observed, "led him to trust too much to his own judgment and he showed a tendency to disregard the advice of colleagues who, while not his equal in some respects, possessed much more political experience and sagacity. . . . His confidence in the product of his own judgment was so profound and his advocacy so determined that the policy was open to little or no discussion, still less could it be recast or toned down in any way to meet the demands or soothe the feelings of dissenting groups or interests."[8] The major foreign policy decision of his brief Ministry of 1920-1 was his opposition to the renewal of the Anglo-Japanese alliance. The proposals which Arthur Meighen put before the Imperial Conference in June 1921 had been worked out by himself and Loring Christie of the Department of External Affairs as early as March, but no members of his Cabinet had been consulted about them or, as one Minister noted on June 5, about "any of the possible matters that may come up" in London before he set out.[9] He took none of his ministerial colleagues with him, and seems to have consulted none while there, so that the first knowledge of what had transpired was conveyed to them by the Prime Minister at a Cabinet meeting after his return. "He appears to have played his part well," Sir George Foster wrote after the meeting, "—a little too advanced on the Jap. Tr. matter in my opinion."[10]

No Canadian Prime Minister has so openly dominated his Cabinet colleagues as R. B. Bennett, the Conservative Prime Minister from 1930 to 1935. The story is often told of his walking alone, lost in thought, when spoken to by a citizen of Ottawa. "Please do not interrupt me," Bennett replied. "Can you not see I am engaged in a Cabinet meeting?" This (doubtless) apochryphal vignette is altogether justified by what is known of Bennett's conduct of government policy at the Imperial Economic Conference of 1932. "Several other Canadian Ministers took part in the proceedings," a New Zealand delegate recalled, "but it was obvious that none of them could agree to any decision without the prior consent of Mr. Bennett."[11] A Canadian observer wrote soon after the Conference opened: "Bennett has one quality which differentiates him from [Mackenzie] King: it is both an asset and a liability. This is his active mind and his readiness to plunge."[12] There is evidence that until the final days before the Conference (it may be the final hours) the Prime Minister was uncertain whether he would "plunge" for high tariffs or for low, and that his "active mind," marvellously untroubled by what his colleagues might think, was still grappling with the drastic alternatives of protection and preference.[13] That on so crucial an issue, ordinarily productive of hours of acrimonious bargaining inside the Cabinet between its protectionist and free-trading wings,[14] the Prime Minister should have felt free to swing from one extreme to the other without fearing ministerial resignations, is indicative at once of his unusually strong position as leader and of his determination to exploit it. (It also illustrates the rarity of resignations from Canadian cabinets on matters of principle.)

As the months and years of his administration passed, the country slipping deeper into depression, Bennett's autocratic methods became if anything more pronounced. Like the "New Deal" type of programme on which he fought (and lost) the election of 1935, his views on the Italo-Ethiopian War, (which broke out in the last months of his administration) were formulated on the spur of the moment. He intended to take a strong stand against Italy, he told his Under Secretary of State for External Affairs, O. D. Skelton, over the telephone on October 10, 1935, and he was " 'not going to wriggle out of it if it meant I didn't get one vote'."[15] It was perhaps unfortunate that the voters of Canada were not prepared to allow him the opportunity of converting conviction into policy.

Bennett was evidently sensitive to criticism that his had been a one-man government for, once back in opposition, he took the first opportunity to deny the charge. Contrasting the 967 Council meetings over which he had presided with the 516 meetings which had been held during an equal period of the preceding Liberal administration, he added: "So far as the conduct of departments was concerned there never was a time in this country when there was greater freedom on the part of those conducting departments, or a time when men enjoyed greater latitude or greater opportunity to make their views prevail."[16] On that score opinions were bound to differ, and the matter will remain in the realm of opinion until the private papers of Bennett and his colleagues are available for examination.*

With the exception of the five years of the Bennett Government and a few days in 1926, Mackenzie King was Prime Minister of Canada

*The Bennett Papers, which are the personal property of Lord Beaverbrook, have been deposited at the Library of the University of New Brunswick.

from December 1921 to November 1948. Over this long period of political leadership, at its close unequalled in the history of parliamentary democracy and since only once surpassed, the nature of his relations with Cabinet colleagues naturally underwent some change. At first, his relative youth, his position as head of a minority government, and the presence in his first administration (1921–5) of a number of colleagues of greater experience and prestige than himself, combined to make Mackenzie King eager to defer to his ministers on most important matters, foreign as well as domestic. When informed (by a newspaper reporter) of the appeal of the British Government for Canadian help to stem the Turkish advance upon Chanak in 1922, his first words were: "That will require the deliberation of the Cabinet before any pronouncement can be made." Asked whether the Government would send troops, he replied: "I would not make any statement without a conference with my colleagues," and, pressed for his own views, only remarked: "I haven't any, apart from those of the Cabinet."[17] At the end of the second day of the crisis he wrote in his diary: "I shall not commit myself one way or the other, but keep the responsibility for prlt.—the executive regarding itself as the committee of prlt."[18] On September 18, the following day, no fewer than three Cabinet meetings were held, to which the Prime Minister referred incoming despatches from the British Government and asked those present to draft a reply. "We debated long over question of giving 'moral support' & approving attitude," Mackenzie King wrote afterwards. "I felt that involved whole question of participation in European wars and held back on it. Cabinet agreed in this."[19] Earlier he had sent a telegram to Ernest Lapointe and W. S. Fielding, the two members of the Government absent in Geneva for the League of Nations Assembly, asking for their views. The reply of his Minister of Finance must have been disconcerting: "We heartily approve attitude British Government respecting Constantinople."[20] But Lapointe's message a day later suggested that Fielding had spoken only for himself: "Be governed by Canadian opinion. . . . Would advise delaying answer and being non-committal."[21] This was preaching to the converted.

The presence within his Government of Laurier's designated successor (who had been Laurier's Finance Minister and was now his), was a factor of some consequence to Mackenzie King in developing foreign and imperial policy during his first administration. Supported by the majority if not the remainder of his Cabinet, the Prime Minister felt able to withhold support from the British Government over Chanak when Fielding wanted to offer it; and he proceeded in spite of Fielding's misgivings to allow Ernest Lapointe to become the first Canadian Minister to sign a political treaty without the covering signature of a British plenipotentiary. When it came to exercising the right of legation, however, Fielding's determined opposition was an important (although not the only) reason for the prolonged delay in appointing a Canadian Minister to Washington.[22] By 1926 this restraint, and others, had been removed. Fielding had resigned in 1925, and the following year Mackenzie King had won a resounding electoral victory of which he was very much sole architect. No longer was he head of a minority government. He was both more experienced and more confident, and with good reason. Henceforth he was to be the unchallenged master of his administration until the conscription crisis of 1944; and from that challenge he emerged more powerful than ever.

The characteristic style of Mackenzie King's handling of foreign policy matters first became apparent during the administration returned to office in 1935, for not until then did major issues of external policy begin to impinge upon Canadian events and a Canadian Prime Minister begin to exercise important, if carefully concealed, initiatives in regard to them. "Under a Liberal regime the Prime Minister states the foreign policy and the Cabinet Ministers state the policy for internal affairs without consultation with any of the members," a disgruntled Liberal backbencher wrote privately at the time,[23] and the acuteness of his analysis was to become evident during the next few years. No Cabinet colleagues accompanied Mackenzie King on his visit to Hitler in the summer of 1937, and none could therefore challenge with an authority based on comparable experience the grievously inappropriate notions of Nazi policy and leadership that their Prime Minister acquired on this mission. During the Munich crisis the secrecy with which Mackenzie King had by this time come to cloak the conduct of external policy assumed almost paranoic proportions. "Laid up at Kingsmere with sciatica, he watched the climax of appeasement," writes Mr. Bruce Hutchison.

He watched it so secretly that, as he told this writer, he did not dare to let his Cabinet colleagues . . . read the coded cables from London. . . . Such was King's control of government and nation, such the numbed state of his colleagues, that he could take foreign policy into his own hands and direct it as he pleased. . . . It can be said on the authority of Ministers who attended the Cabinet in these hours that it never discussed the European crisis. Two ministers raised the question in council. No answer came from Kingsmere. Government, when the nation quivered on the knife edge of war, had moved from the East Block to King's bedroom in the country.[24]

The onset of war made necessary a considerable devolution of responsibility in the conduct of external policy, less through the personal inclination of the Prime Minister than through the pressure of events compelling a division of labour. In the early months of the conflict, no fewer than five different Cabinet ministers set out successively for England on a variety of missions related to the war effort. When Mr. Churchill wished to revive the Imperial War Cabinet of the First World War, Mackenzie King defended his opposition to the proposal on the grounds that "important decisions should not be made by one man but by a government as a whole."[25] In fact, however, not the "government as a whole" but the War Committee of the Cabinet became the effective policy-making body for the duration.

The origin of Cabinet committees in Canada is to be found in the suggestion raised by United Kingdom authorities at the Imperial Defence Conference of 1909 that the self-governing Dominions follow the example of the British Government by creating defence committees within their various ministries. Nothing immediately came of this proposal in Canada, nor of the recommendations of Sir George Murray in 1912 that the burden of individual members in the Canadian Government be relieved by allowing a quorum of Cabinet ministers to dispose of routine business. It was not until October 1917 that the Union Government under Sir Robert Borden divided itself into a War Committee and a Committee on Reconstruction and Development, each of ten members. These Cabinet committees did not long outlast the end of the war, and none reappeared until 1936 when a Defence Committee was constituted composed of the Prime Minister, the Minister of National Defence, and the Ministers of Justice and Finance. It met on only two occasions prior to the outbreak of war, on November 14, 1938, and on September 5, 1939 (the Canadian declaration of war, it will be recalled, came a week after that of the United Kingdom, on September 10), for the purpose of discussing with the Chiefs of Staff proposed defence estimates.

The Defence Committee was replaced following Canada's entry into the war by the Emergency Council (sometimes called the Committee on General Policy), one of six "sub-committees of council" created by an order-in-council (P.C. 2747) on August 30, 1939. It met six times before in its turn being replaced by the War Committee and, like it, was responsible for policy relating to the over-all war effort. A further reorganization of the Cabinet committee system took place in December 1939, and one of the nine committees thus created was the War Committee of the Cabinet.

The War Committee met for the first time on December 8, 1939, and over the next five and a half years was to meet on 343 occasions. Its membership throughout this period varied according to the composition of the Ministry and for other reasons, but always included the Prime Minister (who was also Secretary of State for External Affairs), the service ministers, the Minister of Finance, and, after the creation of the portfolio, the Minister of Munitions and Supply. "The result," the former secretary of the War Committee has commented, "was that, while the War Committee like other Cabinet Committees was never an executive body but was, in fact as in form, purely advisory in character, its prestige was such that its decisions were for practical purposes the decisions of the government."[26] In addition to the regular ministerial members, advisers from the services and from government departments were frequent participants. The Under Secretary of State for External Affairs attended regularly and, when military matters were under discussion (as they usually were), the Chiefs of Staff were normally present. After 1943 the chairman of the Canadian section of the Permanent Joint Board on Defence periodically attended its meetings.

As the war continued, a number of measures were introduced to make the work of the War Committee more orderly and efficient. The most important of these was the creation of the post of secretary of the War Committee in April 1940, to which Mr. A.D.P. Heeney was appointed.* From that date to the Committee's dissolution in June 1945 minutes were kept of its deliberations. In September 1941, following the Prime Minister's first-hand observation of the working of the United Kingdom

*The project of some form of Cabinet secretariat had been in Mackenzie King's mind as early as 1923. In that year he told Sir Maurice Hankey, secretary to the United Kingdom Cabinet, "that he would like to have a Secretary to Canadian Cabinet, and that he would have one 'in his time', but that at present it wouldn't do. His Cabinet would not stand for it, and he stressed the way his Cabinet had to be representative in character and how he didn't have the same freedom as the British Prime Minister to choose. A secretary would cause all kinds of trouble. . . . Hankey suggested that this kind of a Cabinet needed some organization more than the British, but King would not have it then. . . ." R. MacGregor Dawson, "Memorandum of interview with Lord Hankey," 1951.

Since 1945 it has been the practice of Canadian governments to keep a full but impersonal record of Cabinet deliberations, evidently not without justifying Mackenzie King's earlier misgivings. "Ministers are conservative beings, to whom the intrusion of a Secretary taking notes of their discussions was difficult to accept. Even after the War, there was usually one Cabinet a week during the session and certain others where the Secretary was absent and of which no minutes were kept. On these occasions the Cabinet was discussing 'political' (i.e. party) questions or the Secretary or his Department were under discussion. As time went on, these became less frequent and it was very rare, in fact, for there to be an entire meeting without the Secretary. At present . . . all meetings of the Cabinet and its committees are attended by a member of the Secretariat, and minutes are kept." J. R. Mallory, unpublished manuscript.

War Cabinet, several procedures designed to facilitate its business were adopted. Among these were the preparation of proper agenda circulated to members in advance of meetings, together with papers and memoranda related to items on the agenda; regular meetings on Wednesday of each week, in addition to meetings called at the discretion of the Prime Minister; regular attendance by the three service Chiefs of Staff at the first meeting in each month and their submission of military appreciations regularly every month; attendance by ministers not members of the War Committee, at the Prime Minister's discretion, when matters directly affecting their departments were under consideration.*

The end of the Second World War did not bring about the disappearance of Cabinet committees as at the end of the First. Instead, the wartime committees were replaced by others designed to meet the needs of post-war policy. Cabinet committees have now become a normal feature of parliamentary government in Canada. Despite this fact, however, it is impossible to offer an exact description of their operation, for no detailed information has been disclosed and the government is apparently constitutionally unable to disclose it.† Cabinet committees function therefore in some obscurity. We are told on the authority of the Registrar of the Cabinet that most of its committees now are of an *ad hoc* variety, "set up to deal with special problems as these arise or acquire prominence or urgency, and report but to the Cabinet. Their life is usually brief and they die naturally when they have reported. They represent purely internal arrangements made by the Cabinet and are usually not well known to the public, although reference has been made

*This last measure did not guarantee that ministers not members of the War Committee would know what went on in the charmed circle. In February 1942 the Minister of Pensions and National Health, Ian Mackenzie, who as the British Columbia representative in the Cabinet bore the brunt of strong pressure from that province to strengthen Pacific defences, wrote to the Prime Minister: ". . . not being a member of the War Committee, I am not exactly sufficiently conversant with what is transpiring, although the Ministers separately have been very courteous in giving me the necessary information." Ian Mackenzie to Mackenzie King, Feb. 14, 1942; quoted in Col. C. P. Stacey, *Six Years of War: The Army in Canada, Britain and the Pacific* (Ottawa, 1955), p. 170. Mackenzie's lack of information is the more surprising in that prior to 1939 he had been Minister of National Defence, and enjoyed with the Prime Minister "a degree of personal intimacy which would not have been tolerated in another colleague after 1941 [when Lapointe died]." J. W. Pickersgill, *The Mackenzie King Record*, I, *1939-1944* (Toronto, 1960), p. 7.

†In 1957 the Speaker of the House of Commons ruled that "an inquiry into the method by which the government arrives at its decision in Cabinet is out of order. . . . As I understand the situation, the decision of the government is one and indivisible. Inquiry into how it is arrived at, particularly inquiry into the Cabinet process, is not permitted in the House." Canada, *House of Commons Debates*, Nov. 6, 1957, p. 813.

on occasions in Parliament to their work."[27] Thus, in June 1960 reference was made in the House of Commons to the existence of a Cabinet Committee on Emergency Plans, consisting of the Minister of National Defence (chairman) and the Ministers of Finance, Trade and Commerce, National Health and Welfare, Defence Production, and Justice, the Associate Minister of National Defence, and the Minister without Portfolio, whose function was to develop governmental policies to be put into effect in the event of surprise atomic attack upon the North American continent.[28]

Perhaps the most important of contemporary Cabinet committees is the Cabinet Defence Committee, created in August 1945 to consider and advise upon post-war defence problems. Its chairman was originally the Minister of National Defence, a provision designed to gain the support and co-operation of the three services, but subsequently its chairmanship passed to the Prime Minister, the Minister of National Defence acting as vice-chairman. Its meetings are normally attended by the Under Secretary of State for External Affairs and the permanent chairman of the Chiefs of Staff Committee, together with the three Chiefs of Staff, in addition to the ministerial heads of other important departments such as Finance, Trade and Commerce, and External Affairs. A meeting of the Defence Committee was attended by James Forrestal, then United States Secretary of Defense, on August 16, 1948. "One of the deep impressions that I had as a result of this meeting," he recorded afterwards in his diary,

was the contrast to the functioning of our own government. In this group there were the incoming Chief of State [sic], Mr. L. S. St. Laurent, who will succeed Mackenzie King as Prime Minister; the Under Secretary of State for External Affairs, Mr. L. B. Pearson, who will succeed to St. Laurent's job as chief of that Department; Minister of Trade and Commerce C. D. Howe; Minister of Defence Brooke Claxton, and the three chiefs of staff. . . .

This group not merely was the Defence Committee of the Cabinet . . . but they represented the control of the Canadian Parliament, because they are the chosen Ministers of the Liberal Party, which is the party now prevailing in power, as well as the chiefs of their respective government agencies. Therefore expressions of policy at this meeting are the statements of a responsible government. . . .[29]

The single exception to the rule that committees of the Cabinet have their origin and foundation in the conventional working of the parliamentary system is the Treasury Board, a committee of the Cabinet created by legislation (see Revised Statutes of Canada, s. 71) and differing as well from other Cabinet committees in its permanence and in its

staff of experts engaged in its work of scrutinizing departmental estimates. The chairman of the Treasury Board is the Minister of Finance;
with him serve five other Cabinet ministers of whom the Secretary of State
for External Affairs is not one. The fact that its members are Cabinet ministers is sufficient safeguard against the Treasury Board too often thwart-
ing government policy by implacable opposition to extravagance and
waste (as it is charged the United States Bureau of the Budget is prone
to do). But it offers to the Prime Minister and his Minister of Finance an
incomparable instrument with which to pare away at costly departmental projects. A former Finance Minister has described the process:

The staff of the Treasury Board, without reference to the Minister in the
first place, go at those estimates and try to have them reduced. They are
successful to a considerable extent in having them reduced. But various
departments demur, and some go even farther than that and vigorously
and violently protest against the proposed cuts. The matter is then taken
up by myself with the various Ministers, and after a considerable amount of
argument the estimates are still further reduced until they reach the form
in which they appear before the House of Commons. . . .
At times I feel as though I am against the whole world when I try to keep
a lot of these expenditures down. We just do the best we can, that is all,
and keep them down.[30]

The impact of the Treasury Board is felt, naturally enough, in those
aspects of foreign policy that require large outlays of public moneys
such as defence and foreign aid; but it makes its mark on less expensive
matters:

Mr. Martin (Essex East): Is there any likelihood of any mission being
established in Baghdad . . . ?
Mr. Green (Secretary of State for External Affairs): This is a mission
I would like very much to have established, and there are others too I
would like to have established, but in getting these wishes carried out, I
always run foul of the Treasury Board. I do not doubt the leader of the
Opposition had that same problem when he was minister. I would like
to have a mission in Baghdad right now, but so far I have not been able to
make much progress. . . .
Mr. Pearson (Leader of the Opposition): I appreciate the Minister's difficulties with the Treasury Board. I would have thought that perhaps he
would be more skilful than I ever was in overcoming them, but I am sure
the Minister does not need anyone to tell him that while funds for capital
construction abroad do add to the budget and the budgetary difficulties of
the Minister of Finance, over the long run they are economical. . . .
Mr. Green: That is exactly the argument I have been making with the
Minister of Finance. Now that I have some support from the Leader of the
Opposition, perhaps it will be easier to convince him. . . .[31]

The fact, mentioned above, that the Secretary of State for External
Affairs is not among the six Cabinet ministers who are members of the

Treasury Board does not place his Department at too much of a disadvantage in keeping its estimates intact; more important is the personal relationship of the foreign minister with the Minister of Finance and with the Prime Minister. (Before 1946, when the Prime Minister and the foreign minister were one and the same person, the modest demands of the Department were met without too much protest, although, depending on his interests and his temperament, the incumbent of both posts might favour one at the expense of the other.) Nor to be overlooked are the personal relationships between the civil service staff of the Treasury Board and the foreign service officers of the Department of External Affairs. These have sometimes been strained, to the disadvantage of the Department. "Much of the success of our aid programmes and much of the success of our organization as a department," one of its members has written privately, "depend on better relations with Finance and Treasury Board."[32]

Two other Cabinet groupings, not ordinarily thought of as Cabinet committees but having the same purpose of bringing matters of external policy before the ministers directly concerned, are the Canadian members of the Joint United States–Canadian Committee on Trade and Economic Affairs and of the Canada–United States Ministerial Committee on Joint Defence. The former was created by an exchange of notes between the Canadian and American governments in November 1953 stating that the Committee should meet "once a year, or more often, as may be considered necessary." It consisted of those members of the Canadian and American cabinets principally involved in economic affairs, and was thus an attempt to combine in a single piece of intergovernmental machinery two distinct and perhaps incompatible governmental systems, with the danger (as was observed at the time) "that people may be led to expect results from men who are in no position to effect them."[33] On the Canadian side the representatives usually consisted of the Secretary of State for External Affairs, and the Ministers of Trade and Commerce, Finance, and Agriculture. A second and similar Committee was established in 1958 "to consult periodically on all matters affecting the joint defence of Canada and the United States ..., not only military questions but also the political and economic aspects of joint defence problems." The Canadian members of this Committee were ordinarily the Secretary of State for External Affairs and the Ministers of National Defence, Defence Production, and Finance, attended by expert advisers from their respective departments. "There was no long table at which we sat down with minutes and paper before us," the Minister of National Defence reported after the Committee's meeting at Camp David in the fall of 1959. "However, we sat around in an informal group and we had the most intimate discussion on all defence matters."[34]

The proliferation of Cabinet committees and groupings in recent years has had its effect upon the relationship of the Prime Minister to his Cabinet colleagues in the formulation of external policy. To the extent that such committees and groupings impose order and routine and settled procedures, and ensure that different facets of policy come as a matter of course before the ministers nominally responsible for them, it becomes that much more difficult for a Prime Minister to gather the reins tightly in his own hands. The members of the War Committee of the Cabinet, Mackenzie King remarked in 1943, were "immediately concerned with matters relating to external affairs, so that they are in a position to assist me, as in fact they do. They carry much of the responsibility that I have to assume in that particular position [Secretary of State for External Affairs]."[35] Some months after the war had ended he spoke appreciatively once again of the devolution that had taken place:

Thank God, I have around me Ministers who are taking more of [the load] from my shoulders day by day. . . . I have to take responsibility for what is said and done, but if hon. members will notice how matters relating to external affairs have been dealt with in considerable part by one minister after another, they will realize that the burden of the Department of External Affairs is not wholly on the shoulders of any one man, but is shared by a very large part of the Ministry.*

In the larger gathering of the full Cabinet the Prime Minister may more easily have his way or more easily keep matters to himself; in the smaller and more specialized committee of the Cabinet such evasion, while not impossible, is less likely to go unremarked and unchallenged. Indeed, it may be for just this reason that there is not now nor has there ever been a Cabinet Committee on External Affairs, a fact suggestive of the unwillingness of Prime Ministers to allow it to dispose of

*Canada, *H. of C. Debates,* April 2, 1946, p. 492. It is possible, and even probable, that by thus citing the collegial nature of Cabinet decision-making in external affairs, the Prime Minister was attempting to forestall suggestions that he devolve the External Affairs portfolio upon another member of the Cabinet. Mackenzie King's real feelings on the subject of sharing with his colleagues the process of decision-making in matters which, like external affairs, lay close to his own interests, may have been expressed in an entry in his dairy a few days after the sudden death of O. D. Skelton early in 1941. "There must be a purpose," he wrote characteristically of this tragic event, "and, as I see it, it may be meant to cause me to rely more completely on my own judgment in making decisions, and to acquaint myself more meticulously with all that is happening so as to be able to meet each demand as it is occasioned." Quoted in Pickersgill, *The Mackenzie King Record,* I, p. 166.

what Mackenzie King once referred to as "the political side of public affairs in the large sense of the word."[36]

Another potential check upon prime ministerial control, also of fairly recent origin, is the practice of resorting to settled procedures for disposing of certain types of foreign policy decisions. In 1956, for example, the then Secretary of State for External Affairs described the manner in which decisions were made with regard to the export of war matériel. Certain lines of policy had been laid down: no arms shipments of any kind to the Sino-Soviet bloc, no restrictions on arms shipments to NATO allies and most Commonwealth nations. Scope for discretion existed with respect to "areas of tension or strife or what we call sensitive areas" of which there were at that time thirty-four thus designated. To these sensitive areas there could not be exported "arms of such a character that they might increase any temptation to commit an aggression or begin a preventive war." In no case could any kind of shipment of war matériel be made to such areas without the agreement of the Minister of National Defence, the Minister of Trade and Commerce and the Secretary of State for External Affairs. In addition, "if the application is a particularly significant one, either in quantity or because of the political circumstances surrounding it, and even though the three ministers may have agreed to the [export] permit, the matter is referred to the whole Cabinet."[37] Another example of settled procedures is the manner of deciding upon projects for capital assistance under the Colombo Plan. An interdepartmental committee submits recommendations to the Cabinet. "If the Cabinet approves them," the Administrator of the International Economic and Technical Co-operation Division of the Department of Trade and Commerce (then Mr. R. G. Nik Cavell) informed the House of Commons Standing Committee on External Affairs in 1956, "we go ahead." To that date, he added, the Cabinet had approved all the recommendations of the Committee.[38] A third illustration is to be found in the manner of deciding upon whether and where to open up new diplomatic missions, described in 1952 by the Under Secretary of State for External Affairs:

An attempt is made within the Department [of External Affairs] in the first instance to assess that need against expenditure in terms of men—because we are short of qualified men—as well as in terms of money. That assessment then comes up through the Under Secretary to the Minister of External Affairs himself. He examines the proposal in relation to other requirements and demands . . . and he comes to a decision as to what recommendation to make. He then takes it to the Cabinet and the Cabinet decides whether or not post "A" or post "B" or post "C" or all three require to be opened. According to their decision submissions are made to Treasury Board for the appropriate establishments and then amounts appear in the estimates. The process through which we go in this field of activity, I can assure the Committee, is a very careful one.[39]

As the range and complexity of foreign policy decisions increase, they have become more and more the result of settled procedures designed to bring to bear upon them the judgment of ministers and officials from other departments of government in addition to the judgment of the Prime Minister. In the last analysis the firmly held view of the Prime Minister will prevail, but only the most paranoic of prime ministers would wish to disregard too often or too obviously the recommendations of colleagues and officials. In this sense the trend to settled procedures of decision-making may be said to limit the potential scope of prime ministerial discretion in the matters for which they are employed. The procedure for opening new diplomatic missions, described above, is in striking contrast to the earlier practice when the decision to open legations in Tokyo and Paris reflected Mackenzie King's personal and somewhat eccentric opinions about the configuration of world power. Even as late as 1942 the decisions were wholly his. "Robertson and Pearson always wanted to go a little too fast," the American Minister in Ottawa records him as saying. "For instance, they were pressing him to establish Canadian Legations all over the place. He was inclined to think that a Legation would soon be opened in Moscow, and I suggested that Mexico might have some merits. He said yes, but he had no intention of spreading too fast."[40]

PRIME MINISTER AND FOREIGN
MINISTER

The authority of the Prime Minister in foreign affairs has been potentially circumscribed by the assumption in recent years of the External Affairs portfolio by a member of his Cabinet other than himself.

When the Department of External Affairs was created in 1909 it was the expectation of its first Under Secretary, Joseph Pope, that the new portfolio should be held by the Prime Minister; and, as the individual more than any other responsible for its creation, he was vexed when the Department was placed instead under the Secretary of State. This, he wrote at the time, was "a *great* mistake. It should be under the Prime Minister."[41] Despite the assignment of responsibility to the Secretary of State by the Act of 1909 bringing the Department into being, it was Sir Wilfrid Laurier as Prime Minister rather than Charles Murphy as Secretary of State who assumed effective control of the

Department of External Affairs. In 1912 legislation of the Borden Government corrected this anomaly by bringing the Department legally as well as practically within the Prime Minister's authority:

2. There shall be a Department of the Government of Canada to be called the Department of External Affairs, over which the Secretary of State for External Affairs shall preside.
3. The Member of the King's Privy Council for Canada holding the recognized position of First Minister shall be the Secretary of State for External Affairs.[42]

After two years of wartime leadership, Sir Robert Borden found himself increasingly unable to do justice to both positions. His remedy was not to divest himself of the External Affairs portfolio but to create the new post of Parliamentary Under Secretary of State for External Affairs. The Order-in-Council by which this was accomplished (P.C. 1719 of July 15, 1916) recited the following "orders and regulations" in connection with the position:

2. The Parliamentary Under Secretary shall, with respect to the Department of External Affairs, perform such parliamentary duties as may from time to time be assigned to him by the Governor in Council.
3. The Parliamentary Under Secretary shall, subject to such instructions as may from time to time be issued by competent authority assist the Prime Minister in administering the Department of External Affairs, and may, subject to the approval of the Prime Minister, conduct such official communications between the Government of Canada and the Government of any other country in connection with the external affairs of Canada, and perform such other duties in the said Department as from time to time may be directed.
4. In the absence of the Prime Minister, the Parliamentary Under Secretary shall, subject to the direction and approval of the Acting Prime Minister for the time being, preside over and administer the Department of External Affairs; and in such case he shall have authority to report to and make recommendations to the Governor in Council through the Acting Prime Minister.[43]

The terms of the Order-in-Council permitted the Parliamentary Under Secretary of State for External Affairs to assume considerable responsibility. The first occupant of the position, Colonel Hugh Clark, whom Borden appointed in October 1916, did little more, however, than answer questions in the House of Commons, and Francis Keefer, who took over from Clark in 1918, did not enlarge its scope. The office had been authorized only "during the continuance of the war," and was soon afterward allowed to lapse.

In 1943 the position of Parliamentary Assistant to the President of the Privy Council was created. Brooke Claxton was the first to hold the post. The Parliamentary Assistant was responsible to Parliament for the activities of a number of wartime governmental agencies which had originally been placed under Mackenzie King in one or other of his three positions, Prime Minister, Secretary of State for External Affairs, and President of the Privy Council; among these agencies were the Wartime Information Board and the Economic Advisory Committee charged with post-war planning and reconstruction. The Parliamentary Assistant to the President of the Privy Council was thus in fact though not yet in name a Parliamentary Assistant to the Secretary of State for External Affairs. In later years the latter position replaced the former, and, undergoing one more change in title, emerged as that of Parliamentary Secretary to the Secretary of State for External Affairs, today a normal fixture of the Ministry.

In 1918 Sir Robert Borden seems to have been ready to offer the External Affairs portfolio to Sir George Foster, then Minister of Trade and Commerce. "Sent for Foster," Borden noted in his diary on November 1. "He agreed to accompany me to England and to accept External Affairs." This invitation is apparently confirmed by Foster's diary entry for the same date:

My own position will be radically changed. I shall hate to leave my work in T. and C. just as I am getting it into shape for good work. On the other hand there is a vast mass of detail in it and I am 71 years old. I do not now get an hour free from hard grind and I cannot stand it long. So *vale.* The other will bring me into close contact with Empire and international relations and adjustments which will be congenial. I shall be free from detail worries. The next few months in Europe will be very interesting.

For some reason remaining obscure the change did not take place at this time or, indeed, until very much later. R. B. Bennett upon becoming Prime Minister in 1930 had, according to Mackenzie King, "entertained the view that it would be desirable to separate the two offices" but changed his mind soon afterwards.[44] There is no evidence for the contention of Dr. W. A. Riddell that in 1935 Mackenzie King was prepared to offer the External Affairs portfolio to Ernest Lapointe, then Minister of Justice, and was only dissuaded by his dissatisfaction with Lapointe's handling of the "Riddell incident";[45] Mackenzie King himself later stated that "I should have found it perilous and indeed impossible to have separated these two positions at that particular time."[46] On at least two occasions during the Second World War, however, he considered (how seriously is anyone's guess) the possibility of himself holding the External Affairs portfolio in the event of some other member of the Government becoming Prime Minister.* In 1943 he offered the the House of Commons an explanation of "why, to put it in a direct way, I myself have retained the position of Minister of External Affairs while holding the office of Prime Minister at this time of the war." It was not, he insisted, "through any desire on my part to carry the extra portfolio. I would point out that in time of war nine-tenths of the Prime Minister's work is related to external affairs, and it would be making his task in some ways more difficult were he to try to assume the office of Prime Minister without being responsible as well for External Affairs."[47]

In 1946 Canada acquired for the first time a Secretary of State for External Affairs who was not also Prime Minister. This was Mr. L. S. St. Laurent, who for a few months after his appointment continued to hold the Justice portfolio as well as External Affairs.† Since then it has been the rule rather than the exception for the External Affairs portfolio to be the sole responsibility of a member of the Cabinet other than the Prime Minister. Mr. St. Laurent held it until becoming Prime Minister in 1948, when Mr. Lester Pearson became Secretary of State for External Affairs, remaining in that capacity until the defeat of the

*"I said [to the Cabinet] I would be quite prepared to stay on under Ralston, and accept any post he would like to give me, particularly if he thought well of giving me External Affairs. I would feel happier in devoting my entire time to it." King Diary, entry for May 29, 1940, quoted in Pickersgill, *The Mackenzie King Record,* I, p. 83. On July 8, 1942, Mackenzie King told Ralston that "quite frankly, what I would like, above everything else, would be to let someone else take the office of Prime Minister. Let me continue as Minister of External Affairs, and give to the Prime Minister all the help I could." Quoted in *ibid.,* p. 399.

There is some inconsistency between these comments and Mackenzie King's public statements that as Prime Minister it would be necessary for him to retain External Affairs; if he as Prime Minister could not relinquish it, why should some other Prime Minister be able to? Perhaps the answer is that Mackenzie King never seriously contemplated giving up the prime ministership to become foreign secretary or head of any other department, but used the threat of resignation as a means of quieting opposition in his Cabinet.

†Mr. St. Laurent was apparently not the first minister to be approached by Mackenzie King to accept the External Affairs portfolio. While in Paris for the Peace Conference of 1946, King had offered it to the then Minister of National Health and Welfare, Brooke Claxton. According to the obituary notice appearing in the Toronto *Globe and Mail* the day after Brooke Claxton's death on June 13, 1960, "Mr. Claxton wished nothing better [than to become Secretary of State for External Affairs] but he reminded Mr. King that Louis St. Laurent, the Minister of Justice, had decided to go back to his law practice. It was important to the party that he remain in public life. Mr. Claxton suggested that Mr. St. Laurent be offered External Affairs. Mr. King said it would be fruitless, that Mr. St. Laurent was determined to retire, but agreed to try. Mr. St. Laurent accepted. . . ."

Liberal Government in June 1957. The new Prime Minister, Mr. John Diefenbaker, was his own foreign minister until in September 1957 he brought Sidney Smith into his administration and handed the External Affairs portfolio over to him. When Sidney Smith's new career was tragically ended by his death in March 1959, the Prime Minister again assumed responsibility for the External Affairs Department, relinquishing it in July of that year to the then Minister of Public Works, Mr. Howard Green. For a time Mr. Green retained, while Secretary of State for External Affairs, not only his old portfolio but also his position as House Leader; there was some criticism in the House of Commons at this piling on of responsibilities, and within a few months Mr. Green was left free to devote all his time and energy to foreign affairs.

The relationship between a Prime Minister and his foreign minister, "the most fateful . . . of all imposed by the machinery of government,"[48] is seldom free from difficulty and may easily become tensely competitive. Where a Prime Minister is wise enough and generous enough to allow an able colleague sufficient scope for judgment and initiative, or where a foreign minister is content with a technician's role, a harmonious and productive partnership may result. But this rarely happens. "The relations of subordination that bind them together," an authority has written, "the care taken by the minister of foreign affairs in order to keep his own autonomy, the fear of the prime minister that this collaborator may carry him too far towards a policy of which the parliament disapproves . . . , the general tendency to hold numerous international meetings at the highest level, all this creates between these two men, even when they belong to the same political party, a fatal competition."[49] Whether they contrive a mutually profitable division of labour, or whether their energies are dissipated in rivalry, will depend mainly upon their temperaments; especially will it depend upon the temperament of the Prime Minister.

Mackenzie King combined the positions of Prime Minister and foreign minister for all but the last two years of his long sojourn in power. He did so not because he felt foreign affairs to be insufficiently important to warrant another Cabinet minister holding the portfolio but precisely because he felt foreign policy to be too serious a matter to be left to foreign ministers. His attitude resembled that of the Abbé Sieyès towards a second chamber: if it agreed it was superfluous; if not, mischievous. When in 1946 he finally relinquished the External Affairs portfolio, it was without any intention of yielding control of important foreign policy matters; on the contrary, it was in order to devote more attention to them, and to slough off upon the new Secretary of State for External Affairs such mundane matters as the acquisition of new properties abroad for Canadian diplomatic missions then being opened up. The necessary amendment of the Act of 1912 was passed in April 1946, but it was not until September that Mr. St. Laurent took over. To justify his refusal to shed the portfolio at the earlier date, Mackenzie King referred to his own long experience of foreign policy:

This House knows that the problems we have in all these international relationships have not grown up in the last few days or weeks or years; they have come into being over the years, and with respect to them, wide knowledge and information is a very great asset in reaching highly important decisions. The movement of international affairs is so rapid in these days that unless one has some of the direct knowledge of the background out of which these situations have sprung it would be next to impossible . . . to make with any sense of security the decisions which are essential if the proper steps are to be taken. . . . It is not for me to say whether or not a new minister of external affairs coming into office tomorrow would be able, in the critical situations which have to be dealt with at some of the international gatherings which are to take place this year, to render, perhaps, the same service to Canada as one who has known at first hand the international situation as it has grown up over the years.[50]

It seemed likely, therefore, that the new Secretary of State for External Affairs would not be allowed much leeway in those larger affairs of state that the Prime Minister clearly intended to deal with himself; and this proved to be the case.

Two incidents during the short period when Mackenzie King and Mr. St. Laurent worked together as Prime Minister and foreign minister are suggestive of their difficult and unsatisfactory relationship. The first took place soon after Mr. St. Laurent acquired his new portfolio. A telegram from the Prime Minister of the United Kingdom, relating that India was soon to achieve independence on such generous terms that it was expected to remain in the Commonwealth, was received in Ottawa during Mackenzie King's absence. Mr. Lester Pearson, then Under Secretary of State for External Affairs, prepared an answer (to the effect that Canada welcomed the news in Mr. Attlee's message) which Mr. St. Laurent signed, delaying its despatch for the Prime Minister's approval on his return. When presented to him in Cabinet, Mackenzie King "was furious. He remarked that Attlee's cable had been addressed to the Prime Minister of Canada and he assumed that he and no other was still Prime Minister. Since he alone was entitled to answer his own correspondence, he took the draft reply rudely out of St. Laurent's hands and said he would deal with it himself. . . . St. Laurent received this outrageous rebuke in silence."[51]

A similar and more serious episode occurred a few months later. Mr. J. L. Ilsley, then Minister of Finance, leading the Canadian delegation at the United Nations General Assembly, signified Canada's acceptance of membership on the U.N. Temporary Commission on Korea, and Mr. St. Laurent, as Acting Prime Minister in King's absence from Ottawa, approved Mr. Ilsley's decision. On learning of this development on his return, Mackenzie King was so incensed that he despatched Mr. Lester Pearson to Washington to obtain President Truman's approval of Canada's withdrawal from the Commission. (It had been in response to a request from the United States that the Canadian representative had agreed to accept membership.) When Mr. Pearson reported that he had been unable to secure Mr. Truman's agreement to a Canadian withdrawal, the Canadian Prime Minister determined to withdraw in any case. Thereupon a number of Cabinet members, including Mr. St. Laurent and Mr. Ilsley, threatened to resign. Confronted with one of the rare occasions in Canadian political life when ministers have threatened resignation over an issue of foreign policy, Mackenzie King backed down, and settled for a compromise by which Canada remained a member of the Commission on the understanding that it would play as inconspicuous a role as possible. Soon after this incident, Mackenzie King invited Mr. St. Laurent to his Laurier House home and there, "in his most charming manner, remarked that he had not realized how keenly his colleagues felt about the Korean matter. St. Laurent replied that naturally he must resign if King repealed his policy. Resignation, King protested, was unthinkable. If St. Laurent . . . believed in the wisdom of his action, then there was nothing more to be said. . . . This affair marked a watershed in the political lives of King and St. Laurent. King was no longer the dominant power in the Government. . . ."[52]

If Mackenzie King and Louis St. Laurent provided a model of how a Prime Minister and a foreign minister ought not to work together, Mr. St. Laurent as Prime Minister and Mr. Lester Pearson as foreign minister offered a model of how they should. As one who had himself held the position of Secretary of State for External Affairs under the difficult circumstances just described, Mr. St. Laurent had a sound appreciation of its importance while content to leave a large area of discretion to his younger colleague. Mr. Pearson has himself disclosed that during the Suez crisis in November 1956 he was given a free hand at the United Nations. "Mr. St. Laurent was more than a prime minister to me, he was always a very close friend. 'Don't worry', he told me. 'Do what is best. Do the right thing, and I'll back you'."[53] This happy understanding appears to have been the basis of an exceptionally harmonious and fruitful collaboration throughout eight eventful years, for which the Prime Minister, as the senior partner, deserves full credit. Mr. St. Laurent's relationship with Mr. Pearson is well described by words once applied to Mr. Churchill's relationship with Anthony Eden: "[It] was so frank and sagacious, and his own temperament so little inclined to backstairs methods, that there was never any question about what might be called a 'double foreign policy'."[54]

The present Prime Minister has so far displayed in this matter a less sure touch. Mr. John Diefenbaker's spectacular electoral triumphs of June 1957 and March 1958 were due more than to anything else to his own personal appeal, evoking such "hysterical adoration," a correspondent noted in wonder, "that at places like Fredericton, N.B., women were holding up their children to touch the hem of his garment."[55] He was thus less than usually solicitous of colleagues during the normally sordid business of cabinet-making; and as he was widely regarded as an authority on international affairs—he had been since the death of Gordon Graydon in 1953 the official Opposition's foreign policy spokesman—no one was greatly astonished at his decision to become his own foreign minister, at least for the time being.

In September 1957 Mr. Diefenbaker announced that Sidney Smith would enter the Cabinet as Secretary of State for External Affairs. Sidney Smith was then the respected and widely known President of the University of Toronto, with a reputation for vigorous and witty speech in the cause of higher education, often rumoured as a possible leader of the Conservative party of whose membership he had made no secret. All expected him quickly to make his mark as a Canadian foreign minister. In this all were to be disappointed. Sidney Smith was not at home in his new job, and while he had shown some signs of mastering it shortly before his death in office, he never displayed the consistently professional flair of his Nobel prize-winning predecessor. It cannot be said that the Prime Minister made his foreign minister's apprenticeship any easier. Sidney Smith's earliest public utterance as Secretary of State for External Affairs was delivered a few moments after being sworn into the Cabinet, Mr. Diefenbaker standing watchfully at his side. He was asked by newspaper reporters for his opinion of Canadian policy at the time of the Suez crisis. Embarked on an honest if maladroit reply to the effect that he was in general agreement with the St. Laurent–Pearson position, he was interrupted, "rather tartly, it seemed to some listeners,"[56] by the Prime Minister who proceeded to offer his own, very different, version of what the Secretary of State for External Affairs had meant to say. This initial reprimand set the tone of their relationship for its tragically short duration.

In Mr. Howard Green, who became Secretary of State for External Affairs on June 4, 1959, three months after Sidney Smith's death, the Prime Minister had a wholly different kind of colleague. An experienced parliamentarian who had entered the House of Commons with Mr. Diefenbaker in 1935, Mr. Green was noted for an obsessive concern that Canada join some kind of Pacific counterpart of NATO, for a rancorous attack on the Government at the time of the Suez crisis, and for a record, surely unique for a foreign minister, of unbroken domicile in his own country since his return from the Western front in 1918. It was widely noticed, at least during the first year and a half of their new relationship, that Mr. Diefenbaker seemed reluctant to allow Mr. Green the latitude Mr. St. Laurent had permitted Mr. Pearson, that he reserved for himself important pronouncements on world affairs, and on occasion made things more difficult for his foreign secretary to suit his own political advantage. Like Lord Curzon forty years before him, Mr. Green was "to discover the personal embarrassment to which a Foreign Secretary might be subjected by a Prime Minister . . . who took an active and sometimes independent part in the foreign policy of his country."[57]

PRIME MINISTER AND
GOVERNOR GENERAL

Half a century ago, when the conduct of Canadian external policy was both theoretically and practically the concern of the British Government, the Governor General as its representative played as great a part in the external affairs of the Dominion as his own temperament and that of his Prime Minister would allow; and they could allow a great deal. Lord Minto has left a revealing account of what he conceived to be his constitutional role during his governor generalship (1898–1904):

I think what I should like to make most clear [he wrote to his Canadian friend George R. Parkin in 1904] is the position I have taken up with "my ministers" on matters of public importance..viz. always to express my views as openly and as decidedly as I could on all matters upon which I have been consulted—and though it may sound conceited I have been consulted about everything of any moment, and I am sure you will understand the pleasure it is to me that the longer I have been here, the greater weight I have been able to bear..I have however always assumed the position, in matters of importance, that there were two classes into which questions placed before me resolved themselves...viz. Imperial questions, and purely Canadian questions—as regards the former I have always claimed my right to assert myself, i.e. to put my foot down, if I suspected anything detrimental to Imperial interests, whilst as to Canadian questions however important, I have only expressed my opinion as strongly as I could, simply as my opinion, for what it was worth, telling the minister interested that such was my opinion and that he could take it or not as he liked.*

Lord Grey, Governor General from 1904 to 1911, found the area in which he could "put my foot down" somewhat smaller than that available to his predecessor, but did not hesitate to put it down when he saw fit, as when he wrote to the British ambassador in Washington, "with the view of preventing the office of Governor General drifting into a subordinate and undignified position," to request that he be sent "copies of any private communications you may send to the Secretary of the Department of External Affairs."[58] In the main, however, Grey relied, as his successors had necessarily to rely, on influence rather than on constitutional authority. His restless and energetic intelligence lapped into every cranny of Canadian life, suffusing his ministers with schemes, goading them into action and frequently into irritation. "On one occasion (1909) when Grey's enthusiasm for proportional representation threatened to become embarrassing, Laurier 'wished Earl Grey would mind his own business', and King in his diary added: 'The truth is His Ex. is getting into too many things'."[59] But Bryce, in Washington, was more appreciative. "When I look back over these last three years," he wrote to Grey in 1910, "I doubt if any decisions would ever have been got out of Canada but for your action."[60]

Under Grey the influence of Governors General upon Canadian external policy reached a high water mark from which it was to recede for many years. The pressures of war had by 1919 created the practice of direct communication between prime ministers, and although the channel formally ran through the Governor General's office in Ottawa, the hold-up of the British Government's telegram at the time of the Chanak crisis of 1922 (received in the Governor General's office at 10 on the evening of Friday, September 15, deciphered there the following morning and delivered to the Prime Minister's office at 3 P.M. on September 16, two hours after the news had appeared in the Canadian press[61]) helped to make inevitable the changes in the position of the Governor General throughout the Dominions agreed upon at the Im-

*Lord Minto to George R. Parkin, Sept. 26, 1904, quoted in Frank H. Underhill, "Lord Minto on his Governor Generalship," *Canadian Historical Review*, vol. XL, no. 2, June 1959, p. 124. Professor Underhill draws attention to Minto's curious "system of punctuation by means of dots and dashes."

perial Conference of 1926.* Henceforth the Governor General no longer functioned as the representative of the British Government; he was to be no more (if no less) than the representative of the Sovereign. In that capacity he might continue to exercise influence on policy by means of the prerogatives of constitutional monarchy classically defined by Bagehot as "the right to be consulted, the right to encourage, the right to warn."

Warning and encouragement, however, were only useful, indeed they were only practical, on the assumption of adequate consultation. This the Imperial Conference of 1926 recognized and sought to promote by stating in its report that "a Governor General should be supplied with copies of all documents of importance and in general should be kept as fully informed as is His Majesty the King in Great Britain of Cabinet business and public affairs." Whether in fact he would be so informed of course depended not upon constitutional documents drawn up in London but upon the inclination of his Prime Minister. In Canada, the Prime Minister was not so inclined. While Canadian practice did not so obviously follow that of the Irish Free State in seeking to degrade the Governor General's office for political advantage, there was certainly no great effort by Mackenzie King to draw the Governor closely into his confidence or to seek the benefit of his advice. Lord Willingdon, Governor General from 1926 to 1930, complained that "few chiefs of a State have such little knowledge of the work that is being done by his administrators as has the present Governor-General of Canada";[62] Lord Tweedsmuir, Governor General from 1935 to 1940, although on much closer personal terms with his Prime Minister than Willingdon had been, had hardly more influence on policy. The Governors of Mackenzie King's last years in office were ceremonial cyphers. In 1944 King George VI inquired of his Canadian Prime Minister, then in the United Kingdom, "how his uncle was getting on. I spoke of being exceedingly pleased with Lord Athlone. . . . He asked me how often I saw him. I said sometimes quite a little period went by, sometimes, some weeks would go by. It was then that he spoke of seeing Churchill

*The wisdom of one of these changes, that prescribing that the Governor General was no longer to act as the channel of communication between a Dominion government and that of another member of the British Commonwealth, was forcibly suggested by the later experience of New Zealand which alone of the Dominions clung in this respect to the old system until 1941; many serious delays in the transmission of messages between London and Wellington occurred as a consequence. On one occasion "an important London cable of 19 Mar 37 reached Government House on the 20th but the Prime Minister's Department not until the 23rd." F. L. W. Wood, *The New Zealand People at War: Political and External Affairs* (Wellington, 1958), p. 63.

once a week. . . . "* With Lord Alexander, Athlone's successor, Mackenzie King was on friendly terms but again "did not make a practice of consulting the famous soldier, presumably because he was confident that Alexander's advice on Canadian politics would be quite worthless."[63] Lord Alexander, it will be recalled, left his vice-regal post to become Minister of Defence in the Government of the United Kingdom.

The appointment of Mr. Vincent Massey in 1952 and that of his successor, Major General Georges Vanier, in 1959 have to a considerable extent rehabilitated the office. Both had wide experience of Canadian affairs (Mr. Massey indeed having been a member of a Canadian Government) and in particular of Canadian diplomacy, so that their Prime Ministers could not with much plausibility hold aloof on the ground that their Governors' knowledge and judgment of events were too slight to make their counsel worth acquiring. Nor would an increasing number of informed Canadians have been content with a cypher's role. The prestige of the Governor General's office has, for the first time in thirty years, been noticeably enhanced. The appointment of Canadians has contributed to this result, and even more the rare distinction with which the first Canadian appointee, Mr. Vincent Massey, went about his duties. So has the increased popularity of the monarchy itself and its domestication into the Canadian constitution with more frequent (and less stuffy) royal visits.

*Quoted in Pickersgill, *The Mackenzie King Record*, I, p. 694. The weekly meetings with Mr. Churchill, King George added, were sometimes alone, sometimes with the Chiefs of Staff, sometimes with members of the War Cabinet. Mackenzie King "asked him if his presence caused the men to discuss matters less freely. He said not at all. They spoke quite freely back and forth. He found it very helpful." *Ibid.*, p. 694.

Chapter Two

THE BUREAUCRACY

THE SENIOR CIVIL SERVANT

It is a paradox of bureaucratic history that no sooner had the principle of an official, permanent and neutral public service been firmly established in the constitutions of Western democracies than the line between political and administrative activity began to be so smudged and blurred that today it is doubtful whether a frontier exists, let alone whether the boundary may be precisely delimited. No sophisticated student of politics is any longer shocked by this, nor does he hanker for a golden age of administration from which patronage and politics have been forever banished. The day of "the administrative eunuch with neither policies nor politics"[1] is over, if it had ever dawned; the administration of things, in splendid defiance of the Marxian prediction, has come to mean the government of men. The civil servant, more especially the senior civil servant, has been drawn ever more intimately to the centre of the political process. The range and complexity of technologies modern governments must master, the wants of citizens grown accustomed to their welfare state, the trend towards mobilized if not garrisoned communities in an era that is neither war nor peace, all have increased his influence upon affairs.

In Canada, the senior civil servant's involvement in the policy process has been as close and continuous as anywhere in the world. The longevity of governments has brought him into prolonged and often familiar contact with political superiors. The state's uninhibited participation in taming and harnessing the resources of the more forbidding half of the continent has placed a premium upon his managerial talents. The still more specialized problems of defence in the missile age have cast doubt upon the validity of the classical formula "layman on top, expert on tap" to the extent that the political layman is concerned about national, as distinct from his own, survival. Such are the circumstances offering the senior Canadian administrator a position of power and influence greater, perhaps, than that of his counterpart in other democratic bureaucracies. Students of the political process in Canada are all agreed upon his importance, if they are just beginning to penetrate the mysteries of decision-making in which he is so crucially involved.

It might be thought, recalling the waning influence of the career diplomatist (see below, chapter VII), that the senior Canadian administrator exerts his authority only in questions of internal policy. This would be a major misinterpretation of his role. For at the summit of the civil service the divisions between foreign and domestic affairs all but disappear. At this exalted level the gaze of the civil servant sweeps across the whole horizon of public policy. Thus the senior members of the Department of External Affairs, with their commanding position on interdepartmental committees and their unique relationship with the Prime Minister's office (see above, chapter I), are assured of opportunity to influence decisions in areas far more extensive than a recital of their nominal responsibilities might suggest. In the same way, key members from other departments and agencies of government bring their experience to bear upon problems of external policy which in a more rigid division of labour would be the sole prerogative of foreign offices. The mutuality of these intrusions helps to allay the resentment they might otherwise arouse.

The group whose members stray so frequently into each other's jurisdictions is not and could not be a large one. Its numbers have varied over the years: perhaps a dozen or so in 1945, perhaps triple that today. It is a group without fixed composition, just as it is a group without defined duties. Within it are usually to be found the deputy ministers and on occasion the associate and assistant deputy ministers of certain important departments—External Affairs, Finance, National Defence, Trade and Commerce, Transport—together with the senior officials of the Bank of Canada, the secretary of the Cabinet, perhaps the principal private secretary of the Prime Minister. Its members have been described as an "under Cabinet."[2] It is an apt term, for this is the group to which responsible ministers of the Crown turn, individually and collectively, for continuous advice and guidance on matters of high policy. It thus comprises a kind of civil service ministry, and to its members might well be applied Sir James Stephen's description of higher public servants in England a century ago, "statesmen in disguise."

Below the "under Cabinet" may be found a larger group of officials, usually of the rank of assistant deputy minister or head of a major branch or division, likewise engaged in general administration and properly described as members of the senior civil service. The number of such officials has greatly increased over the years—indeed the whole group is largely a product of the period since the end of the Second World War—but it is still a small and select sector of the public service as a whole. Its present membership has been estimated variously as between 150 and 250.* It may be best described as "the bureaucratic élite." To identify its members with the "under Cabinet" would be to exaggerate their responsibilities, but it is from the bureaucratic élite that "under Cabinets" of the future are recruited.

Where departmental divisions are barriers rather than aids to action, the "under Cabinet" and the bureaucratic élite usefully dissolve them. This may be done by the interdepartmental committee, meeting at the level of deputy ministers or heads of division, habitual resort to which is so distinctive a feature of public administration in Canada (see below, chapter VI). But the interdepartmental committee as such cannot be expected to secure that broad comprehension of national interest which is its ostensible purpose and which it may achieve at its best. At its worst, however, it is a forum for departmental lobbying, for postponement and procrastination, for pitching discussion and decision at the lowest common denominator of understanding and agreement.

A valuable aid to interdepartmental liaison of a more helpful kind is the practice of posting key officials to other departments and receiving in return key officials from them. "We feel that in many cases these officials are interchangeable," Mr. L. S. St. Laurent remarked soon after becoming Prime Minister, "and can be moved to new posts either in other departments or with special government agencies."[3] The practice seems to have been inaugurated during the Second World War among actual or prospective members of the "under Cabinet," and since then two or three very senior civil servants indeed have rotated every three or four years among the most important administrative posts—the under secretaryship of state for External Affairs, clerkship of the Privy Council, chairmanship of the Civil Service Commission. It has also been encouraged within the ranks of the less senior bureaucratic élite, particularly among the Departments of External Affairs, Trade and Commerce, and Finance. But civil servants who find useful experience in departments other than their own are still the exception, and the characteristic complaint continues to be the classical complaint that the public service offers rather less than private enterprise the oppor-

*Keith B. Callard, *Advanced Administrative Training in the Public Service* (Toronto, 1958), p. 22, cites a figure of "possibly . . . 150"; John Porter, "Higher Public Servants and the Bureaucratic Elite in Canada," *Canadian Journal of Economics and Political Science*, vol. XXIV, no. 4, Nov. 1958, pp. 497–501, offers a larger estimate more carefully computed. Taking as his bureaucratic universe "twenty-one deputy ministers, and twenty others at the deputy minister level; twenty-nine associate and assistant deputies, and sixty others at that level; seventy-seven below these ranks . . . at the director level . . . ; and senior executives of Crown Corporations," Professor Porter arrives at a figure of 243. Of these 202 offered fairly uniform biographical data, and these officials form his "bureacratic élite."

tunity to make the most of one's talents in whatever branch they are most urgently needed or best rewarded. Canada has developed more hesitantly than United States business the interchangeable executive along with the interchangeable part, moving imperturbably and effectively from one enterprise to the next; the interchangeable civil servant is as yet an ideal and in some quarters he is not yet that. "It seems to me that the Canadian service is much too highly fragmented," a former member of the "under Cabinet" commented in 1957. "There are far too many pigeon holes and blind alleys. . . . Too much talent gets lost and frustrated within these narrow confines. . . . I expect someone will say, 'Look at yourself. You seem to have got around.' That is true, but I have resigned three times."[4]

Perhaps the chief catalyst of co-ordination at the higher levels of the civil service is the way its members spend time together outside their offices, "having lunch at the Chateau, or on a Saturday at Madame Burger's."* A former member of the "under Cabinet" has stressed the importance of this extra-bureaucratic environment:

In informal gatherings at lunch, at dinner, at receptions, at evening parties and at the fishing club, the leading advisers of the Government . . . make a practice of consultation. . . . It is taken for granted at most Ottawa social gatherings that the wives gravitate to one end of the room while their husbands collect at the other for that infinitely fascinating occupation of "talking shop". From observation and from conversation with civil servants in other countries, I have come to the conclusion that this close contact and constant exchange of views among leading civil servants in Ottawa is in many respects unique. In Washington interdepartmental consultation hardly exists except in formally constituted committees. In London there is greater informality during working hours than in Washington, but after hours civil servants depart for their homes in widely separated suburbs of the city and have relatively few social contacts.[5]

The system works effectively enough to cure the usual bureaucratic malaise of dissipating rivalry and competition, but in doing so it may produce undesirable side-effects. The senior civil servant may view such a vast panorama of government business that he becomes incapable of that close scrutiny of detail or that specialized knowledge without

*Callard, *Advanced Administrative Training in the Public Service*, p. 1. "The Chateau" is the Chateau Laurier Hotel, "Madame Burger's" a restaurant in Hull, Quebec, a few minutes' drive across the Ottawa River. A typical meeting of this kind was described in 1942 by the American Minister in Ottawa who having attemped without success to track down some members of the "bureaucratic élite" at the Rideau Club on the previous day, "tried my luck at the [Chateau Laurier] cafeteria today and lunched with Jack Pickersgill (Private Secretary to the Prime Minister), Jim Coyne (Assistant to Donald Gordon in Price Control), Saul Rae and Escott Reid of the Department of External Affairs." Nancy Harvison Hooker, ed., *The Moffat Papers* (Cambridge, Mass., 1956), p. 382. The luncheon yielded more political information for the Minister than half-a-dozen formal interviews.

which no enterprise, public or private, can fully succeed. A member of Parliament has described senior public servants in Canada as "a bunch of mandarins who, by being all-around gentlemen, sort of crossword puzzle experts, have never got around to having enough expert knowledge in any one sector to develop or elaborate policy."[6] The description is doubtless overdrawn, but it suggests a tendency of which the "mandarins" themselves are not unaware. Another hazard is that debate between spokesmen of different departments may be sapped by familiarity or inhibition. Professor Wheare has written convincingly of the need in effective committee work for the talents "of being unable to see the sense in what is being done, of questioning the whole basis of organization, of brushing difficulties aside, of ignoring logical argument, and of pressing a point beyond what most men consider a reasonable limit."[7] These are not the ordinary bureaucratic virtues, and they are likely to be in acutely short supply in a bureaucracy whose members (to adapt the famous phrase of Jinnah) occasionally intermarry and habitually interdine. The extent to which close personal association of the members of the senior civil service makes for a dangerously monolithic approach to public policy is hard to determine. One of the members of the group has recalled after leaving it that "on many matters it was considered undesirable to try to reach common views for presentation to the Ministers. . . . To have attempted to do so might have given a quite unjustified authority to the resulting piece of paper or have glossed over differences of interpretation that Ministers . . . should be aware of."[8] Against this encouraging testimony may be set the disturbing evidence of the former chairman of the Chiefs of Staff Committee that the Committee had been " 'packed' to protect the government against the receipt of unpalatable advice, rather than present the military case objectively and fearlessly on its merits."[9]

Related to this danger is another which might be called, however inelegantly, the "politicization" of the senior civil servant. It is of course a commonplace that the senior civil servant can no more avoid politics that he can avoid policy; nor is it desirable that he should. "In the formulation of policy," writes Professor Wheare, "a Higher Civil Servant is advising and assisting a Minister not only to carry through a policy which is the policy of a majority party in the House of Commons, but also to defend that policy against the criticisms and attacks of the party or parties in opposition. He works in the midst of party politics. He must be aware of party politics; indeed he ignores it at his peril. A first requirement of a Higher Civil Servant is a political sense."[10] Yet no aspect of his work requires more discretion or carries greater risk. An obsessive concern with party politics displayed under a single government over a long period of time may tempt him to place the party before the public interest; or if he is not so tempted a new set of political masters may regard him notwithstanding as too closely associated with the old to be of much use to them. "The one thing that I don't like," Mackenzie King wrote in his diary on the occasion of appointing General A. G. L. McNaughton as commander of the Canadian Army in 1939, "is the school from which he comes, which was the school of MacBrien, of Bennett, and Herridge. . . . No better evidence could be given of our disinterested action than in giving this command to one who comes . . . from that particular group."[11]

The quasi-political nature of the services rendered by senior Canadian administrators to the politicians set in authority over them is recognized by the special manner of their appointment. Unlike other civil servants, who are appointed by the Civil Service Commission, deputy ministers are called to their exalted positions by the Governor-in-Council on the advice of the Prime Minister. An incoming administration is thus not only able but to some extent expected to reappraise its predecessor's "under Cabinet" in the light of its own intended policies, and to replace any obvious misfits by officials enjoying its confidence and eager to do its bidding. It would be altogether improper to regard this procedure as a throwback to the patronage system of Laurier's day and a major exception to the principles of civil service neutrality and permanence. If it results in changes of personnel, those changes are expected to be few and obvious. But following the General Election of 1957 which returned the Conservative party to power after twenty-two years in opposition, the belief was widespread that the "under Cabinet" which had served Liberal masters for so long and so well (not least of its services being to contribute from its ranks the Secretary of State for External Affairs and the Minister of Citizenship and Immigration*) would prove unacceptable to the new Government. Distinguished heads, it was confidently predicted, would soon roll; indeed, in some quarters the cry was that they should be made to roll, the *Globe and Mail* of

---

*Respectively, Mr. Lester Pearson (who had been Under Secretary of State for External Affairs at the time of his entering politics), and Mr. J. W. Pickersgill (previously Clerk of the Privy Council). In 1948, in announcing Mr. Pearson's Cabinet appointment, the Prime Minister remarked that the civil service should be regarded as "the stepping stone to the Ministry," a doctrine immediately stigmatized by a leading constitutional authority as asserting "a constitutional principle as novel as it is subversive of parliamentary government" and, later, as "untrue, vicious, and unnecessary." Eugene Forsey, "Mr. King and Parliamentary Government," *Canadian Journal of Economics and Political Science,* vol. XVII, no. 4, Nov. 1951, p. 454.

Toronto arguing after the impressive Diefenbaker victory of 1958 that the time had come for "the dismantlement of what has come to be called, in Ottawa, the 'Establishment'."[12] But while some senior officials left the public service after the new administration took over, there is no evidence that any were actually dismissed. The transition, in retrospect, took place with far less friction and recrimination than had been expected, and such desire as there may have been to replace members of the "Establishment" found an outlet in the hiring of new personnel rather than in the firing of the old.[13]

THE UNDER SECRETARY OF STATE
FOR EXTERNAL AFFAIRS

Senior officials of the Department of External Affairs have on the whole been more secure in their positions throughout changes of government than have their colleagues in such departments as Trade and Commerce, perhaps because foreign policy has been less controversial than commercial policy. But tranquillity has not always been their lot. During the early 1920's, when the nature of Canada's position within the British Commonwealth of Nations was still unsettled and what is now of largely antiquarian interest was capable of stirring the Dominion, a change in government produced the resignation of the most able member of the Department of External Affairs. When Mackenzie King assumed his duties as Prime Minister and Secretary of State for External Affairs in December 1921, he found that Department to consist of three administrative (non-clerical) officers: Sir Joseph Pope, its Under Secretary; W. H. Walker, Assistant Under Secretary; and Loring C. Christie, Legal Adviser. Pope and Walker had been in the Department since its creation in 1909 and in the public service since 1878 and 1887 respectively; they were elderly men, no longer able to keep fully abreast of affairs. The major burdens of the Department had devolved upon Christie, an exceptionally able official whose formal title of Legal Adviser conveyed most imperfectly the scope of his actual responsibilities. The two prime ministers whom he had previously served relied on him for advice and assistance in policy formulation at the highest level: Sir Robert Borden's report on the Washington Disarmament Conference was largely Christie's work, while the policies argued by Arthur Meighen at the Imperial Conference in 1921 had their origin in his memoranda. "On matters of external affairs," Meighen wrote to Christie some years afterwards, "I value your views more highly than any other I know."[14] It was no doubt because of the high esteem in which Christie was held by Conservative leaders both in Canada and in the United Kingdom that Mackenzie King at the outset of his administration regarded him with considerable mistrust, remarking in his diary in 1922 that the Department of External Affairs was "a Tory hive." Shortly after becoming Prime Minister, Christie later recalled, Mackenzie King

called on me to say at great length that my relations & work with him would be exactly the same as with you [Borden] and Mr. Meighen. . . . [But] during the year that followed I saw him on business possibly a dozen times, including meetings in the corridor, & scarcely ever more than a few minutes. . . . I had very little to do—and thus though it was decided that I should not go to the Genoa Conference or to Geneva on the ground that there was important work at home, the important work never turned up, and all I did throughout the year might have been done in three weeks. Long afterward I recalled that at our original interview he had talked about his political creed at great length, contrasting it with Mr. Meighen's & so on, and that at one or two appropriate pauses I had either been silent or sought to talk about the Department. . . .15

If by tactics of enforced inactivity Mackenzie King had in fact sought to compel Loring Christie to resign from the Department of External Affairs, he was altogether successful, for early in 1923 the Legal Adviser tendered his resignation which was accepted.* For the next year Mackenzie King laboured with foreign and imperial affairs without any expert assistance from the Department. He turned from time to time to O. D. Skelton, then Dean of Arts at Queen's University, Kingston, Ontario, and well known as the biographer of Laurier, and in 1923 took him to London as his adviser for the Imperial Conference. King had been anxious as early as 1922 to bring Skelton into the

---

*In 1935 Christie was brought back into the Department of External Affairs by R. B. Bennett after consultation with Mackenzie King to ensure that his position would not be jeopardized by a Liberal administration. In 1939 Mackenzie King appointed him Minister to the United States. The *Financial Post* of Toronto (Sept. 23, 1939), commenting on this appointment, recalled that when Mackenzie King had come to power in 1921, "Mr. Christie's advice was no longer sought; he found himself sidetracked in his office in the East Block. . . . Mr. Christie—a lifelong Conservative—was not deemed the best Counsellor in foreign policy for a Liberal Administration." Upon reading this article Christie wrote privately to the associate editor stating that relations between himself and the Prime Minister had never been other than friendly, and that his resignation in 1923 had been due wholly to personal reasons (Loring Christie to K. R. Wilson, Oct. 4, 1939, Christie Papers). This version is clearly at odds with Christie's letter to Borden quoted in the text; but it is surely the earlier version, written thirteen years closer to the event, which is to be believed. It would not have been helpful as Minister to the United States to have in circulation rumours that he was at one time forced out of the Department of External Affairs by his Prime Minister. Christie's untimely death took place in Washington in 1941.

Department;* on July 10, 1924, he was officially appointed Counsellor; and in 1925, on the retirement of Sir Joseph Pope, he was made Under Secretary of State for External Affairs, a position occupied continuously by him to his death in 1941.

In O. D. Skelton, Mackenzie King had found a deputy minister in whom he could repose as much trust and confidence as his nature could allow. Skelton's influence upon the formation of external policy was very great. During the early 1920's, not yet a member of the Department of External Affairs, Skelton "strengthened and refined" King's views on inter-imperial affairs;[16] during the later 1930's his great experience was thrown, although not in the end decisively, into an attempt to protect Canada from involvement in a European war.† The intimacy of their association might be thought to have diminished Skelton's usefulness to a succeeding government, just as Christie's role

*On January 21, 1922, Mackenzie King wrote in his diary: "An excellent address [by Skelton]—pointing out that foreign policy was an extension of domestic policy & that as we had gained control of the one so we must gain control of the other. . . . Skelton's address would make an excellent foundation for Canadian policy on External Affairs, and Skelton himself would make an excellent man for that Department. . . . I told him that he might be wanted there some day. . . . He certainly has the knowledge & the right point of view." Quoted in R. MacGregor Dawson, *William Lyon Mackenzie King: A Political Biography*, I, *1874–1923* (Toronto, 1958), p. 454.

†During the week between the British and Canadian declarations of war on Germany in September 1939, "King was engaged in another struggle with neutrality under the most wrenching personal strains of his career. Skelton, his trusted adviser on foreign affairs from the beginning, insisted with all the power of his experience and integrity that Canada must remain neutral. . . . Skelton argued that the surrenders and hypocrisy of appeasement, from Ethiopia onward, had undermined all the moral purpose for which the war ostensibly was to be fought. Since no moral question was involved, Canada, like Ireland, should keep out. Being a North American nation, it might exercise some mediation in the course of a conflict morally chaotic. . . . King told Skelton bluntly that his counsel, whatever else might be said of it, was impossible." Bruce Hutchison, *The Incredible Canadian* (Toronto, 1952), p. 250. Loring Christie, who had re-entered the Department in 1935 to become, next to Skelton, its most important official, also argued in this vein, although advocating passive belligerency rather than neutrality. "What is the safest attitude of government in Canada at the moment when the blind European preventive war plunge has been taken and Canada is instantaneously precipitated into the legal status of war?" he inquired in a memorandum written soon before Munich. "To preserve the greatest caution and slowness, realizing there is for Canada no strategic necessity for rapid mobilizations or other action. To give no lead to take the people into Europe. . . . To make it clear that Canada is not a participant in the same sense or on the same kind of unlimited scale as the European allies, but is only what for short may be called an 'associate'—a North American associate . . ." ("Notes on the Canadian Position in the Event of a German-Czech Conflict Involving Great Britain," Sept. 8, 1938, Christie Papers). The influence of Skelton and Christie did not go unremarked at the time. See H. D. Hall to J. W. Dafoe, July 1, 1936; Dafoe to P. J. Noel-Baker, May 29, 1937, Dafoe Papers.

as policy adviser to Borden and Meighen made him suspect in the eyes of Mackenzie King. In this regard, however, R. B. Bennett was to display a larger spirit than his predecessor. Skelton did not share many of the ideals of his new chief, but Bennett, after an initial and wholly natural period of reserve, came to recognize the quality of his judgment and advice.

O. D. Skelton was the last Under Secretary of State for External Affairs to hold this important post for so long a continuous period. With the succession of Mr. Norman Robertson to the under secretary-ship in 1941 following Skelton's death, the practice was begun of rotating three or four senior members of the Department between the under secretaryship and two or three other important diplomatic posts—the mission in Washington, the office of High Commissioner in London and, after 1952, the position of permanent ambassador to the North Atlantic Council. The same officials, in keeping with the prevailing philosophy of public administration, might serve also in key government posts outside the Department, perhaps as Clerk of the Privy Council or chairman of the Civil Service Commission. The revolving under secretaryship has certain obvious advantages the most important of which, in the context of the present discussion, is to reduce to the minimum the temptation for the Under Secretary to become a party politician in disguise rather than a statesman in disguise. For the Minister it prevents the excessive dependence or personal animosity which prolonged association with a single deputy may develop. For the Under Secretary it provides the stimulus of a new but not an unfamiliar assignment. For the Department it offers periodically fresh direction and minimizes the danger of internal rivalries and cliques. If the device is to work well (and there is general agreement that so far it has worked well) much depends upon the compatibility of the senior officials who take turns at the top. The position of a relative newcomer to the "under Cabinet," doing an initial tour as Under Secretary of State for External Affairs, could become difficult if not untenable if former under secretaries in ambassadorial posts were unready to defer to his judgment or abide by his decisions. It may be for this reason that the deputy minister in most foreign offices is a long-term appointment, in the United Kingdom his relative administrative longevity being emphasized in his title, Permanent Under-Secretary of State for Foreign Affairs.*

*The author of the volume on the Foreign Office in the New Whitehall series, himself a former Permanent Under-Secretary of State for Foreign Affairs, has pointed out that "the official use of the word 'permanent' in this connexion is perhaps somewhat misleading, with its suggestion of hoary and impregnable bureaucracy. There is of course nothing permanent about the tenure of the office so far as the individual incumbent is concerned—he rarely holds it for more than

THE HEAD OF MISSION

Heads of diplomatic missions comprise another category of senior public servants appointed by the government of the day rather than by the Civil Service Commission. Like deputy and associate deputy ministers, they must command the confidence of their political chiefs if they are to perform useful service, and there is general agreement that a new government, should it be seriously dissatisfied with the diplomatic appointments of its predecessor, ought to be able to replace them with its own. It is equally understood, however, that frequent resort to such a practice is prejudicial to the public interest, and that an effective safeguard against abuse is to select heads of diplomatic missions from the ranks of the senior civil service, only occasionally handing out ambassadorships as political rewards.

Two of three early diplomatic appointments were offered in part as political consolation prizes. Mr. Vincent Massey, who went to Washington as Canada's first Minister to the United States, had been a member of Mackenzie King's Cabinet unable to secure a seat in the House of Commons; Herbert Marler, who became Canada's first Minister to Japan, had been in precisely the same predicament. On the other hand, Canada's first Minister to France, Philippe Roy, had since 1911 performed quasi-diplomatic duty as Canadian Commissioner in Paris and might on that account be regarded as a career appointment. The trend since these early days has been steadily in the direction of developing a career diplomatic service in which the most able members of the Department of External Affairs could look forward with some assurance to becoming heads of missions. "I cannot conceive of any training better adapted to qualify a man [for an ambassadorship]," Mackenzie King remarked in 1942, "than that which he may receive as a permanent official in the Department of External Affairs."[17] At the same time there has been a conscious effort to make outside appointments at the heads of missions level both to take advantage of the talents of gifted outsiders and to reduce the dangers of inbreeding. "You cannot do much better than the inspired amateur," Mr. Lester Pearson remarked when Under Secretary of State for External Affairs; but he conceded that "all amateurs are not inspired."[18]

---

four or five years at the end of his career." Lord Strang, *The Foreign Office* (London, 1955), p. 153, n. 1. Even this qualified description, however, sufficiently distinguishes the office from its Canadian counterpart, for it is not the practice in Ottawa to reserve the post for the last few years of the incumbent's career. The present (1961) Under Secretary of State for External Affairs, Mr. Norman Robertson, held the same position as long ago as 1941, serving, in the interim, in most of the other key bureaucratic positions.

The general principles then and since governing appointments of heads of diplomatic missions were stated in 1947 by the Under Secretary of the Department:

In the United States diplomatic service the very top posts have rarely, if ever, been held by career men. That I think is not good for the morale of the Foreign Service. On the other hand, the British diplomatic service is sometimes criticized as too much of a closed corporation of officials recruited from a limited class of persons. I think the Canadian service has given evidence that it will avoid these extremes. This will mean rejecting the view on the one hand that a man who has successfully manufactured safety pins can be equally successful in conducting delicate and complicated negotiations between governments, and, on the other, avoiding the equally dangerous delusion that because a man has not passed a Foreign Service Examination and learned how to sign his letter "I have the honour to be, Sir, with all Truth and Respect, Your Lordship's Humble and Obedient Servant", he has not therefore qualified to manage an embassy.[19]

This view was reaffirmed in 1954 by the Acting Under Secretary of State for External Affairs who remarked, in response to a question whether it was the Department's policy to draw all heads of missions from its own personnel: "It may be desirable to have a few exceptions. There are some posts where perhaps it is most desirable to have a man with a broad experience in business."[20] In recent years the exceptions have been few; in 1956, of forty-four appointees then heads of diplomatic missions, thirty-two had come up through the Department of External Affairs; eight had been appointed from other government departments; only four had been drawn from outside government service.[21] The number of outside appointees is too small to justify conclusions about favoured occupations. Some have been friends of the administration; some have been business men; a very few, distinguished men of the arts. Appointments from the military are not unusual; as Mr. Lester Pearson observed in 1949, "in certain countries the use of a military title does not do one any harm."[22] Most military men appointed to diplomatic posts have had considerable experience in public administration, and it would be wholly proper to describe as career appointments those of General A. G. L. McNaughton (permanent representative on the United Nations Security Council and later chairman of the Canadian section of the International Joint Commission), General Maurice Pope (head of the Canadian Mission in Germany and later ambassador to Spain), and General E. L. M. Burns (representative to the ten-nation disarmament conference at Geneva in 1960). The appointment of Brigadier General Victor Odlum as High Commissioner in Australia in 1942 was not, however, a career appointment in this sense, and he found the transition to diplomatic life somewhat difficult. "I have not yet learned to deal with delicate matters on paper in a correct diplomatic language," he wrote to his Prime Minister soon after arriving in Canberra. "My whole training has been to keep silent on a subject or to approach it openly and directly. . . . I have a rooted objection to dealing with certain religious and racial questions on paper. . . . When men of great eminence talk to me in confidence I do not know how to give you the picture without breaking that confidence. . . ."[23]

Members of the C.C.F. (Socialist) party have been concerned with the danger of developing an ambassador corps based on class and social position, its leader, Mr. M. J. Coldwell, remarking in 1942 that "we have had enough of diplomacy by well-to-do aristocrats."[24] Government spokesmen have agreed, while denying that the condition exists. "Striped pants are not a garment but a state of mind," Mr. Lester Pearson observed in 1954. "That state of mind, I hope and believe, does not exist in the Canadian External Affairs Department or in its Foreign Service."[25] There has been some tendency in Parliament to refer to the need to diversify the professional and occupational background of Canada's heads of missions; the Conservative foreign policy critic, the late Gordon Graydon, was prone to speak at length on the need to appoint "a distinguished member of the agricultural vocation."[26]

An exception to the generally accepted principle of the desirability of drawing heads of missions from career personnel is the position of High Commissioner in the United Kingdom. The High Commissioner has sometimes been regarded by the government of the day as being in a category different from that of other heads of diplomatic missions. When the Conservative Government came to power on August 7, 1930, it found that it had inherited as its High Commissioner in London the appointee of the defeated administration, Mr. Vincent Massey, as the result of an order-in-council passed only a few days earlier on July 24. Although the Prime Minister was later to insist that he had accepted Mr. Massey's resignation, not compelled it, the account given by R. B. Bennett himself of his interview with Mr. Massey on August 13 suggests that an element of compulsion was not lacking:

I put to Mr. Massey [Bennett told the House of Commons] the circumstances in connection with the duty on agricultural implements and his expressions of opinion concerning the then Prime Minister [Arthur Meighen] and the government of the day [1925]. I put his statements to him fairly; I put to him the communications which he had had with the then leader of the opposition [Mackenzie King]. I put the fact to him that within a few months later he accepted office under the man whom he had thus described. . . . Then I turned to him and said, as I now say to his spokesman in the House: "Can you possibly represent the administration of this day, anywhere, at any time, in any place?" Do hon. members think he could? Would any man give such a man a power of attorney to act as his representative, in view of those facts? . . . How could I carry on? How could any Prime Minister carry on business in London with that man as his representative? . . . How could one open his heart to him?[27]

On the day following the interview Mr. Massey submitted his letter of resignation; soon afterward the Prime Minister appointed as High Commissioner in London the former Conservative Premier of Ontario, Howard Ferguson.

In the extensive parliamentary discussion which followed, R. B. Bennett and Mackenzie King sought respectively to justify and condemn what had been done by advancing conflicting theories concerning the nature of the office. According to Bennett, the High Commissoner in London was "not a diplomatic officer in the sense in which that term is used with respect to external affairs. His position with respect to the government is one of the most confidential character and in my judgment the High Commissioner for Canada should be in touch with the government of the day in Ottawa in such a way as to indicate that it has his confidence and he has the confidence of the government."[28] According to Mackenzie King, the high commissionership was "the highest of all diplomatic offices which can be held by anyone belonging to this country" but in no other way distinguishable from those of "our ministers at Washington, Tokyo and Paris. . . . All the qualifications of character, ability, tact and judgment, which are essential in a minister or an ambassador abroad, are equally essential, if indeed not more necessary, in a representative of Canada in Great Britain. . . . I cannot see how my right hon. friend can draw an essential distinction between the two classes of positions."[29] Mackenzie King did not have to put his doctrine to the acid test of retaining as High Commissioner an individual for whom he had little affection or respect, for when the results of the General Election of 1935 became known, Howard Ferguson submitted his resignation directly to the outgoing Prime Minister, leaving Mackenzie King free to appoint Mr. Vincent Massey. Mr. Massey held the high commissionership until the end of the Second World War, when it became, along with the embassies in Washington and Paris, one of those important diplomatic posts among which the three or four senior officials of the Department of External Affairs circulated every few years. In 1957, however, when a Conservative Government came to power in Ottawa for the first time since 1930, the incoming Prime Minister reverted to the earlier quasi-political conception of the office of High Commissioner in London by appointing a leading member of his party and the former Leader of the Opposition.

It remains to be seen whether upon Mr. George Drew's eventual retirement the high commissionership will once again be held by a career official.

THE FOREIGN SERVICE OFFICER

If the heads of Canada's diplomatic missions have been recruited increasingly from the ranks of the Department of External Affairs, their qualities are bound to be those sought and developed by the foreign service itself, thus reflecting the Department's policies of recruitment, training and promotion.

Although Joseph Pope's memorandum of 1907 advocating the creation of a Department of External Affairs was acted on in 1909, not until many years afterwards was effect given to one of its principal recommendations, that there should be recruited for the Department "a small staff of young men, well educated and carefully selected." Even by 1925 the Department could muster no more than three administrative officers in Ottawa, and the shortage was so acute that the Prime Minister and Secretary of State for External Affairs, Mackenzie King, complained that he had no one to assist him in preparing despatches and accordingly had to bear the burden of their composition himself.[30] It was at this time that N. W. Rowell, a former Liberal member of Borden's Union Government whom Mackenzie King was then unsuccessfully trying to bring into his own, wrote to him on the subject of the Department's personnel problems. "I cannot see how it is possible for Canada to deal intelligently with large questions of Imperial and international policy," Rowell observed, "without having a real Department of External Affairs, and having in that Department competent and trained men who would be familiar with the problems requiring consideration and decision by the Government. I do not undervalue what we have, but in my view it is inadequate to meet the present situation."[31] O. D. Skelton, who had himself joined the Department only a few months previously, remarked, on being shown Rowell's letter by the Prime Minister, that it was "essentially right . . . as to the inadequate staffing of the Department. With only Mr. Walker, Mr. Désy and myself (corresponding to Mr. Walker, Mr. Christie and Sir Joseph [Pope] formerly) to deal with wider questions, and with the pressure of correspondence, interviews, and administration, it is absolutely impossible, even with 7-day weeks and 16-hour days, to secure the independent and exact knowledge of external affairs which has now become desirable. However, we should not seek to expand too rapidly."[32] In replying to Rowell, Mackenzie King wrote that he was heartily in agreement with your view that it is not possible to carry on the work adequately without an increased staff, and a consequent measure of departmentalization. We have not done as much in this field as I should myself have liked. My former deputy [Pope], while a very distinguished and competent public servant, naturally, with fifty years' service behind him, looked somewhat askance upon extensive plans of reorganization. Further, the insistent demand for economy in public expenditure, which has come from so many people who do not like to pay the piper for the railway tunes and the war tunes they called, has made expansion in any Department, and not least in the Prime Minister's Department, or Department of External Affairs, a matter requiring special consideration.

A distinct beginning has been made, however. We have recently appointed a very promising counsellor, Mr. Jean Désy, a graduate of the best diplomatic school in Europe, l'Ecole des Sciences Politiques, and latterly Professor of International Law at the University of Montreal, and I hope to add a promising young University graduate every year or two as the work of the Department grows.[33]

The "promising young University graduates" thus recruited in the later 1920's—it was the only significant intake until the later 1930's—more than made up in quality for their very small number, for it was at this time that the Department gained the services of Lester Pearson, H. L. Keenleyside and Hume Wrong. "Dr. Skelton's young men," as they were known, came in time to exert a remarkable and beneficial influence on the fortunes of their country, and indeed of the world.

A second ripple of recruitment took place in the period 1935-9, staffing the new legations opening up in Western Europe and further augmenting the embattled few in the East Block at Ottawa; by 1939 it brought the total number of foreign service officers in the Department to thirty-three. These new recruits, like the distinguished entrants of a decade earlier, came to the Department by the difficult road of a civil service examination. There was at this time of depression and unemployment no shortage of candidates; in one year there were "200 applicants and only 20 qualified and only 4 of the 20 were called in."[34] During the war the acute shortage of personnel was to some extent alleviated by those who came forward from civilian life for temporary service in the Department; for such special assistants the requirements of the civil service examination were waived. It was also decided to dispense with the regular pre-war examination procedure during the first year or two of post-war recruitment. "It seemed quite unfair," the Associate Under Secretary of State for External Affairs explained to the House of Commons Standing Committee on External Affairs,

to ask people who had been in the armed forces perhaps for five years to pass a fairly severe examination of academic standards. We substituted for it a simple examination designed to show whether the candidate had any capacity for thinking for himself and expressing what he thought, and very little more. . . . The main test was to ask the applicants to write an essay on a choice of about ten different subjects on widely selected scientific, literary, historical and military subjects. . . . They are written in English or in French, and they have to write the examination in . . . three hours. That is the simple test, and it is surprisingly effective. . . . On that basis we were able to decide that a large number of candidates were obviously unsuited, and we dropped them. The remainder are brought up for interview by the Board which the Civil Service Commission and ourselves jointly co-operate on.[35]

During the year when this temporary system was in effect (1945–6), 1,000 applicants wrote the foreign service officer examination, of whom a few more than forty were accepted. Asked whether the Department intended to revert to the pre-war system "of having the various examinations so stiff that even the foreign secretary of many nations could not qualify," the Associate Under Secretary replied: "I should not say that we would revert exactly to the pre-war system. I should hope not. That would be rather an urge to adhere to past practices in a changing world; but we will no doubt stiffen the examinations as we get further away from the particular problem of not imposing a handicap on those who have been in the armed services and are a long way from school and university. . . ."[36]

This prediction proved wholly correct for a time. During the decade 1946–56 the two hundred or so university graduate or graduating students ordinarily applying for admission each year were reduced to a hard core of about fifteen succesful candidates by a three-stage process of selection, the first stage of which was a written examination whose formidability may best be judged by the reader:

FOREIGN SERVICE OFFICER, GRADE I
DEPARTMENT OF EXTERNAL AFFAIRS
Written Examination, 1952
PAPER I. TIME: 3 HOURS

The purpose of this paper is to test your capacity to analyze a theoretical problem lucidly. The examiners will base their judgment on the manner in which you present your views and on the cogency of the views themselves.

Discuss *one* of the following:

1. What is the best balance of work and leisure; how should the question of leisure time be approached in modern society?

2. "The form of government of any country is determined by tradition, physical environment and the stage of its economic development".

3. "A Nation, in its influence upon civilization, is not an aggregate of its living people, for they are but part of the whole continuing and historic people. Nor is it a State, for the State is artificial. A Nation is an Idea".

4. "Without justice, what is political rule but brigandage and rapine?" ("Remota justitia, quid sunt regna nisi magna latrocina?")

5. "The first requirement of a sound body of law is that it should correspond with actual feelings and demands of the community, whether right or wrong".

6. "There is no such thing as a science of economics; every system of economic thought is in large measure subjective in that it is posited on desired social goals".

PAPER II. TIME: 3½ HOURS

The purpose of Parts A and B of this paper is to test your interest in, and understanding of, some of the following problems and your ability to discuss them clearly and in logical fashion.

In parts A and B candidates must do three questions with at least one from each part. Part C, which is designed to test the candidate's ability to comprehend the meaning of written material, is compulsory for all candidates.

Part A. Questions on Canada

1. Discuss the feasibility of Canadian membership in the Sterling Area.

2. Discuss some of the implications of recent trends of domestic and foreign investment in Canada.

3. Discuss the contribution to political thought and action in Canada of one of the following: Henri Bourassa, J. S. Woodsworth, Goldwyn [*sic*] Smith, J. S. Ewart.

4. Discuss the relationship of Canadian trade unions to the political life of Canada.

5. Discuss the role of the Federal Government in fostering cultural activities.

6. Discuss Canada's role in the evolution from "British Empire" to "Commonwealth of Nations".

7. To what extent do you think the British North America Act restricts the Government of Canada in the conduct of its external affairs?

Part B. Questions on International Affairs

8. How do you account for the appearance of Titoism in Yugoslavia? What are the chances of similar developments in the European Satellites and China?

9. Discuss the movement toward European integration, and assess its prospects.

10. Discuss the role of Christian Democracy in Europe today.

11. In your opinion, in the present international situation do "neutralist" or "no foreign entanglements" policies contribute to world peace? Discuss, using examples drawn from foreign policies of governments in both Europe and Asia.

12. "Stalin has none of Hitler's compulsion to go to war; indeed, the compulsion is all the other way, taking into consideration his own nature, the categories of Marxist thinking, Soviet geography and resources, the nature of the Russian people, and the miserable and unreliable state of the Soviet Union today". Comment.

13. Assess the role of either the United Nations or NATO in preserving international peace and security.

14. Do you think it is desirable to establish at the present time an International Court of Criminal Jurisdiction?

15. Discuss two representative authors from any one of the following countries: France, Germany, U.S.A., U.S.S.R., United Kingdom, Canada, and indicate why you consider them representative.

Part C. Read the passage contained in Appendix A [an extract from Arnold Toynbee, *A Study of History,* vol. I, pp. 299–301] and answer the following questions which are based on it.

1. Summarize in one paragraph of not more than one page in length the theory presented in this passage.

2. The author suggests that in the historical process there is one vital unknown element. Define, and if you agree or disagree with his theory, give your reasons.

3. From the above passage, what does the phrase "Uniformity of Nature" mean to the author and to what extent does it satisfy the author's view of the origin of a civilization?

4. Relate the idea of "Integration of Custom" to "Differentiation of Civilization".

5. In your opinion is the author subscribing to a deterministic theory of history? In a short paragraph, defend your answer.[37]

An examination of this kind favoured, and was no doubt intended to favour, university graduates in such courses as history, political science and economics, and law; and, moreover, university graduates from the stronger universities. In the House of Commons Standing Committee on External Affairs, where officers of the Department were questioned on the theory and practice of its recruitment programme, there was some disposition to express the kind of views found in the Wriston Report on the United States Foreign Service.[38] "I do think we ought to have people in our diplomatic service besides those who are postgraduates of universities across Canada," the Opposition foreign policy critic, Mr. Gordon Graydon, remarked in 1953. "I would like to see the Department of External Affairs a little better balanced up with practical, sound, common sense people."[39] Perhaps because of a fear that the departmental examination displayed a donnish preciosity on the part of the departmental examiners, perhaps because a wider basis for recruitment was felt to be desirable, certainly because of a growing scarcity of good candidates, the written examination underwent an important change in 1956. In that year the so-called "objective-type" examination was introduced: "the Civil Service Commission thinks [it] is useful," a spokesman of the Department explained, thus allowing the implication that his own Department was less certain of its utility. At the same time the written examination was itself shortened and simplified:

FOREIGN SERVICE OFFICER, GRADE I
DEPARTMENT OF EXTERNAL AFFAIRS

1957. TIME: 2½ HOURS

Answer any *two* questions

1. "It is not the terms of the Charter that block the development of the United Nations into a peace-enforcing authority, but the facts of international life in our age". Discuss.

2. A Canadian statesman recently declared that a *Canadian* foreign policy is not necessarily "the same as an *independent* policy". Discuss this statement in relation to Canada's membership in the Commonwealth, the United Nations and NATO.

3. "The problem of disarmament is the problem of security". Is this dictum of the 1930's still valid?

4. What would be some of the results of the application to the contemporary world of the principles of Adam Smith?

5. The guiding principle of Soviet foreign policy has sometimes been described as "all mischief short of war". How characteristic in your opinion is this of the policy of the U.S.S.R. today?

6. What features of Canadian life should a government-sponsored information and cultural programme try to project abroad?

7. Discuss "colonialism" as a factor influencing the policies of countries of East and South-east Asia.

8. Do you believe that the policies pursued by Western democracies since the Second World War bear out the statement made by Walter Lippmann that "faced with these [interdependent] choices between the hard and the soft, the normal propensity of democratic governments is to please the largest number of voters. The pressure of the electorate is normally for the soft side of the equations"?

9. What would be the views on the idea of the integration of Western Europe of any *three* of the following: Machiavelli, the Duc de Sully, Napoleon, Bismarck, Woodrow Wilson?

10. Is Canada a "welfare state"? Should it be?

11. Suggest means by which international law could effectively make for a more orderly world.

12. Discuss some of the implications of industrialization of *either* the Province of Quebec *or* the four western provinces.[40]

Candidates successful in the written examination are called for an oral examination convened in the main cities of Canada and, if sufficient numbers warrant, in some of the larger cities of the United States, the United Kingdom and Western Europe. The examining board normally consists of five members, two examiners from the Department of External Affairs, two outside examiners representing the business and university communities, and a representative of the Civil Service Commission who acts as chairman. An effort is made to secure continuity of representation on the board of examiners, the Civil Service Commission representative and one departmental examiner ordinarily attending all oral examinations in a given year. The examiner's task is the difficult one common to most oral examinations of this kind, to try to assess, on the basis of an interview usually lasting no more than an hour, the candidate's "intellectual capacity, integrity, initiative, personality and appearance."[41] The opinions of one of the Department's most experienced examiners, set down in 1947 as a guide for prospective applicants, disclose something of its assumptions and criteria:

Quand il s'agit de jeunes qui sortent de l'université, l'expérience est plutôt courte et n'offre guère l'occasion de poser beaucoup de questions. Aussi les membres du jury trouvent-ils des questions générales pour faire parler le candidat. Il importe de savoir s'il pense vite ou lentement, s'il pense juste ou non, s'il s'exprime bien, s'il se tire avec ingéniosité de situations imprévues. Tout au cours de sa carrière, il se trouvera dans des situations semblables. Aux conférences internationales, il n'aura pas toujours la réponse exacte aux problèmes qui se posent. Il devra improviser. Parfois il devra temporiser et toujours se tirer d'une passe difficile avec élégance. L'examen oral permet de découvrir certains traits profonds du caractère du candidat.

Certains candidats se présentent avec l'idée bien arrêtée et bientôt évidente de ne pas se compromettre. Ils ne répondent que par monosyllabes aux questions qui leur sont posées. Ou bien ils répondent en Normand. D'autres, au contraire, savant tout, on réponse à tout. Parfois ils ne semblent pas se rendre compte le moins du monde du but de l'examen oral et de la portée des questions. Un jour, un membre du jury posait à un candidat la question suivante: "Si, demain, un gouvernement mondial était établi, qui serait le meilleur premier ministre: un avocat, un homme de science, un théologien ou un diplomate". Il s'agissait de savoir quelle était l'échelle des valeurs du candidat, quels étaient les facteurs qui, à son avis, avaient le plus d'importance dans le gouvernement des hommes. Le candidat fut complètement désemparé. Il refusa de répondre en disant qu'il s'agissait là d'une question purement théorique. Il suggéra même par son attitude qu'il trouvait la question saugrenue et ridicule.

Les candidats feraient parfois meilleure figure s'ils se souvenaient que l'examen a pour but de faire voir leur tournure d'esprit. Ils feraient bonne impression en étant sincères, en se montrant tels qu'ils sont. S'ils pensent lentement, ils auraient tort de vouloir faire croire qu'ils sont rapides; ils se peut que leur lenteur soit compensée par plus de précision, plus de profondeur. Un membre du jury avait posé une question assez difficile à un candidat. Celui-ci, au lieu de se lancer dans de vagues considérations, répondit qu'il n'avait jamais sérieusement réfléchi à la question mais que si l'on voulait bien lui donner deux minutes pour réfléchir il essaierait de donner une opinion qui vaudrait mieux que les banalités qui lui viendraient peut-être tout d'abord à l'esprit. Même si ce qu'il avait à dire plus tard ne fut pas très brillant, il avait mérité une bonne note pour son bon sens, sa prudence. En une autre occasion, un membre du jury demanda à un candidat de lui résumer la question de Palestine. Celui-ce répondit qu'il achevait ses études de droit, si je ne me trompe, qu'il avait à peine eu le temps de lire le journal à l'occasion et que ses notions sur la question étaient trop vagues pour lui permettre de donner une opinion valable. Cette sincérité était encore, dans les circonstances, la meilleure politique. Un secrétaire qui reconnaît son ignorance dans une matière donnée aura tout probablement le courage de l'étudier si cela est nécessaire et, après quelques jours, il sera plus utile que celui qui se contente de notions vagues et s'illusionne volontiers sur l'étendue de ses connaissances.[42]

A candidate who impresses his board favourably during the oral examination is then rated on the basis of his military, business or professional experience, if any, and if he obtains a sufficiently high final mark on all three phases of the competition is graded according to rank and placed upon an eligible list from which appointments to the Department are made as vacancies arise.

The kind of junior foreign service officer that this winnowing is designed to select is typically a graduating student from a university honours course in the humanities or social sciences. He cannot ordinarily be older than thirty years of age, nor may he be younger than twenty-three. He is therefore without much outside experience, and certainly is unlikely to bring to the Department a great deal of specialist knowledge. The role of specialists within the Department has been the subject of much discussion, and properly so. The guiding principle of personnel policy, unimpaired since the days of O. D. Skelton, is that the ideal foreign service officer is someone of all-round ability, capable of performing widely differing assignments at short notice, rather than a highly skilled specialist paying little attention to matters lying outside his field. To this principle the senior administrators of the Department have displayed what at times has seemed an almost perverse attachment, an observer remarking in 1952 that "the man who studied public opinion and wrote a book with George Gallup, Mr. Saul Rae, was moved from the Head of the Information Division . . . , the personnel expert T. W. L. MacDermott was transferred from Head of the Personnel Division, . . . and one official . . . remarked rather proudly . . . that most of the members of the Department who can speak Russian are not working on the Soviet Union."[43] (The deleterious consequences of the generalist approach, which has undergone significant modification in recent years, are noted in chapter v.)

Their devotion to the generalist ideal has caused the senior administrators of the Department to look with some suspicion upon the device of lateral entry, that is, the recruitment of specialists at intermediate or senior levels of advancement. An exception to the rule took place in 1956 when the Department asked the Civil Service Commission to conduct examinations for a small number of specialists in Slavonic, Arabic and Chinese languages and affairs, and in international law and economics. "There were a lot of applicants," a departmental official commented on this experiment, but a good many of them did not appear to have the qualifications which people in our service already possessed. . . . On the whole we find it best to recruit at the bottom—at grade one level—and to promote people as their ability develops and as they acquire experience. . . . If we are looking for, say, a Foreign Service Officer Grade 4 I think you would probably get better results from a man who had come in as a Grade One officer and worked his way up, spending a number of tours of duty abroad and in this country and gaining a certain amount of expertise and knowledge during that period. I think such a man would have more to offer, as a general rule, than a man who came in because he was, let us say, a good economist or an expert on Slavonic languages.

He conceded that "there is a danger of having a closed corporation. I think we are aware of that and trying to meet it."[44]

The recruiting policy of the Department of External Affairs is usually defended on the ground of the superiority of the generalist concept, but there are two practical considerations by which it could as well or better be justified. To a much greater extent in Canada than in the United States or the United Kingdom there is a shortage of qualified specialists in various aspects of international affairs from whom recruits at more senior levels might be drawn. Secondly, the opportunities for advancement of specialists within the Department are necessarily more restricted than in the far larger State Department or Foreign Office. Both these handicaps to specialist recruitment will become less severe with the passing of time.

Since entry to the foreign service is restricted by inclination and necessity to young and inexperienced applicants, the quality of the senior officers of the Department of External Affairs depends to a greater than ordinary degree upon the quality of in-service training and sound promotion policies. Provision for training foreign service officers within the Department is not elaborate, and is confined mainly to the early probationary period of their careers. "We have classes in French for candidates who come in without adequate knowledge of French," the Acting Under Secretary of State for External Affairs informed the House of Commons Standing Committee in 1954. "We do, also, in the case of incoming officers for the first year, put them through a sort of course of training. We send them to different divisions of the department for short periods. We provide courses of lectures. We bring in people from other departments to lecture to them—as well as people from our own Department. Other than that we do not provide special classes or facilities for junior officers to get ahead. We expect them really to learn on the job."[45] Officers failing to measure up to expectations during this initial training period may be released from the Department at this time; this does not often happen, but it does happen. "It is an *ad hoc* way to look at the problem of training," the Under Secretary admitted in 1958, "but, on the whole, bearing in mind that there [are] seldom if ever more than 20 new Foreign Service Officers in any given year, we do not think it would be appropriate to set up too elaborate a school."[46]

There is some opportunity for the foreign service officer to receive specialized training later in his career, particularly training in more difficult languages. A promising officer may be sent for a year to the Middle East Centre for Arabic Studies run by the United Kingdom Foreign Office in the Lebanon, to the School of Oriental and African Studies in the University of London, or the Department of Slavonic Studies at Cambridge University. There has been some discussion of regular sabbatical leave for study and research, but neither senior nor junior members of the Department seem to have followed up the suggestion very energetically. The Department annually appoints one or two members to the National Defence College at Kingston, Ontario, the Imperial Defence College in London and the NATO Defence College in Paris.

Finally, promotion. Do the best men (and women) get to the top? Do they get there soon enough? A former public servant, speaking from long and intimate experience, thought it a legitimate criticism of the Canadian civil service generally that "there is too much of what the Germans call *Gleichschaltung*—too much holding back to the pace of the average. . . . Our present procedures are based on the assumption that the messenger boy might become the deputy minister. By all means let that be so, but if he has the capacity, do not require him to move consecutively from grades one to ten at every stage. If he survives that weary process, the chances are that he will no longer make a good deputy minister."[47] Foreign service officers have suffered rather less in this respect than other members of the public service. During the Second World War, and immediately afterwards, the Department of External Affairs had too few able personnel to fill the rapidly growing number of key positions opening up abroad and at home; individuals of proven performance and greater promise were moved into posts of great responsibility at a comparatively early age, rising in their forties to become assistant, associate and deputy ministers, and heads of missions. But with the pause in the Department's expansion, incoming recruits could look with less assurance than the hopeful entrants of 1946–9 for rapid elevation to policy-making positions. It became harder in a Department of three hundred foreign service officers than in a Department of thirty to keep sight efficiently of younger people of ability, and an element of luck entered inevitably into posting and promotion. It would be wrong to suggest that morale has suffered on this account alone, for the discontent of which tangible evidence may be found in resignations at all levels in recent years must be related to other factors—the improved salaries offered by Canadian universities, the diminished prestige of the foreign service following Mr. Lester Pearson's resignation as Secretary of State for External Affairs in 1957, the strain of working with politicians who have for twenty years been unused to office, and the toll on health and spirit of frequent postings to politically and climatically uncomfortable environments.* Yet the shortage of room at the top has made for some malaise. For the first time in its history the Department of External Affairs experienced difficulty in securing its normal quota of candidates for the foreign service officer competition in 1960.

THE ATTACHÉ

Not least among the pressures assailing the professional diplomatist has been the gradual usurpation of his investigative and reportorial functions by specialists inside his embassy and outside, enjoying or claiming diplomatic status, stuffing the pouches with their reports, frequently by-passing altogether the normal channels of diplomatic communication.† Jostled and hemmed in by specialists, the traditional foreign service officer may well wonder what is left for him to say once the commercial,

*"I regret that our bag of July 12 [1960] contained no political reports," a foreign service officer wrote to his regional desk officer in the East Block from his mission in Southeast Asia. "This was primarily due to the absence of the Ambassador [on home leave] and to the pressure of administration, Colombo Plan matters, etc., which had fallen to me for about three weeks, in addition to my normal duties. During that time, poor X was out with a combined attack of amoebic dysentery, tapeworm and roundworm. But X is now better, and, although he has yet to recover from residual anaemia, he is back at work. Y is now suffering from bacillary dysentery but seems to be able to put in a normal day." As members of the public service foreign service officers may participate in a health insurance plan at favourable rates, but the Department of External Affairs is unable to assume financial responsibility for treatment of illnesses incurred as the result of serving in unhealthy environments. Military attachés, on the other hand, receive the protection to which they are entitled as members of the armed forces, a circumstance not improving morale among their diplomatic colleagues undergoing comparable hardships.

†The dislike shown by career diplomatists for attachés from outside the foreign service is nothing new. "Three attachés, my dear Palmerston," wrote Sir Frederick Lamb from Vienna in 1838, "are as much as this place can bear; more would be like keeping a pension for grown-up pupils." From Lisbon Lord William Russell sent a similar protest: " When they are so numerous the Chancery becomes a sort of Coffee House where the dispatches are read and criticized like newspapers." Quoted in Sir Charles Webster, *The Foreign Policy of Palmerston, 1830–1841,* I (London, 1951), p. 70.

military, press, labour, finance, agricultural, science, and technical assistance attachés have had their say; or, if something in his own despatches has escaped their notice, whether his political superior can possibly find time to read it. The Canadian diplomatist has enjoyed in this regard an experience happier, on the whole, than that of his colleagues in government service elsewhere. The range and number of specialists, while expanding, are not oppressive, and leave him ample scope for significant activity. The machinery for co-ordinating his work with that of functional diplomatists, while not yet perfect, has worked effectively, both in the embassy and at Ottawa, to prevent the kind of inter-agency rivalry that elsewhere reduces the status and morale of the regular foreign service.

The commercial attaché is at once the oldest and most important type of functional diplomatist in the Canadian public service. In relation to him, indeed, the foreign service officer of the Department of External Affairs is something of an interloper, for commercial representation overseas preceded by several decades the exercise of the right of legation. That relations between commercial and diplomatic representatives have been largely devoid of personal rivalry and jurisdictional squabbles owes much to the tradition of interdepartmental co-operation and interchange of personnel. "A man can transfer entirely from the trade commissioner service to External Affairs," remarked the Under Secretary in 1948. "We have made a trade commissioner an ambassador. We have made one a consul-general. We have transferred a trade commissioner to an embassy as first secretary. We have transferred a trade commissioner to be a second man at Canada House."[48] It will be noted that these are examples of one-way traffic from Trade and Commerce to External Affairs; there has been less, if any, flow from External Affairs to Trade and Commerce, a fact reflecting the greater prestige of diplomacy as against commercial representation, and also the pressure exerted by C. D. Howe, when Minister of Trade and Commerce, to find suitable employment for a backlog of senior officials of his Department.

The overseas representatives of the Department of Trade and Commerce are more widely dispersed than those of the Department of External Affairs. In those countries where there is a trade commissioner but no diplomatic representative, the trade commissioner's work may reach into the political sphere, most usefully, perhaps, by providing diplomatic intelligence. Where there is diplomatic as well as commercial representation, the trade commissioner and his staff work closely with the embassy or legation, without being wholly subservient to it. "It is not true that trade commissioners and diplomatic missions report only through or to the Department of External Affairs," the Under Secretary explained in 1952.

We do not seek to channel their reports too rigidly through the head of mission, although the head of mission would be aware of what is being reported. I would put it this way: if the commercial secretary in Havana were to be writing upon the general commercial policy of the government of Cuba, a despatch of that character I should think should more properly be sent by the Ambassador—sent forward to the Department of External Affairs and then distributed to departments of the government including Trade and Commerce who are interested in matters of policy. If, on the other hand, the commercial man were reporting on some detail regarding sugar, for instance, I think the appropriate course would be for him to address his despatch or report to the deputy minister of Trade and Commerce and send a copy of it to the head of mission. I think that satisfies both the proprieties and the practicalities.

Asked whether he considered "the time has arrived when External Affairs should take over the trade commissioners and include them in their department from the point of view of policy, administration, and generally speaking for the good of the country and economy," Mr. Arnold Heeney replied: "That suggestion has been canvassed from time to time both from within the Department of External Affairs and the Department of Trade and Commerce. . . . I am afraid that to answer the question would require a degree of diplomatic skill of which I am not capable."[49] Whatever the merits of this proposal, it would have had at least the effect of removing one source of irritation and grievance—the uncertainty about whether in the absence of the head of mission a foreign service officer of the Department of Trade and Commerce or of the Department of External Affairs should assume the responsibilities of chargé d'affaires.

A far more important problem of jurisdiction is which of the two departments, if either, should be responsible for foreign aid programmes. Canada first entered the field of external assistance to under-developed countries in 1949 through the United Nations programme of technical assistance, and for this reason administration of foreign aid became at the outset the responsibility of the United Nations division of the Department of External Affairs. The inauguration of the Colombo Plan a year later placed the Department's facilities under considerable strain, and it was at this juncture that the powerful and energetic Minister of Trade and Commerce, C. D. Howe, expressed the readiness of his Department to take over the administration of Canadian participation in the Colombo Plan and all other foreign aid programmes. The Department of External Affairs rightly sensed that this interest had been aroused by the commercial and trading possibilities of the venture, but its misgivings, if such there were, vanished at the prospect of relief from administrative burdens rapidly becoming intolerable. Membership on an interdepartmental committee* would, it hoped, enable it to keep a watchful eye on the administration of the programmes and to see that foreign policy aspects were kept well to the fore.

Under the capable direction of the first Administrator of the International Economic and Technical Co-operation Division of the Department of Trade and Commerce, Mr. R. G. Nik Cavell (who was chairman of the interdepartmental committee), this system worked more or less satisfactorily for several years. But the process of clearing proposals with three departments (External Affairs, Trade and Commerce, and Finance), two Crown corporations (Defence Construction, Ltd., and the Canadian Commercial Corporation) and Treasury Board became increasingly irksome. Co-ordination between officials at home and in the field left much to be desired, largely because of the inability of the cumbersome bureaucratic apparatus at Ottawa to delegate sufficient discretionary authority to the men on the spot, with the result that decisions were unduly delayed and opportunities for constructive action needlessly lost.† Finally, the Asian beneficiaries were beginning to complain privately that commercial advantage rather than disinterested philanthropy seemed too often to motivate the donor.

The resignation of C. D. Howe as Minister of Trade and Commerce in June 1957, followed not long afterwards by that of Mr. Cavell as Administrator, offered the new Government an opportunity to re-examine the administration of foreign aid programmes. Three choices lay before it. One was to do what might be done to improve the existing system, without altering its main administrative features. A second was to create a new Department of Foreign Aid, distinct from the Departments of

---

*Composed of the head of the Economic Division, Department of External Affairs; Director, Trade Commissioner Service, Department of Trade and Commerce; Deputy Governor of the Bank of Canada; Assistant Deputy Minister of Finance; and Administrator of the International Economic and Technical Co-operation Division, Department of Trade and Commerce.

†"Most capital and especially technical assistance administration can be carried on at highest efficiency in the countries to which the aid is directed rather than at desks, however intelligently manned, ten or fifteen thousand miles away. . . . An indefensible amount of time is now spent in lengthy and tedious correspondence between field technicians, Canadian missions abroad, and the three Ministries . . . on points of appalling triviality." Keith Spicer, "Some Remarks concerning Canadian Assistance under the Colombo Plan" (unpublished manuscript); and "The Administration of Canadian Colombo Plan Aid," *International Journal*, vol. XVI, no. 2, Spring 1961, pp. 169–82. I am grateful to Mr. Spicer, who conducted extensive field research for his doctoral thesis on Canada and the Colombo Plan, for placing his paper at my disposal.

Trade and Commerce and External Affairs, with its own autonomous corps of career officers. So radical a reorganization might be undertaken in the hope of allaying suspicions of recipients of aid administered by departments primarily interested in trade or diplomacy, improving the morale and effectiveness of field officers by making foreign aid their sole responsibility,* and providing better facilities for creative exchange of ideas between the Ottawa planners and the overseas experts.

The reorganization actually undertaken was far less radical. Responsibility for foreign aid was restored to the Department of External Affairs, just as, five years earlier, the United States foreign aid agency, the Foreign Operations Administration (which had replaced the Mutual Security Administration in 1953), had been abolished and replaced by the International Cooperation Administration under the direction of the Secretary of State. A statement issued by the Prime Minister on August 25, 1960, explained the new arrangements in the following terms:

In recent years the responsibilities for Canada's economic assistance have been divided between the Department of External Affairs and the Department of Trade and Commerce, with co-operation by the Department of Finance.

Recently the idea of economic assistance to underdeveloped countries has acquired a new significance and attraction for a lengthening list of prospective recipients and potential donors.

It has been decided that the administration and operation of aid programmes, in the interests of efficient and expeditious administration and to assure a sound and productive use of the aid programmes, should be placed under one head. An external aid office will be established in charge of an officer to be known as Director-General of External Aid Programmes. Under the direction of the Secretary of State for External Affairs, his responsibilities will be as follows:

(a) The operation and administration of Canada's assistance programmes covered by the general aid votes of the Department of External Affairs;

(b) To keep these programmes under constant review and, as appropriate, to prepare recommendations on them and related matters to Cabinet; to prepare submissions to Treasury Board on financial questions relating to economic assistance;

(c) To ensure co-ordination in the operations of other Departments and agencies of government concerned with various aspects of economic assistance programmes;

(d) To consult and co-operate as appropriate with international organizations and agencies;

*"Although present Canadian aid administrators abroad are generally of the highest individual calibre, few . . . are enthusiastic about the aid aspect of their work, and some of them frankly consider it an annoying impediment to the pursuit of their principal career." Spicer, "Some Remarks concerning Canadian Assistance under the Colombo Plan."

(*e*) To consult and co-operate as appropriate with Canadian voluntary agencies active in underdeveloped countries;

(*f*) To co-ordinate Canadian efforts to provide emergency assistance in the case of disasters abroad; for this purpose to achieve the necessary liaison with the Canadian Red Cross Society and other appropriate Canadian organizations;

(*g*) To be responsible for the internal administration of the External Aid Office; and

(*h*) To perform such other duties as may be required in relation to Canada's external assistance programme.

It has been decided to appoint Mr. H. O. Moran, recently High Commissioner to Pakistan, as Director-General in the External Aid Office, with effect from September 1st.

Unlike his commercial counterpart, the military attaché is a comparative newcomer to Canadian missions abroad. In 1927 the Canadian Government unanimously decided against appointing military officers to the High Commissioner's office in London or to the newly opened legation in Washington.[50] It was not until Colonel G. P. Loggie was assigned to Canada House in 1937 as ordnance representative of the Department of National Defence that any of Canada's missions acquired an official remotely resembling a service attaché. The creation in September 1939 of the Canadian Military Headquarters in London was thought to make unnecessary the appointment of military officers to the High Commissioner's office, and this did not take place until the disbanding of C.M.H.Q. at the end of the war.

Canada and the United States, having not yet appointed service attachés to their missions in Washington and Ottawa, carried on their pre-war military conversations largely through Canadian staff officers who travelled to Washington for the purpose. The mission of the Chief of the General Staff (Major General E. C. Ashton) and the Chief of the Naval Staff (Commodore P. W. Nelles) took place in January 1938 under conditions of great secrecy, General Ashton leaving Ottawa one day, Commodore Nelles the next. Travelling separately, in civilian dress, they arrived at the Canadian legation, their identity unknown (or at least undisclosed) to any of its staff save the Minister himself.[51] They proceeded to discuss with their American counterparts, General Malin Craig and Admiral William D. Leahy, plans for the defence of North America in the event of war with Japan. In April 1938 Colonel N. O. Carr of the Department of National Defence discussed with various United States technical and supply officers in Washington the matériel which a belligerent Canada might acquire from the United States in the event of delay in or failure of delivery from the United Kingdom, and in November of the same year a third discussion on military matters took place between Major General T. V. Anderson of the Department of National Defence and American officers.

Shortly after Canada's declaration of war, there was discussion in the Department of External Affairs of appointing a naval attaché to the Washington legation. (The Navy may have been chosen as the senior service, or because naval problems were most pressing at the time.) It was, however, an R.C.A.F. officer, Air Commodore W. R. Kenny, who became the first Canadian service attaché in Washington, taking up his duties in February 1940. Air Commodore Kenny was instructed to deal with all service matters, but the burden of dealing with army and navy, as well as air force, affairs was from the start a heavy one. The air attaché, reported the Canadian Minister in July, "can perhaps at the moment handle the specific requests for information and action which reach him, but he cannot under such conditions find the time or opportunity for contacts and studies and reports of a general nature which are so useful." He recommended that the Government appoint a naval attaché to the legation, inasmuch as the United States administration was considering sending a naval attaché to Ottawa.[52] The following month a naval and an army attaché were posted to Washington.

Even though all three services now had their representatives in the United States, the Canadian Government felt it still lacked access to the inner councils of the Grand Alliance. Accordingly it pressed for the creation of a Canadian joint staff mission at Washington, similar to the British. This request was opposed by the United States War and Navy Departments "on the grounds that representation through the Permanent Joint Board on Defense and the British Joint Staff Mission met all the Canadian needs for liaison, and that an undesirable precedent would be established for similar requests by other dominions and the American republics."[53] This explanation did not give much satisfaction in Ottawa, and on August 18 the Prime Minister told the American Minister "that the prolonged refusal of Washington to approve a military mission was the only aspect of U.S.–Canadian relationships that seriously troubled him."[54] The Minister, Pierrepont Moffat, made an earnest but unsuccessful attempt to impress his military colleagues with the adverse political effects of their position, but both the United States Chief of Staff and the Secretary of War felt "that foreign political considerations inimical to our military interests should not be allowed to determine the attitude of the War Department."[55]

The entry of the United States into the war spurred a renewed Canadian effort to win acceptance by the United States of a joint military mission at Washington, which in the Canadian view the creation in

December 1941 of the U.S.–U.K. Combined Chiefs of Staff made all the more imperative. Mackenzie King took advantage of Mr. Churchill's presence in the Canadian capital to raise the matter with him:

Said quite openly to him the problem we faced was that while we had been in [the war] during two and a quarter years, things would be so arranged that the U.S. and Britain would settle everything between themselves, and that our services, Chiefs of Staff, etc. would not have any say in what was to be done. That in the last war, there had been a Military Mission at Washington. People thought, in Canada, there should be a Military Mission there now, watching Canada's interests. That he would understand our political problem in that regard.

I got the Chiefs of Staff later to explain the position. He said he thought we should be entitled to have representation there, but expressed the hope that we would take a large view of the relationships of the large countries, to avoid anything in the way of antagonisms.[56]

A fortnight later he told the American Minister that he "was very critical of the attitude of many of our technicians, particularly in the Army and Navy, for trying to settle in two-way discussions matters that directly affected Canada and should be carried on in a three-way discussion."[57]

These persistent complaints eventually were rewarded. In July 1942, after a record of negotiations described by an official historian of the United States Army as "one of the least happy aspects of the U.S.–Canadian World War II relationship,"[58] a Canadian Joint Military Mission, with self-contained naval, army and air force staffs, was created in Washington. (The extent to which it succeeded in prying strategic secrets out of the Combined Chiefs of Staff is discussed below in chapter v.)

The chairman of the Canadian Joint Military Mission was Major General Maurice Pope, who in addition to being a military representative on the Permanent Joint Board on Defence, had since March 1942 been the representative in Washington of the War Committee of the Cabinet "for the purpose of maintaining continuous contact with the U.K.–U.S. Combined Staffs and the Combined Planning Committees, and to represent the War Committee before the Combined Staffs when questions affecting Canada were under consideration."[59] The original intention had been to appoint General Pope as the representative of the Chiefs of Staff Committee rather than as the representative of the War Committee but, according to General Pope's own account, "the Navy and Air Force would have none of this" since it appeared to offer the Army a privileged channel of communication.[60] But to have offered equal status to all three services would have encountered American opposition. Asked "whether he thought it would have been possible to secure recognition for three Canadian Service representatives in Washington at the same level and with the same status that had been accorded General Pope," the American Minister in Ottawa "said emphatically that, in his judgment, it would not have been possible, and that if [the Canadian Government] had endeavoured to insist on separate top level representation for the three Defence Departments, none of these Washington representatives could have enjoyed the position *vis à vis* the Combined Chiefs of Staff which he expects General Pope to fill."[61]

The number of service attachés posted to Canadian diplomatic missions was greatly increased following the Second World War. By 1948 the Department of National Defence was represented in Belgium, Czechoslovakia, Denmark, France, Germany (Bonn and Berlin), Italy, Japan, the Netherlands, Sweden, Turkey, the United Kingdom, the United States, the U.S.S.R. and Yugoslavia, although in some cases the representative was responsible for more than one of these countries. The manner of appointing service attachés was described in 1948 by the Under Secretary of State for External Affairs:

If the defence services feel that it would be desirable from their point of view to have a service attaché at a diplomatic mission they approach the Department of External Affairs to get our general views on the desirability or otherwise. We normally say, if they wish to send a service attaché, that is all right with us. . . . There have been one or two occasions where we thought on certain grounds it was undesirable to have a service officer at a diplomatic post,* but normally we do not object. The final appointment is made by the Department of External Affairs after agreement in the appointment has been reached with the Department of National Defence.[62]

The service attaché, once posted to a diplomatic mission, is under the authority of the head of mission and subject to removal from the post at the discretion of the head of mission.[63] Like the commercial attaché, he has a dual responsibility, to the head of mission (and through him to the Department of External Affairs) and to the Department of National Defence. He is required to send reports of general interest to the Canadian government through the head of mission to the Department of External Affairs, furnishing copies of such reports to National Defence Headquarters; only reports of other than general interest are sent directly to his own Department. On one occasion during the Second World War the service representatives in Washington failed to follow

---

*One such occasion arose in 1947, when the R.C.A.F. wanted to appoint an air attaché to the High Commissioner's office in New Delhi. The "certain other grounds" on which this proposal was thought undesirable presumably included the prospect, if it were adopted, of making a similar appointment in Karachi.

this procedure. At a meeting of the War Committee of the Cabinet on May 14, 1943, Mackenzie King

"spoke out very strongly against some of the officials of the Defence Department not forwarding to me, as Prime Minister [and Secretary of State for External Affairs], important documents which came from our military staff at Washington. . . . I said that no document in the public service should be concealed from the Prime Minister. . . . I made it clear that a direction was to go from the War Committee to the Chiefs of Staff and stated . . . that I was to have for my personal possession, these different communications, that I might be in a position at any time to take full responsibility for what I had done. . . ."[64]

The service attaché, in a word, is in every way impressed by the principle of civilian supremacy that distinguishes the relation between soldiers and governments in Canada (see below, chapter III).

The Canadian government has responded to the increasing specialization of modern diplomatic activity by appointing to its major missions attachés who perform other than commercial or military duties. Press attachés have been a normal part of the personnel of the Washington embassy and of Canada House, London, since 1941, and the subsequent appointment of labour, agricultural, financial, scientific and other specialists has turned these missions into miniature replicas of the federal government at Ottawa. There has not, however, been that extreme proliferation of overseas representation which characterized the conduct of United States foreign policy during the 1950's, when as many as fifty different agencies of the administration maintained their own functional diplomatists abroad, often with only the most tenuous connection with the head of mission.[65]

THE DEPARTMENT OF EXTERNAL
AFFAIRS

One of Joseph Pope's first official acts upon becoming Under Secretary of the new Department of External Affairs he had done so much to bring into being was to cast about for some principles of departmental organization. A study of the Australian Department of External Affairs (created in 1901) did not prove helpful. "Their Department seems to have a much wider sphere of activity than is contemplated for the Canadian one," was the comment of W. H. Walker, the senior of two "chief clerks" with which the Department had been provided, "and while the information supplied [by the Australian Government] is interesting so far as it goes it does not seem to me very helpful towards

establishing an organization or procedure for the new Dep^t."[66] Some
years earlier the Prime Minister while in London had taken "pains to
learn how these things were dealt with there,"[67] and it was accordingly
to London that Sir Wilfrid Laurier decided to send Pope in 1910 "to
look into the Foreign Office system and to collect back records."[68] Pope
was chiefly interested in the latter part of the assignment and spent
several happy weeks at Whitehall busily copying documents. There was
indeed little to be done at this stage about the organization of a Department consisting of a Deputy Minister, two clerks and a secretary, a
budget (for 1909–10) of $14,950, and an office over a barber shop.
An important and far-reaching step was taken in 1913, probably without realization of its beneficial consequences, when the office of the
Canadian Commissioner in Paris was brought under the jurisdiction
of the Department of External Affairs. A precedent was thus created
which, followed in 1921 by the merging of the High Commissioner's
office in London with the Department and later of the missions in
Washington, Paris and Tokyo, forestalled the development of a foreign
service separate from the foreign office as in the United States until
1954.

No further thought appears to have been given to departmental
organization until 1920 when Loring Christie (who had entered the
Department during the First World War and quickly occupied its new
post of Legal Adviser created in 1913) was sent to London "to
investigate the organization of the British foreign office . . . for the
purpose of gathering information which would help . . . in a reorganization of [the] Department of External Affairs."[69] Nothing came of this
investigation, perhaps because, as Mackenzie King wrote afterwards,
the Under Secretary of the Department, "with fifty years' service behind
him, looked somewhat askance upon extensive plans of reorganization."
Sir Joseph Pope's successor, O. D. Skelton, while not averse to such
projects, was not inclined to rush into them, nor did the size of the
Department (which in 1925 contained no more than the three administrative positions with which it had started out fifteen years earlier)
require them. A study was undertaken of procedures employed in the
foreign services of the United Kingdom, the United States, France, Australia and the Irish Free State. In response to a suggestion that the
Department of External Affairs, like the British Foreign Office and
the American State Department, should be organized along regional
lines, Mackenzie King wrote as follows:

A regional basis . . . works adequately only when the staff is sufficiently
large to ensure in each of these regional divisions a number of men who
have specialized in the different subjects and topics that arise. The alternative

procedure, namely, division according to subject rather than by region, has a good deal to be said for it. Probably in the early years of the expansion of the Department we should have to try to combine both methods. At the present time, for example, the Assistant Under Secretary, Mr. Walker, deals with all consular and passport matters and confidential prints, while the Counsellor, Mr. Désy, is taking charge of League of Nations matters and will probably be given special responsibility for the share in the negotiations of commercial treaties which it is my intention that the Department of External Affairs should take in future.[70]

This fusion of regional and functional responsibility was accordingly put into effect. The result was described in 1930 by the Under Secretary:

The work in the Department, so far as our limited staff will permit, is divided partly by subjects and partly by countries. For example, one officer looks after passports; another looks after consular relations; another, the legal aspect of affairs. . . . We also attempt to divide according to countries. One [officer] must specialize in British Empire relations; another must be familiar with the League of Nations and continental affairs; another is familiar with conditions in the United States, and so on. Our staff is not large enough to permit as great a degree of specialization as we would like, but we hope that it will gradually be made more adequate.[71]

While a gradual move in the direction of increased specialization has taken place as the Department has grown to one hundred times the number of its original personnel, the basic principles of departmental organization have undergone little change. The fusion of responsibilities for policy and administration, originally the product of necessity, has been thought a virtue in its own right serving to break down departmental barriers and to offset the development of an inner circle of political officers untroubled by the menial chores of keeping house. Thus one of four assistant under secretaries was until recently responsible for the consular, information, legal and American affairs divisions; another, for the Commonwealth, the United Nations, the Far Eastern and the historical divisions; a third for the two economic and the two defence liaison divisions. There is continuous tinkering with the organizational structure. "We allocate our functions and change around our divisions perhaps once every six months to correspond with the work in hand, which changes in character all the time," the Associate Under Secretary explained in 1945, and changes, he might have added, to accord with the interests and capacities of the senior officials who happen to be at home rather than in the field. He went on to describe the organization of the Department as it existed at that time:

To start at the top, there is Mr. Robertson, Under Secretary, while I [Hume Wrong] am the Associate Under Secretary. I have the special responsibility of supervising the political divisions of the Department while Mr. Robertson, in addition to his legal responsibilities as deputy minister, supervises the other divisions of the Department directly. Then the next two senior members of the staff are Mr. Read, Legal Adviser, and Mr. Beaudry, Assistant Under Secretary. There are three divisions dealing with political questions. . . . The first of the three divisions deals with questions of international organization and general matters affecting the peace settlement. The other two are geographical. They deal with political affairs in certain areas. One takes in Europe and the Commonwealth. It is a large assignment. The other, the American continents and the Far East, on the political side. Then we have a legal division which is again extremely active at the present time and rather hard pressed. It looks after the functions you would expect a legal division to do, including the drafting of international instruments. . . . Then there is an economic division which has to work very closely with the other divisions. . . . It handles the current economic business passing through the Department and is responsible for conducting a good deal of liaison business with the other Departments at Ottawa. Then there is the diplomatic division which deals with the diplomatic corps in Ottawa and its problems, and has general responsibility for certain other questions such as passports and questions of immigration. . . . We have recently established an information division. . . .[72]

Within a year a new treaty division was added, as well as a new administrative division; by 1948 the Department's organizational chart bore little similarity to that in use in 1945. The first political division, formerly dealing with international organization, had become the United Nations division; the second political division, formerly dealing with both Commonwealth and European affairs, had given way to a European division and a British Commonwealth division; the diplomatic division had issued in a protocol division and a consular division; while to deal with the Department's rapidly growing staff and the problems of its posting overseas a new personnel division had been added. Finally, the Associate Under Secretary had been replaced by two assistant under secretaries. "The general scheme of organization," the Under Secretary explained in 1948, "is that the three geographical divisions . . . are under the direct supervision of the assistant Under Secretary of State in charge of the political side of the Department. Certain other divisions, the United Nations, the consular, the legal, the economic and the information divisions report directly to me. The personnel division and the administrative division are under the charge of the assistant Under Secretary of State in charge of administration."[73] In 1949, the year of the Atlantic Pact, the defence liaison division was created, "having to do," the Under Secretary stated, "with matters in which we are interested jointly with the Department of National Defence."[74]

During the next decade eight more boxes were added to the departmental organization chart, bringing the total number of divisions from twelve to twenty; a press office, an inspection service, and a political co-ordination section were also acquired. On the geo-political side the number of divisions rose from three to five, Far Eastern and American affairs finally acquiring divisions of their own, while in 1957 a new Middle Eastern division was "entrusted with the serious problems which have of late brought east and west face to face in that troubled area," and charged with providing "advice . . . on the political aspects of Canadian participation in the United Nations Emergency Force."[75] In 1960 a Latin-American division came into being, and consideration was being given to the formation of an African division to end the existing anomaly of dealing with Africa south of the Sahara, so much of it lying outside the Commonwealth, through the Commonwealth division. The despatch in August 1960 of some five hundred Canadian troops as part of the United Nations presence in the Congo Republic could be expected to produce greater attention to African affairs within the Department, whose first African desk officer was appointed only in 1957.

To secure the optimum liaison among the different divisions of their Department, its senior officers have resorted to a variety of formal devices. The practice of weekly meetings of division heads was discontinued some years ago, and the principal method of co-ordination is now the regular morning conference between the Under Secretary and the assistant under secretaries. But the most important catalyst of communication continues to be supplied by the traditions and *esprit* of the foreign service officers themselves. The Department is still small by the standards of Washington or London, and as less than half of its members serve at any given time in Ottawa it is possible to get to know all one's colleagues slightly and some of them well. But in the last analysis much depends upon the receptivity of those at the top to the ideas of those further down. Generalization is hazardous, but it is true to say that senior officials of the Department profess their readiness to entertain suggestions of their juniors, and that—a more revealing test—most of the juniors appear satisfied that access to the higher echelons is as easy as might reasonably be hoped for.

A different aspect of communication is that between members of the Department and their political masters. All members of the Department could find in Mr. Lester Pearson (who had been one of them for twenty years) an accessible and receptive audience. Perhaps in this respect his successors were bound to suffer by comparison. But there was some feeling in the Department that, by 1961, making every allowance for the different background and personality of their new Minister, its resources were not being exploited as fully as these deserved.

Chapter Three

THE MILITARY
ESTABLISHMENT

THE CIVIL-MILITARY TRADITION

That the influence of the military establishment upon national policy has increased, is increasing, and ought to be diminished, most liberal-minded people find it easy to agree. The widespread acceptance of this proposition in Canada must not however be thought to stem solely from a commitment to liberal democracy; its greatest support is found, or used to be found, in the authoritarian, anti-liberal setting of rural Quebec. Rather, it is the result of a variety of historical circumstances placing the military profession in low estate.

For more than one-third of the Canadian people, suspicion of the military mind and of the military virtues derives directly from the central circumstance of their history. French-speaking Canadians are a conquered people, conquered by British arms. That the cry of battle on the Plains of Abraham has been hushed for two centuries has not deprived *la conquête* of the quality of a Sorelian myth, a myth which in the hands of ultra-nationalist leaders remains a potent if waning force for national disruption. Cut off from his motherland by distance and by his distaste for the republican institutions and manners of modern France, the French Canadian was still less capable of responding sympathetically to the imperialism agitating the British Isles at the turn of the century. "The new Britain of Mr. Chamberlain," wrote Henri Bourassa in 1901, "is in sore need of soldiers and sailors to prop the fabric raised by her frantic ambition. Being actually denuded of troops at home, she turns in distress to her colonies. . . . Under miscellaneous names and variagated uniforms—Royal Rifles, Mounted Infantry, Strathcona Horse, Yeomanry—they extort from us whatever they may get in the shape of human material for their army. . . ."[1] Bourassa's interpretation captured accurately enough the mood of his compatriots. The Prime Minister himself took up the cry, expressing the feelings of a great many more than those whose mother tongue was French. "There is a school abroad, there is a school in England and in Canada, a school which is perhaps represented on the floor of this parliament," Sir Wilfrid Laurier declaimed in the House of Commons in 1902, "a school which wants to bring Canada into the vortex of militarism which is the curse and blight of Europe. I am not prepared to endorse any such policy."[2] It was no wonder that successive officers of the British Army, sent from London to take charge of the Canadian militia, came into conflict with the Canadian Government and were eventually recalled at its request. The most celebrated of these episodes were those involving Major General E. T. H. Hutton and Major General The Earl of Dundonald; the former was recalled in 1900, the latter in 1904. In neither case was the motive of the Canadian Government pitched at the highest level of principle, for the most irritating aspect of the General Officer Commanding was his propensity to reduce its powers of patronage in militia affairs. But the Hutton and Dundonald incidents established at the outset of the Dominion's modern history the principle of civilian control over the military establishment. Less happily they reinforced civilian prejudices against the military mind. Both traditions were to persist strongly down the years.

The First World War did as little in Canada as elsewhere for the reputation of the military. More than half a million Canadians fought in France and Belgium; more than fifty thousand died there. "It was European policy, European statesmanship, European ambition, that drenched this world in blood," the Canadian delegate told the First Assembly of the League of Nations,[3] and he might with more justice have included European generals. "The narrowness of his training in the regular army and his lack of adaptability to new conditions militated against his usefulness," Canada's wartime Prime Minister, Sir Robert Borden, wrote afterwards of the British commander of Canadian forces in France until May 1916;[4] and what he saw and learned of still higher levels of command disturbed him even more. No attempt was made by the British Prime Minister to conceal from him the "constant mistakes [of the generals], their failure to fulfil expectations, and the unnecessary losses which their lack of foresight had occasioned." Borden asked Lloyd George "why he had not dismissed those responsible . . . ; and he replied that he had endeavoured to do so but did not succeed in carrying the Cabinet; the high command had their affiliations and roots everywhere; and it was for the purpose of strengthening his hand in dealing with the situation that he had summoned the Dominion Ministers to the Imperial Cabinet." If such was Lloyd George's purpose, the Canadian Prime Minister, for one, did not let him down. On June 13, 1918, Borden spoke to the Imperial War Cabinet. "Gave illustrations of incompetence, lack of system, disorganization, lack of foresight, etc." As the Canadian Prime Minister began speaking, the Chief of the

Imperial General Staff attempted to leave the room but Lloyd George directed him to return and to listen. "Sir Henry Wilson," Borden noted laconically in his memoirs, "was handicapped by his intense vanity and by his love of intrigue."[5] Official dissatisfaction with the High Command was more than equalled by the feelings of the Canadian people, well summed up in a letter to F. S. Oliver from his brother in British Columbia: " . . . the British generals one and all are the most incompetent lot of bloody fools that have ever been collected together for the purpose of sacrificing armies. . . ."[6]

No Canadian general rose high enough in the hierarchy of command to bear direct responsibility for the strategic conduct of the war, but this did not protect the commander of the Canadian Corps in 1917–18, Sir Arthur Currie, from the slurs and accusations which were to hound him later in public life.[7] The only British general to become a Canadian hero, General J. H. G. Byng, Viscount Byng of Vimy, on assuming the governor generalship of the Dominion in 1921 encountered considerable hostility precisely because of his military career.

Finally, the mass of French-speaking Canadians, rallying with surprising enthusiasm to the call to arms in 1914, were quickly alienated by the tactlessness and stupidity of the Canadian Government in relegating French-speaking officers to minor positions, assigning French-speaking soldiers to English-speaking regiments, using in rural Quebec methods of recruitment appropriate to urban Ontario. Enthusiasm soured into sullen resentment and then, in 1917, threatened civil war when the Government decided to impose conscription for overseas military service.[8] The crisis of Quebec during the First World War cast a long and sombre shadow upon the relations of soldiers and governments in years to follow.

SOLDIERS AND GOVERNMENTS:
THE YEARS BETWEEN THE WARS

In 1919 Sir Arthur Currie was appointed Inspector General and Military Counsellor to the militia forces of the Dominion, his first duty being to develop plans for the reorganization of the Canadian militia. He offered three principal recommendations. The existing Department of Militia and Defence should become a Department of National Defence for the three military services, Navy (hitherto the responsibility of the Department of Marine and Naval Services), Army and the nascent Air Force. Second, the Minister of National Defence, together with the Prime Minister and Minister of Finance, in consultation with the Chiefs of

Staff, should form a Committee of State to study all aspects of national security policy. Third, there should be created a Defence Committee of twenty-five members of the House of Commons, empowered to summon before it as witnesses the senior officers of the three services.

Of these three recommendations, the third has yet to be implemented in its original form, although special defence committees of the House of Commons have been created from time to time (see below, chapter IV). The second was put into effect only in 1936, "at the earnest solicitation of the Canadian General Staff."[9] The first proposal, a single ministry for the three services, was not new; it had been first put forward in 1909 by Sir Frederick Borden, Minister of Militia and Defence in the Laurier Government. When it was finally acted on in 1922, the chief incentive was economy rather than efficiency. "What I do want to accomplish, if I possibly can," the Minister of Militia and Defence proposing the necessary legislation frankly conceded to the House of Commons, "is to have a well organized, snappy defence force that will be a credit to Canada without being too expensive."[10]

Machinery for national security policy was developed even more slowly at higher service levels. From June 1927 the Chiefs of Staff could meet formally in their own committee (known as the "Joint Staff Committee" until January 1939 when, following the appointment of one of its members, the Senior Air Officer, as Chief of the Air Staff, it acquired its present title of "Chiefs of Staff Committee"). But it was not until March 1938 that a group of sub-committees and a secretariat, similar to those functioning in the United Kingdom under the Committee of Imperial Defence, were created under the Defence Committee of the Cabinet to plan for various defence measures in the event of war. "The central organization for the coordination of defence," the official historian of the Canadian Army remarked, "was thus gradually improving."[11] But the operative word is "gradually."

Such pre-war preparation for defence as had been accomplished by September 1939 had been due almost entirely to the insistent pressure of the military establishment upon governments reluctant to commit resources to what they regarded as a sterile and unnecessary enterprise. Although the Minister of National Defence privately described the condition of the Dominion's defences in 1936 as "most astonishing and atrocious,"[12] the Government of Mackenzie King did little to improve them. Politicians, taking their cue from public sentiment as politicians must, could perceive neither prestige nor necessity in policies designed to defend the realm. For the realm seemed unassailable. The world was still wide. To the oceans and the Royal Navy might now be added as purveyor of security the great and friendly guardian to the south. Canada was a "fire-proof house, far from inflammable materials";[13] its fortunate inhabitants peered disapprovingly at the distant continent from which invasion seemed so improbable, and rejoiced at the moral virtues of their North American civilization. "We think in terms of peace," the Canadian delegate had informed the League of Nations Assembly in 1924, "while Europe, an armed camp, thinks in terms of war."[14] Canada and the United States, Mackenzie King told the same long-suffering body a few years later, had ceased "to rely on Force, we have looked to Reason as the method of solving our differences."[15] Soldiers, whose sense of duty and professional instinct alike impelled them to bring the forces at their disposal to a peak of efficiency and strength, could hardly accept such assumptions. Their duty was to defend the realm; and if their planning for a time disclosed a curious conception of whom it was necessary to defend it against (for as late as 1926 "Defence Scheme No. 1" for use in the event of armed attack by the United States was circulating under top secret classification among Canadian military districts[16]), their assumptions proved in the event to be more relevant than those of their civilian masters.

The differing perspectives in which the Canadian Chiefs of Staff, on the one hand, and the members of the Government together with key officials in the Department of External Affairs, on the other, saw the worsening crises in Europe and the Far East produced a certain tension between the two groups, similar to that prevailing between military and civilian authorities in nearly all the democracies during the years between the wars.[17] The service chiefs thought their political masters altogether too optimistic about the prospects for Canada's remaining outside a European war and, in the event of the Dominion's involvement, altogether too craven concerning the extent of its participation. The Government thought the military unduly impressed by the danger of war, regarding its estimates of Canadian defence needs as both greatly inflated and politically unrealistic. It was also concerned lest pre-war planning and military liaison with the United Kingdom place in jeopardy Canada's right to decide the nature and extent of participation in any future war. An illustration of this concern is offered by the decision of the Cabinet early in 1937 to have the Minister of National Defence examine what were known as the "liaison letters" with a view to determining whether the practice was harmful and ought to be ended. The liaison letters consisted of correspondence between senior staff officers of the Department of National Defence and their counterparts in the United Kingdom; it dated from 1910, but it was of course the more recent correspondence in which the Canadian Government was interested. The Minister, Ian Mackenzie, duly went through the material. In his report to the Cabinet he conceded that much useful information had been exchanged in this way, but noted, with evident concern, a tendency on the part of certain senior Canadian army officers to assume that in the event of war an expeditionary force would be despatched from the Dominion. He thought that discussion of high policy in the liaison letters was a dangerous practice, and recommended that any correspondence between the General Staffs in Ottawa and London pass in future through the Department of External Affairs, so as to be subject to political surveillance. This henceforth became established procedure, doubtless to the irritation and possibly to the disadvantage of the officers concerned.

THE SECOND WORLD WAR:
THE PRINCIPLE OF CIVILIAN
SUPREMACY

The outbreak of the Second World War naturally increased the influence of the military establishment upon national policy, if only because the military establishment was enlarged twenty-fold. And yet the distinguishing characteristic of civil-military relations in Canada from 1939 to 1945 was the extent to which, with one threatened exception to be discussed below, the civilian authorities remained firmly in control of the country's war effort. Canadian experience in this respect differed markedly from that of the United States where, according to one authority, "so far as major decisions in policy and strategy were concerned, the military ran the war."[18]

The official historian of the Canadian Army in the Second World War has remarked that the Prime Minister "did not often express a direct opinion on a purely military question."[19] But the crucial point is that there was very little connected with the Canadian war effort that Mackenzie King was disposed to view as "a purely military question" and therefore beyond the range of his own knowledge and judgment. In part this was a reflection of his temperament and style of leadership—his fussing over detail, his reluctance to delegate responsibility—but in the main it was because over every major military decision of the war, particularly those decisions concerning the disposition of troops for battle, there loomed insistently and obsessively the question of conscription. Mackenzie King's first major policy statement of the war had been to assure Parliament and the nation that "the present Government believe that conscription of men for overseas service will not be a necessary or an effective step. No such measure will be introduced by the present Administration."[20] This was not a policy of which, all else being equal, commanders of Canada's armed forces could in their hearts approve; five years later, when it seemed to presage military disaster, they were to use drastic means to change it, in the event successfully. But in the interval the commitment to voluntary enlistment conditioned every decision of wartime policy, leading the Canadian Government to scrutinize the political implications of military operations more closely, perhaps, than any of the Allies.

Unlike the United States, Canada did not enter the war as the result of treacherous and costly attack on its own territory, rendering it ready to make any sacrifice needed for revenge and retribution. "I am taking the word of the General Staff," a member of the United States House of Representatives had remarked at the time of Pearl Harbor. "If they tell me this is what they need for the successful prosecution of this war and for ultimate victory, I am for it."[21] No such Ludendorff philosophy was to be found in the Canadian House of Commons in September 1939, or, for that matter, in the Canadian Cabinet. At its meeting of September 5 the Cabinet Defence Committee instructed the Chiefs of Staff, about to prepare their estimates for military expenditure, to hold them " to very moderate levels";[22] when estimates to the amount of $500 million were accordingly submitted, the Cabinet promptly cut the sum in two, and told the Chiefs to work to the reduced figure. The appropriation of $250 million was judged sufficient to raise, equip, train and despatch to the United Kingdom an army division, and to begin intensive air training in Canada. A start on this programme having been made, the Government was dismayed to receive from the United Kingdom a proposal that the Dominion should become the centre for training Australian, New Zealand and British airmen as well. "There was general regret," Mackenzie King wrote in his diary, "that it had not been made at the outset so that our war effort would have been framed on these lines instead of having to head so strongly into expeditionary forces at the start." But he was quick to perceive a related advantage for the longer term: "With concentration of Canadian energies on air training and air power and therefore less pressure for a larger army, there would also be less risk of agitation for conscription."[23] Accepted in principle by the Cabinet, the British Commonwealth Air Training Plan, after long and acrimonious negotiation with the British authorities, was to make its great contribution to Allied victory; the original expectation of the Canadian Government that participation in the plan would suffice as Canada's part in the war effort did not outlast the end of the "twilight war" by many weeks.

By February 1940 some 23,000 Canadian troops had been disembarked in the United Kingdom. The Commander of the 1st Canadian Division was Major General A. G. L. McNaughton. His nomination by the Prime Minister was an act of the highest political importance, and Mackenzie King so regarded it. As an officer with the Canadian Expeditionary Force during the First World War, General McNaughton had been haunted by the needless slaughter of his troops; as president of the National Research Council he had become convinced that science and technology, pressed into military service, could prevent a repetition of the carnage in any future conflict. No strategic doctrine could better suit the requirements of a manpower policy based on voluntary enlistment, and Mackenzie King was immediately attracted by the suggestion put forward by Norman Rogers, his Minister of Labour, on September 22, 1939, that McNaughton should command the first expeditionary force of the Second World War. In an interview with the Prime Minister on October 6, McNaughton expounded his views on how the war ought to be fought: the main commitment should be "along the lines of [industrial] production, and . . . every effort should be made to arm and equip the troops to spare human lives." This conception was wholly gratifying to Mackenzie King, and McNaughton's command was announced later in the day. "There could be no question about McNaughton being the best equipped man for the purpose," Mackenzie King wrote in his diary. "I have done my best with my colleagues to remove prejudice which I know there has been against him on account of his tendency to organize matters to the maximum with respect to possible conflict. . . ."[24] Shortly before proceeding overseas, "Andy" McNaughton was quoted in a newspaper despatch as saying: "If I am known for anything it is for the urgent insistence on using guns rather than the lives of our troops and for a proper co-ordination of all arms."[25] Under such an officer, the Prime Minister felt, the problem of reinforcements was unlikely to become acute, and the pledge not to conscript for overseas service and the unity of the nation in wartime could both be maintained.

The confidence reposed by Mackenzie King in his commander did not, however, go so far as to allow him complete discretionary authority to commit his soldiers to battle. This General McNaughton discovered to his chagrin when, faced with the need for troops to forestall enemy action in Norway, the British War Office turned to the G.O.C. 1st Canadian Division on April 16, 1940. In less dire circumstances the

British Government ought more properly to have communicated directly with the Canadian Government in such a matter, but in view of the stress of the moment, the need for secrecy, and above all the need for speed, its overture to General McNaughton is wholly understandable. Having ascertained from Canadian Military Headquarters in London that it lay within his legal competence, General McNaughton agreed to commit Canadian forces to the Norwegian theatre before consulting with Ottawa. Thirty hours elapsed between this commitment and the receipt at the Department of National Defence of a telegram from the Canadian commander stating that he had designated some thirteen hundred of his men to proceed as part of a British force to attack Trondheim. In the absence from the country of the Prime Minister, the matter was dealt with by the Acting Prime Minister and Minister of Finance, Colonel J. L. Ralston. On the evening of April 17, he, the Postmaster General (Mr. C. G. Power) and the Chief of the General Staff considered McNaughton's message. They agreed that there was no alternative to approval of Canadian participation, but strongly objected to the manner in which the decision to commit troops had been taken. On Ralston's instructions a telegram was sent ("during my absence," Mackenzie King later minuted, "without knowledge or authority"[26]) approving the expedition but observing "that such a commitment should not have been entered without prior reference to National Defence and approval of Canadian Government."[27] A more detailed observation was sent to the High Commissioner in London:

We would have expected that Canadian Government would have been informed by United Kingdom Government immediately participation referred to was required. . . . We feel that when consultation commenced intimation should have at once been given by yourself or G.O.C. to afford Canadian Government reasonable opportunity pass on a disposition of such importance to Canadian people as diversion of a portion personnel of present formation to a special Mission of this kind which is a radical departure pre-considered policy and plan.[28]

When, later in the same year, it was rumoured that there was a proposal to send Canadian troops from the United Kingdom to fight the Italians in North Africa so as to gain battle experience, the matter was referred to the Canadian Government. The Prime Minister was much opposed to the idea. "I strongly stated my view [to the War Committee of the Cabinet]," Mackenzie King's diary for December 4, 1940, reads in part,

that we owed it to our men to seek to protect their lives. . . . I thought the logical thing was to have Canadians continue to defend Britain . . . and not to begin to play the role of those who want Empire war. Clearly, the Army people wish this, and Power, I am afraid, has come around to their point of view and has rather sanctioned it with them. . . . [I] insisted on a message being sent to Ralston that no final disposition of troops was to be made until our War Committee had had a chance of getting both sides. Also letting him know, as matters stood, we were opposed to our people being sent to the Suez. . . .[29]

It was later known that there had been no intention of sending them.

In the spring of 1941, the Minister of National Defence stated in the House of Commons that the decision to commit troops outside the United Kingdom was a decision to be taken by the Government of Canada, not by the General Officer Commanding. General McNaughton, who had felt keenly the implied rebuke in the cables from Ottawa about the Norwegian operation the previous April, took no more kindly to this statement, and when the Prime Minister visited England in the summer of 1941 used the occasion to raise with him the whole question of his authority to dispose of the troops under his command. "Question of restriction on use of troops," his memorandum of their conversation reads. "Ralston's statement in Commons which we felt had tied our hands. His attitude in the Norway affair. . . . Warning that I would *not* accept censure, and that he should be very certain that he was right before he gave it."[30] The War Committee of the Cabinet discussed the matter on September 10, and it was there remarked that "while troops could not be sent out of the United Kingdom on the sole authority of the Corps Commander under the law as it stood, it might be desirable to extend his authority to include operations based on the British Isles."[31] In October, the Minister of National Defence had further discussions in England with General McNaughton, resulting in Ralston's cabling Ottawa that it was desirable to widen the discretionary authority of the Corps commander (as McNaughton had by this time become) "to cover future *minor projects* of . . . temporary nature. . . . Extreme need secrecy argues against prior submission each case of such plans to Governmental authority. Recommend War Committee of Cabinet now forward McNaughton general authority to act in such cases subject to his own judgment. He will notify Minister by most secret means in general terms prior to event where practicable [italics added]."[32]

To this procedure the War Committee agreed on October 29, 1941. But the first occasion for the exercise of the new authority of the Corps commander was the projected raid on Dieppe, an operation even in the planning stage not properly described as a "minor project." Accordingly, when General Montgomery first broached the proposal to him on April 30, 1942, General McNaughton thought it wise to consult with the Canadian Government. "Plans are now being made," he cabled, "which involve operations of type indicated but on a scale which cannot properly be classed as 'minor'," and requested that the word "minor" be deleted from the phrase "minor projects of a temporary nature" then setting the limit beyond which his discretion was not to be exercised. The War Committee considered this request on May 1, and agreed to authorize General McNaughton to proceed with the Dieppe operation on the understanding that both he and the United Kingdom authorities approved of the plan. McNaughton's affirmative decision was relayed to the Government on May 15, and the destiny of the ill-fated venture was sealed.[33]

The firm control exercised by the Canadian Government over the commitment of its troops to military operations may be illustrated further by the procedures followed prior to the disposition of forces to the Far East, the Mediterranean, the Northeast Pacific and North-west European theatres of war.

The request for "one or two Canadian battalions from Canada" to reinforce the British garrison in Hong Kong was telegraphed to the Canadian Government by the Dominions Office on September 19, 1941, following approval of the overture by the British Prime Minister who had in turn accepted the advice of his Chiefs of Staff. The proposal was considered by the War Committee of the Canadian Cabinet on September 23, but decision was deferred pending consultation with the Minister of National Defence (then absent in the United States) and examination by the Canadian General Staff. "On 2 October the Minister of National Defence reported to the Cabinet War Committee that the United Kingdom Government's suggestion had been referred to him and approved, after examination by the General Staff. The Committee confirmed the approval for the dispatch of the two battalions, noting that the actual units would be selected by the Minister of National Defence in consultation with the General Staff."[34] (The lack of adequate intelligence facilities leading to this disastrous decision is noted below, in chapter v.)

The commitment of Canadian troops to the campaign in Italy was a more complicated decision, for certain differences of opinion appeared between the Government and the army command. The former was by the summer of 1942 becoming increasingly responsive to public pressure favouring a more active military role for Canadian troops overseas. Two very different motives must be distinguished. The argument that at least some Canadian forces ought to have large-scale battle experience before exposure of the whole Army to the ordeals of the projected but frequently postponed cross-channel invasion was a military argument, and on the face of it sound. But there was also a political argument to the effect that continued inactivity of Canadian troops was damaging to the prestige of the Dominion and might adversely affect its influence on the shaping of post-war policy. The Government, while appreciating the first, did not overlook the second. When the Minister of National Defence met with the British Prime Minister in the United Kingdom in October 1942, Ralston sought to impress Mr. Churchill with the urgency of its request that Canadian soldiers be used in battle at the earliest opportunity. Months of inactivity passed. In March 1943 the Canadian Prime Minister cabled to Mr. Churchill to express his Government's regret at the decision not to employ Canadian troops in the coming Mediterranean campaign, and urged its "earnest re-examination."[35] But the Canadian commander, anxious to preserve his Army intact, viewed with displeasure any project that threatened to divide it, and shared not a bit his Government's concern with the political implications of the decision. "I do not recommend that we should press for employment merely to satisfy a desire for activity or for representation in particular theatres," General McNaughton signalled on March 20. This recommendation the Government felt obliged to disregard. Strong diplomatic pressure was brought to bear upon Mr. Eden and Mr. Churchill, resulting in a directive from the latter to the Chief of the Imperial Staff to include the Canadians in his next operation.

This proved to be the Sicilian campaign. General McNaughton, acquiescing in the diversion of his forces, insisted on his right to pass upon the feasibility of the operation from a military standpoint; after three intensive days of study and consultation he reported to Ottawa that he regarded Operation Husky as "a practical operation of war." On receiving this assurance, the Canadian Government authorized the participation of the 1st Canadian Division, which embarked at the end of June, and landed on the beaches of southern Sicily on July 10.

The Allied conquest was achieved in thirty-eight days. In the urgency of the need to follow up the successes in Sicily with a strike across the Straits of Messina to the Italian mainland, the precise role of the Canadian forces had been neglected. Would they, having gained battle experience in the campaign just concluded, be returned to the United Kingdom to reunite the Army and share with those who had remained the lessons learned in combat? Or would the 1st Division press on to Italy, and perhaps be joined there by more Canadian forces from the United Kingdom? Asked on July 29 for his recommendation to the War Committee, General McNaughton stated to the Minister of National Defence that "the important thing for Canada at the end of the war was to have her Army together under the control of a Canadian," and that he "was opposed to the dispersion of the Canadian Army. . . .

If the Canadian Government decided upon dispersion, then . . . it would be wise to put someone in control who believed in it."[36] This development was not, indeed, far off. The War Committee favoured increased Canadian participation in the Italian campaign. On August 16 Mackenzie King discussed the matter with Mr. Churchill in Washington. The British Prime Minister told him

that the question had been raised by McNaughton, I gathered, as to whether our men going to Italy was to be regarded as part of the one operation. He asked me if I could say that it was. I told him I had always understood that Sicily was simply a step to invading Italy, and to the invasion of Europe from the South. I would, however, like to confer with the Minister of Defence before giving a definite word. He said to me they may be landing there at any moment. They are probably already almost there. I said I would have the matter checked up, but I felt quite sure that the Government had always regarded the whole operation as one. Apparently McNaughton has questioned this.[37]

Mackenzie King consulted Ralston, who informed him that after examining the record he was satisfied that Canadian troops had been committed for the Italian as well as for the Sicilian campaign. General McNaughton was advised of this interpretation. On October 12, 1943, the War Committee formally endorsed Operation Timberwolf, involving the build-up of the 1st Division to corps strength by diverting to Italy troops from the United Kingdom. This endorsation was not without its effect in bringing about, before the year's end, General McNaughton's relinquishment of his command.

The decision to use Canadian troops in the campaign to expel Japanese forces from the Aleutian Islands in the Northeast Pacific was one in which the military played an important and what the Prime Minister regarded as an improper part. The matter was first raised when General John L. DeWitt, Commanding General of the United States Western Defence Command (including the Alaska Defence Command), visited Major General G. R. Pearkes, the Canadian G.O.C. Pacific Command, at Vancouver on April 19, 1943. The two officers discussed the possibility of a combined Canadian-American assault upon the Japanese garrison on Kiska; General Pearkes' report of this discussion, however, made no mention of proposed Canadian participation.[38] On May 8, the chairman of the Canadian Joint Staff Mission in Washington, Major General Maurice Pope (who also was a member of the Canadian section of the Permanent Joint Board on Defence and acted as the War Committee's representative to the Combined Chiefs of Staff), discussed the project with the Secretary of the United States section of the P.J.B.D., Mr. J. D. Hickerson of the State Department:

Hickerson . . . said he proposed telling me of something that had been on his mind for some time. In doing so, however, he wished me to understand that he had no knowledge whatever of the plans of the U.S. Joint Chiefs of Staff. It was obvious, however, that sooner or later the general position would be such as to enable them to mount an operation to drive the Japanese out of Kiska and Attu. When that time came, Canadian troops, in his view, should participate. . . . He had no idea of the forces that would be involved and from his own point of view a mere token force would be adequate. In any event he proposed to take such action as was in his power to see that an invitation be extended to the Canadian authorities.[39]

General Pope observed that "should the idea commend itself to the Canadian Government, it would appear to be more appropriate for us to intimate to the U.S. Joint Chiefs of Staff that we were desirous of associating ourselves in such a project rather than to sit quietly awaiting an invitation to do so."[40]

This conversation General Pope duly reported to the Chief of the General Staff in Ottawa, Lieutenant-General K. Stuart, and on May 12 General Stuart authorized General Pope to raise the matter with the Chief of Staff of the United States Army, General George C. Marshall. But this authorization had been given without previous consultation with the Canadian Government. "In Stuart's message," General Pope recalled afterwards,

there was a phrase which ran generally "that he had not yet consulted the Minister in this respect". In the light of this governing phrase, the "heresy" of his instructions struck in my mind with the clarity of the click of a pebble thrown against a rock. . . . For, more or less in the words of an External Affairs telegram that once came to my notice, "the right to dispose of its fighting forces is one that the Government especially reserves to itself".[41]

Despite his misgivings about how the matter was being handled, General Pope called on General Marshall. "While he undertook no commitment of any kind, [Marshall's] manner seemed to indicate agreement in principle" to Canadian participation in the Kiska operation; on May 24, General Pope was informed by Marshall that the United States officers commanding in Alaska were "delighted at the prospect of having units of the Canadian forces associated with . . . present and future operations in the Aleutian area." Marshall had authorized the American commander, General DeWitt, to confer immediately with General Pearkes to work out arrangements.[42]

It was only after this conference between the Canadian and American commanders had taken place that the War Committee of the Cabinet learned, at its meeting on May 26, of any plans to employ Canadian troops in the Alaskan theatre. "Personally," Mackenzie King commented after the meeting, "I think the Minister of Defence should have been the one to be taking, if anything of the kind were contemplated, the initial step in discussion with the War Committee of the Cabinet," and the editor of his diary remarks that his "initial irritation that this Canadian participation in the expedition had been suggested to the Americans by the military authorities coloured his whole subsequent attitude to the Kiska expedition."[43] At the War Committee meeting the next day (May 27), Mackenzie King

objected strongly to our Chiefs of Staff and others of the High Command in Canada negotiating with corresponding numbers in the U.S. before the Minister had a full knowledge of what was proposed, the War Committee included, and, most of all, myself as the Prime Minister. It was fully apparent that Stuart had gone ahead with his own officers and Pearkes, on the Pacific Coast, and that he, Pearkes, had gone further with his corresponding number in the States, in agreeing to a course of action which would involve our troops being engaged actively with U.S. troops against the Aleutian Islands. I did not object to the project as such, but pointed out that the procedure was entirely wrong; that the Government would be in an indefensible position if it were allowed to go further without being wholly regularized. . . . It was finally agreed that the communication would have to come from either the President to myself, or Stimson to Ralston, to get matters on Ministerial level and out simply of the military level; indeed this whole thing has worked from the bottom up instead of from the top down. . . .[44]

Neither the Prime Minister nor the Minister of National Defence were mollified by the news, reaching them on May 28, that Canadian forces were actually *en route* to Attu. Even though it developed that the forces concerned consisted only of eight officers proceeding to the Aleutians as observers, the Prime Minister continued to feel "incensed that our forces should have been drawn into this business, without knowledge on the part of or request from the Joint Chiefs of Staff at Washington. I would have insisted on a cancellation of the whole thing, were it not that . . . to have cut it off would have raised a serious situation re relation to U.S. and Canadian armies on the Pacific, and probably involve Stuart's resignation."[45]

Mackenzie King's instructions that any proposal to associate Canadian forces with an American expedition against Kiska would have to come from either the President or the Secretary of War were easier to issue than to implement. The task fell to General Pope in Washington, and he has recorded that he learned of his assignment "with mixed feelings," and advised General Stuart "that the U.S. Army might prove tough to move in this matter." When General Pope informed his friend and colleague on the P.J.B.D., Mr. J. D. Hickerson, "that Canada wanted a Stimson to Ralston invitation to collaborate, he laughingly told me to forget whatever Calvinistic tendencies there might be in my system and not to set out in an attempt to reform U.S. Army procedure." The United States Deputy Chief of Staff, visited by General Pope at the Pentagon in the absence of General Marshall, was at first hostile to the request but eventually agreed with another American officer present that there was "no reason why Mr. Stimson should not address a general invitation to Mr. Ralston provided all details were settled through the military channel"; he also told General Pope that "he did not want this approach to Canada to go anywhere near the State Department."[46] The episode illuminates the differing conceptions of civil-military relations prevailing during the Second World War at Ottawa and at Washington.

The desired letter from Secretary Stimson was duly despatched, and after considering it on May 31, the War Committee approved in principle the participation of a brigade group in the Kiska campaign. It instructed the Canadian commander that "the operational control exercized by the United States Commander shall be observed in letter and spirit as fully as if he were a Canadian officer," but also empowered him to withdraw his troops at his discretion and to resort directly to the Canadian Government. It was only at the very last moment, the day before the invading force set out from the American-held island of Adak, that the War Committee, having just received an appreciation from its military adviser, the Vice-Chief of the General Staff, that the proposed expedition represented in his view "a practical operation of war," finally authorized the Canadian forces to proceed.[47]

On landing at Kiska on August 15, the invaders found no Japanese whatever in occupation, and succeeded only in inflicting a few casualties upon their own side. Thirty-four thousand men had attacked an empty island. But if in the light of this anti-climax the caution of the Canadian Government appears excessive, it was not without reason. It was determined not to repeat the disaster at Hong Kong; and a large number of the four thousand Canadians taking part were conscripted men.

The Canadian Government was particularly anxious that the procedure whereby the Canadian commander submitted directly to it his independent appreciation of any operation in which the use of Canadian troops was proposed, so as to allow the War Committee to approve or reject participation as it saw fit, should be followed in the plans for the cross-channel invasion definitely projected for the summer of 1944. On February 21 of that year the Minister of National Defence

cabled a request for such an appreciation to Canadian Military Headquarters in London. "The reason for it," he explained, "is the necessity
for being in a position to assure Canadian homes that Canadian staff
and commanders are assured of timely opportunity to get all the information they need so as to be in a position to exercise their judgment for
the benefit of the Canadian troops for whom they are responsible to
Canada."[48] General McNaughton's successor as commander of the 1st
Canadian Army, to whom this request was referred, was of the opinion
that the Canadian Government's assent to the forthcoming operation
was implicit in its decision in January 1944 to place the 1st Canadian
Army "in combination with" the 21st Army Group, the Allied invasion
force led by General Montgomery. This view the War Committee declined to accept. "The Canadian Government," Ralston wrote to
General H. D. G. Crerar on April 27, "has responsibilities to the people
of Canada and before troops are embarked on the proposed operation
the Canadian Government would expect a report by the Army Commander advising whether or not he is satisfied that the tasks allotted are
feasible operations of war and whether in his opinion the plans formulated for Canadian formations with the resources which are to be made
available can be carried out with reasonable prospects of success. . . .
This is wholly a matter between the Army Commander and the Canadian Government."[49] General Crerar accordingly expressed his satisfaction with the battle plans assigned to the Canadian forces. On May 24
a directive approved by the War Committee was despatched to the
Commander of the 1st Canadian Army. Three of its provisions are of
particular interest:

8. You and the Comd of any Canadian force not operating under your
command . . . continue to enjoy the right to refer to the Government of
Canada in respect to any matter in which the said Canadian Forces are,
or are likely to be, involved or committed or in respect of any question of
their administration. . . .
9. In deciding whether to exercise the authority to withdraw the Canadian
Force [from the 21st Army Group] . . . you will consider all the circumstances including, but not in any way to be restricted to, the following:
(a) Whether in your opinion the orders and instructions issued to you
by the Commander Combined Forces represent in the circumstances a task
for the Canadian Forces which is a practicable operation of war;
(b) Whether in your opinion such task with the resources available is
capable of being carried out with reasonable prospects of success;
(c) Whether in your opinion such orders, instructions or task are at
variance with the policy of the Canadian Government;
(d) Your appraisal of the extent of prospective losses to the Canadian
Force in relation to the importance of the results prospectively to be
achieved;

(e) The effect of such withdrawal in preventing the success of the operation as a whole;

(f) All other factors which you may consider relevant. The authority to withdraw should normally be exercised by you only after reference to the Canadian Government, but, where the exigencies of the moment do not permit such a reference, you have, in deciding whether or not to exercise this authority, full discretion to take such action as you consider advisable. . . .

13. You will keep the Minister of National Defence constantly informed. . . .[50]

It did not prove necessary in the event to exercise either the right of reference or the right of withdrawal; but the Canadian Government's insistence on their explicit formulation and acceptance by the British military authorities at this critical juncture of the war is evidence of the extent to which political considerations were constantly kept to the fore.

The machinery for the political direction of military affairs with which Canada entered the Second World War was the result of legislation dating from 1922 for which, as we have seen, the inspiration had been more that of economy than of efficiency. The centralization of authority under a single Minister of National Defence responsible for all three service arms quickly proved under the pressures of war too great to be borne by any one man, especially after the complex arrangements involved in the British Commonwealth Air Training Plan were added to the load. On March 30, 1940, Mackenzie King urged his Minister of National Defence, Norman Rogers, to consider devolving some of his duties. "I favoured keeping the three branches of the Defence Department under one Minister," Mackenzie King recorded in his diary, "but matters would have to be so arranged as to relieve him [Rogers] of all detail re air development." He asked Rogers whether he felt that Mr. C. G. Power, then Postmaster General, would work well with him. (Mr. Power had been Mackenzie King's first choice as Minister for National Defence at the outset of the war, but was passed over in favour of Rogers when Power himself pointed out that it might be unwise to have the Minister of National Defence from Quebec since this would be sure to raise the conscription issue right away.) Rogers suggested that Mr. Power "should be made an Assistant Minister of Defence, to handle the air work and to be able to answer questions in Parliament."[51] His suggestion was adopted in a slightly different form; on May 22 royal assent was given to an amendment of the Department of National Defence Act (1922) providing for the appointment of a Minister of National Defence for Air. Mr. Power assumed the new portfolio on the following day.

On June 10, 1940, the Minister of National Defence was killed in an air crash. Rogers' successor was J. L. Ralston, and it was Ralston who suggested that Mr. Power combine his portfolio of Minister of National Defence for Air with a new portfolio, that of Associate Minister of National Defence. This post was created by a further amendment to the Department of National Defence Act (1922) on July 12, and Mr. Power was assigned to it, retaining his other portfolio. The amendment specified that the Associate Minister was "entitled to exercise all the powers of the Minister of National Defence." At the same time the post of Minister of National Defence for Naval Services was created, and assumed by Mr. Angus L. Macdonald. A further provision of the amendment was that in the absence of one of the service ministers his powers were to be exercised by another: "if the Minister of National Defence and Associate Minister were absent, the Naval Minister would administer the whole Department, and if he too was absent this authority passed to the Air Minister. Thus the ministers became familiar with their colleagues' functions and duties, with resultant advantages to the public service."[52] It is evident that the system could work well only if the individuals concerned were personally on the best of terms, and on this point one of them, Mr. Power, has since written: "The three were bound together by ties of intimate friendship. . . . Macdonald and Power . . . had such admiration and respect for Col. Ralston that they had no difficulty whatsoever in granting him the primacy over both, and by consent if not by law he was looked upon by all as the senior Minister."[53] This highly effective team remained intact until November 1944, when Ralston and Power resigned, for opposite reasons, over conscription.

Co-ordination of the armed services on matters of high policy was the function of the War Committee of the Cabinet. Where service issues were mainly concerned, the instrument of co-ordination was the Defence Council which, as re-organized on September 13, 1940, consisted of the Minister of National Defence (chairman), the Associate Minister and the Ministers for Naval Services and Air (vice-chairmen), and the three Chiefs of Staff and the deputy ministers for the three services. According to the official historian of the Canadian Army in the Second World War, this institution "was an effective organ of interservice coordination."[54]

Additional apparatus for strategic planning and co-ordination was provided after its creation in August 1940 by the Permanent Joint Board on Defence. Although it was confined to tendering advice to the Canadian and United States governments on defence problems pertaining to the North American continent,* all but two or three of its thirty-three wartime recommendations, many of crucial significance, were accepted. The Canadian section, like the American, was composed of four service personnel and two civilians, but it would be misleading to suppose that the larger service representation led to greater service influence. One of the two civilians in each section acted as its chairman —the Canadian, O. M. Biggar, the American, the redoubtable Fiorello LaGuardia; the other, a senior foreign service officer enjoying the confidence of his government, acted as secretary—the Canadian, H. L. Keenleyside of the Department of External Affairs, the American, J. D. Hickerson of the Department of State. The War Committee of the Canadian Cabinet decided on June 5, 1943, to allow the chairman of the Canadian section to appear at its meetings when the Committee thought his attendance desirable, and this procedure further strengthened civilian influence on the Board. During the early period of its history, the wartime secretary of the Canadian section has recalled, there was a certain tension on the Board, not (as might be expected) between the two national sections, but between the military members of both sections, on the one hand, and the civilian members, on the other. "There was a noticeable tendency among the service members to look on the civilians as ignorant of military affairs and, in consequence, as something of a burden to the Board. The civilians for their part felt that some of the service representatives were handicapped by a too strict adherence to conventional service procedures and to traditional lines of thought. . . . These mutual hesitations and reservations among the members of the Board rapidly disappeared."[55]

More difficult problems of political-military relations were created by dispersal of the various authorities concerned with the Canadian Army. No fewer than three separated centres of command were involved: National Defence Headquarters in Ottawa; the Canadian Military Headquarters in London, England; and the senior Canadian Field Headquarters which, though intended to follow the fighting in Europe, was throughout the greater part of the war located cheek by jowl with C.M.H.Q. Between the defence establishment in the Canadian capital

*On one occasion, when it appeared that the Board had exceeded its advisory function, the Canadian Prime Minister was highly critical, telling the War Committee of the Cabinet on May 27, 1943, that it "had no right to take any step which entered the field of strategy and operations. That the Americans were to report to their Government on matters of defence, and Canadians to our Government but it was for the Governments to consider their recommendations, and to decide on operations, etc." Quoted in J. W. Pickersgill, *The Mackenzie King Record*, I, *1939–1944* (Toronto, 1960), p. 515.

and the overseas Army some difference in perspective was inevitable. Men close to, if not actually engaged in, combat traditionally entertain strategic concepts other than those of the men in government offices. "Even on the administrative side," the Army's official historian has noted, "despite the benefits of cable and telephone, the effort to bridge 3,000 miles of ocean was fraught with difficulties. Geographic remoteness helped to produce different types of thinking on military problems and Canada's military leaders became increasingly aware of the necessity of closer liaison between the staffs 'on the spot' and those in Ottawa."[56] One relatively minor incident illustrates the problem. In January 1944 the Chief of Staff at C.M.H.Q., London, General K. Stuart, signalled the General Officer Commanding, 1st Canadian Army in Italy, concerning the replacement of one of the senior commanders. His recommendation differed from that of the Minister of National Defence, previously expressed by Ralston to General Stuart; and the Minister naturally felt he should at least have been consulted before Stuart sent his message. He thereupon wrote privately to him:

. . . Speaking generally, I would like it, particularly in matters on these high levels where questions are bound to be a mixture of policy and military considerations, if we could have an exchange of views and comments before the matter becomes "set" in a definite recommendation. . . .

I am sure you would be the first to say yourself that it is just good teamwork anyway, quite apart from the "drill", for us here [in Ottawa] to be kept up-to-date and even ahead of time if possible with information in which we would be interested. . . .

. . . Of this you can be sure, that you can never err on the side of giving us too much or too early information.[57]

As planning for "Overlord" reached its final stages, the overseas Headquarters became steadily more apprehensive over the manpower situation. A sharp conflict of opinion developed between senior officers at C.M.H.Q. and Field Headquarters and the staff officers at N.D.H.Q. in Ottawa, who were attempting to reconcile as best they could the military requirements of the forthcoming operation with the Government's determination not to resort to conscription for overseas service. "I am afraid that the telegrams that have passed within the last week or two," the Minister of National Defence wrote to the Chief of Staff in London on March 26, 1944, "have appeared more like those emanating from partisans on opposite sides than from co-workers in a common cause."[58] General Stuart, caught in the cross-fire between the civilian and staff planners in Ottawa and the officers overseas, saw the problem with commendable clarity. On April 1 he wrote to the Chief of the General Staff in Ottawa:

In the past, CMHQ has not understood and has not been sufficiently sympathetic to the broad problems and repercussions other than military that face NDHQ. . . . NDHQ on the other hand has I think tended to emphasize the broader aspects of the problem at issue. Both of these are perfectly natural developments and both are perhaps aggravated by the fact that the two parts of NDHQ are 3000 miles apart. The problem is not only to reconcile the figures involved [i.e., the different estimates of reinforcements required and of numbers likely to be made available under the existing system of voluntary enlistment] but of greater importance to reconcile the two points of view. Representatives of NDHQ are now here [in London] and are engaged in the process of reconciling the figures involved and I am in the process of attempting to broaden the viewpoint of CMHQ in order to bring it as close as possible to that of NDHQ. I am confident of success at this end provided there is some give and take at both ends. CMHQ has at times been unnecessarily alarming in its presentation of alleged facts and I suggest that NDHQ has perhaps been unnecessarily violent [in] its unexpressed but implied reactions.[59]

Some weeks later General Stuart reported to the Minister of National Defence that he felt considerable progress was being made in overcoming "the CMHQ viewpoint" and its "tendency to write alarmist cables."[60]

The difficulty of maintaining productive and harmonious relations between defence planners at home and military authorities abroad was immeasurably increased by the emergence of a fundamental difference of outlook between the political and military branches of the defence establishment in Ottawa. So long as the General Staff at N.D.H.Q. remained sympathetic and responsive to the political directives of the Government, any tension between Ottawa and the overseas Headquarters could be contained within the bounds of national safety. But once differences developed within the defence establishment at home, the prospect of a crisis of immense gravity presented itself. As early as 1941 there is evidence of acute disagreement between the Prime Minister and his military advisers. On June 10, after a meeting of the War Committee of the Cabinet, Mackenzie King requested the Minister of National Defence and the Minister for Naval Services to remain afterwards.

When alone, I said to them that I thought one or the other should be prepared to take on the business of government. That I felt things were getting now where it was almost impossible for me to hope to lead the Administration longer. That I thought there was such a difference growing up between the Defence Department and the Civil Government in matters of policy generally that I could no longer hold the two together. That I could see there was a growing pressure for conscription. That I would be pleased to be out of the fight altogether before that battle came; also that I could not countenance this country being committed to projects it was incapable of carrying out, and assume responsibility for anything of the kind. . . .[61]

Towards the end of the year Mackenzie King privately expressed the opinion that "back of all else, I am positive, is the Army's desire to maintain a foremost position, a certain jealousy of the Air Force and Naval Services." Ralston, he noted a few days later, "is becoming very rigid and I find it difficult, except because of commitments he has already made to some in the Department [of National Defence], to understand his attitude. . . . However, we have reached the end of this year of my life with the Government still intact."[62]

The conscription crisis, which had never been far from the surface of events since the outbreak of war, burst upon the nation in the autumn of 1944. Despite earlier assurances from the military planners that the voluntary system of recruitment would be sufficient to sustain the troops fighting in Western Europe, it was becoming tragically apparent at the scene of combat that it would not. This intelligence reached the Canadian public when a widely known sports promoter of pre-war days, home wounded from the front, told a press conference on September 18 that reinforcements joining Canadian fighting units were "green, inexperienced and poorly trained," and that casualties as a result had been unnecessarily high. The Minister of National Defence, Colonel Ralston, immediately set out for Europe to see for himself. From officers in the field he learned that the situation was as desperate as rumour maintained, and he returned to report his shocking news to the War Committee on October 19, together with his firm recommendation that the Government immediately put into effect a policy of conscripting men for overseas service in order to bolster the flow of reinforcements.

There followed a Cabinet crisis of unprecedented severity in Canadian political life. What is relevant to the present discussion is the part played in the ultimate decision by the senior officers serving at National Defence Headquarters. Even when faced with the opposition of half a dozen of his most influential ministers and the possibility that they would resign, Mackenzie King remained confident that the military situation could be successfully dealt with by voluntary enlistment. What shattered that confidence was the threat not of ministerial but of military resignations. The Army High Command had worked loyally if reluctantly with General McNaughton (brought into the Cabinet to replace Ralston) in his unsuccessful effort to induce large-scale voluntary enlistment. By the middle of November, senior officers of the Army had become convinced that, whatever exertions might be made, the effort would not succeed. They stated as much to their new Minister at a meeting with him in Ottawa on November 14. Although they agreed to do their best to secure the 15,000 men required by the end of the year, "it was clear that emotionally most of them preferred to see the appeal fail so that an adequate supply of men could be made available through conscription."[63] The day before this meeting, General McNaughton had told Mackenzie King that he thought some of his senior officers were "plotting" conscription.[64] In spite of this misgiving, and in the face of the unmistakable opposition of the senior officers to continuing the voluntary system, the Minister saw fit to issue a press statement declaring that "the information given me by the O.C.s confirmed my belief more than ever that continuation of the voluntary policy will provide the reinforcements."[65] Four of the officers present at the meeting promptly telegraphed to McNaughton to protest that nothing that had been said could have properly encouraged him in this belief.

One of the protesting officers was General G. R. Pearkes, a Victoria Cross winner of the First World War, the G.O.C. Pacific Command in charge of the 6th Division of drafted troops. (Thirteen years later he was himself to become Minister of National Defence.) On returning from the Ottawa consultation, he called his officers to a meeting in Vancouver, where they proceeded to give interviews to newspapermen telling of their failure to persuade substantial numbers of their men to volunteer for overseas service and of their doubt whether the Government's policy could ever succeed. This device was clearly intended to bring pressure on the Government from a public by now thoroughly aroused and alarmed. Learning of the interviews, the Prime Minister wrote in his diary: "It is quite apparent that there is a conspiracy. . . . One after the other has been coming out and saying that the N.R.M.A. men were just waiting for the Government to do its duty and send them overseas. That looks like the Army defying the civil power. These men in uniform have no right to speak in ways which will turn the people against the civil power."[66]

A much graver event soon followed. On the morning of November 22, the day Parliament opened, the Chief of the General Staff, Lieutenant-General J. C. Murchie, and other senior officers met with their former commander, now their new Minister, at National Defence Headquarters. To General McNaughton the C.G.S. presented, on behalf of the military members of the Army Council, a brief memorandum. Its key provision read as follows: "After a careful review of all the factors including the latest expression of their views by the District Officers Commanding, I must now advise you that in my considered opinion the voluntary system of recruiting through Army channels cannot meet the immediate problem."[67]

Was this prosaic document an ultimatum? The officers presenting it regarded it as such. "While there was no explicit agreement among them that they would resign if their advice was not followed, at least one or two of them understood that if the Minister remained adamant, resignation would be the next step."* The recipient certainly believed he had been served with an ultimatum. As soon as the officers withdrew, General McNaughton telephoned the Prime Minister:

He said he had quite serious news that the Headquarters Staff here had all advised him that the voluntary system would not get the men. He had emphasized it was the most serious advice that could be tendered. . . . He expressed the opinion that it was like a blow in the stomach. He also said that he had the resignation of the Commander in Winnipeg. That if the Commanders, one after the other, began to resign, the whole military machine would run down, begin to disintegrate, and there would be no controlling the situation.

Instantly there came to my mind the statement I had made to Parliament in June as to the action the Government would necessarily take if we were agreed that the time had come when conscription was necessary. It is apparent to me that to whatever bad management this may have been due, we are faced with a real situation which has to be met and now there is no longer thought as to the nature of the military advice tendered, particularly by Gen. McNaughton. And if so tendered by Gen. McNaughton who has come into the government to try to save the situation, it will be my clear duty to agree to the passing of the Order in Council and go to Parliament and ask for a vote of confidence. . . .[68]

In this way there was formed in the mind of the Prime Minister, in a matter of minutes, the most important decision of the Canadian war effort.

Confronted by what the Prime Minister some days afterward obliquely described as a threat of "anarchy," the anti-conscriptionist members of the Cabinet (with the exception of Mr. C. G. Power who resigned) supported Mackenzie King's dramatic *volte-face*. An order-in-council providing for the immediate drafting of 16,000 N.R.M.A. men for overseas service was approved on November 23. There was

---

*R. MacGregor Dawson, "The Revolt of the Generals," *Weekend Magazine*, vol. X, no. 44, 1960. Mr. Bruce Hutchison, whose investigations first brought the story out into the open, has written: "The final threat [of resignation] was not put in writing along with the officers' memorandum and, in that tense hurried interview, no one seems to remember exactly what was said or who said it. There can be absolutely no question, however, from the information given me quite voluntarily from military sources, that the resignations would have been wide spread and distinguished enough to produce disastrous consequences." Bruce Hutchison, "Mackenzie King and the 'Revolt' of the Army," *Maclean's Magazine*, May 15, 1953.

still Parliament to face, and the prospect that French-Canadian Liberal members might refuse to accept the new policy. The Prime Minister's motion of confidence was carried on December 7 by a vote of 143 to 70, 34 French-speaking Liberals voting against it less out of a sense of betrayal than because of specific pledges against conscription given earlier to their constituents. The threat of civil war had passed, and the members of the Army High Command were spared the ordeal of having to decide whether to carry out the desperate strategy of resignation in wartime.

Some 12,000 conscript soldiers were sent overseas, of whom some 10,000 reached Europe and some 2,500 saw action. That winter the general reinforcement situation improved, and the war in Europe ended before further crises could appear. But the "revolt of the Army" was to have its effect upon civil-military relations in Canada for many years after the German surrender on May 5, 1945.

CIVIL-MILITARY RELATIONS IN
THE NUCLEAR AGE

In 1918 the Armistice was widely believed to presage an era of peace, if not for turbulent Europe at least for North America. A mood of isolationism set in; two decades passed before it was finally dispelled. The mood of Canadians at the end of the second of their two world wars was very different. The hope that international politics might in future see that unity of great powers assumed in the Charter of the United Nations they knew, as soon as any people, to be pitiably slim. Disclosure late in 1945 of Soviet espionage in the Canadian capital revealed, at least to members of the Government, the reckless perfidy of Marshal Stalin's politics; if public disillusionment did not come until the extinction of liberal democracy in Czechoslovakia in February 1948, it came then with sobering clarity. "It is an appalling thought," the Minister of National Defence reflected in the House of Commons in June of that year,

that although hardly three years have gone by since V-E Day . . . many nations should now be engaged in spending money on armaments on a scale never before known in the history of the world in peacetime. . . . The Soviet Union has flouted [its] war-won friendships, obstinately obstructed every move to arrive at understanding, and promoted chaos and disorder and the darkness of the iron curtain. . . . It has produced an attitude in Canada towards defence which is quite different from any that we ever had before in peacetime. Of one thing I am sure, and that is the determination of the Canadian people to defend our country against any attack. . . .[69]

Nor was this a partisan view. "Those who were asleep from 1935 to 1939," declared an Opposition spokesman in the same debate, "are asleep no longer. We know the issues."[70]

To their military advisers, the Chiefs of Staff and senior officers of the three services, the Canadian Government and people turned for advice and guidance about what to do to protect themselves from their new enemy. At the disposal of that enemy was an arsenal of weapons ranging from short-wave radio transmitters to (after 1949) the atomic bomb and (after 1954) the hydrogen bomb; weaponry and strategy had become intricately interwoven, the line between military and political decisions blurred beyond recognition. The result, in Canada as in all Western nations, was to compel senior military officers to exercise judgment in areas lying far beyond their traditional competence.

They have become increasingly concerned with international affairs, that is to say, with the premises of military policy, with the purposes for which and the terms on which military forces will be deployed. They have moved upstream toward the fountain springs of national policy. Second, their support functions—supply, finance, research and development, public relations, manpower management, and the like—have grown more numerous, difficult and important. They have moved downstream to a point where the river widens into a bay far broader than any they have ever travelled before.[71]

A military establishment struggling with these unfamiliar responsibilities could count itself fortunate to enjoy the support and sympathy of the civilian community for whom it stood on guard. The professional soldier never ranked high among the heroes of a country not noticeably disposed to hero-worship, but at any rate he emerged from the Second World War in greater public esteem than he had a generation earlier. "The old attitude there used to be towards sailors and soldiers is a thing of the past," remarked the Minister of National Defence in 1950. "Our sailors, soldiers and airmen have attained and earned the respect of the community."[72] In particular, they had earned the respect of the French-speaking community. Nothing in the traditional values of French Canada conflicted with the traditional values of military life; indeed, its severity, its regularity, its discipline and dedication accorded remarkably well with the kind of society extolled by the defenders of the established order in Quebec. But the commitment of French-speaking Canada to the defence of the realm was bound to be something less than total so long as the enemy contrived to envelop its sinister purpose in the mantle of an ideology not without its own attractions; as Mussolini's Italy and Pétain's France for a time and to an extent managed to do. Once, however, the enemy was identified as international communism, the French-speaking Canadian demonstrated as much capacity for sacrifice as his compatriot in Toronto or Vancouver. Of 10,587 men enlisting in the special volunteer force for service in Korea, 3,134 were from the province of Quebec, a proportion slightly higher than that of the population of Quebec to the population of the whole country; moreover, the proportion of French-speaking Canadians in the special force was almost exactly the same as that of French-speaking Canadians to the total population.[73] If, therefore, Canada continued to share with Iceland the doubtful distinction of being the only member of the North Atlantic alliance not to have introduced compulsory military service, it reflected not so much the unwillingness of Canadians to sacrifice for freedom as the unwillingness of their Government to risk opening the old wounds of the conscription issue. On the wisdom of its diffidence opinions differ, and will differ for a long time; but there can be no question that conditions were more favourable for the experiment during the administration of Mr. L. S. St. Laurent, a Canadian of French descent, than during that of his successor.

All these circumstances assured the military establishment of greater influence on national policy than it had previously enjoyed in peacetime. The proposal to invite European forces from NATO countries to take up operational duties along the northern radar warning lines, favoured by the Department of External Affairs as improving the cohesiveness of the alliance and offsetting United States influence in Canada, was objected to by the Chiefs of Staff and on that account discarded. The decision to create a North American Air Defence Command (NORAD) owed much to the chairman of the Chiefs of Staff Committee, General Charles Foulkes, turning his powers of persuasion upon inexperienced ministers immediately after the change of government in 1957. The proposal to acquire tactical atomic weapons for continental defence and for Canada's forces in Western Europe indicated the influence of the Department of National Defence as against that of the Department of External Affairs whose Minister, Mr. Howard Green, made no secret of his distate for nuclear armaments of any kind. The precise manner and extent to which military influence shaped these and other crucial measures cannot yet be ascertained, but there can be no doubt that it was decisive on several occasions.

But despite the new importance of the military establishment in the making of national policy, the traditional ideal of civilian supremacy was in no way impaired. On the contrary, firm civilian control appeared all the more essential in an era when even the most distant paramilitary skirmish ran the risk of thermonuclear catastrophe. "The professional soldier is answerable to the government," the Leader of the Opposition declared to an approving House of Commons in 1953. "The professional soldier must take his direction from the government; he must carry out policies established by the government. It is not for him to tell the government what it will do; it is for the government to say what the staff officers will do. . . . That has been the policy of the supervision of our defence forces ever since we have had defence forces."[74] The Prime Minister did no more than express the general will of his countrymen when he expressed dismay at the "vocal rocket rattling" of "those in positions of military authority," adding that he could "think of no more sterile or irresponsible use . . . of office than a tendency to brandish the symbols of military power."[75] That in this matter the Government was prepared to practise what it preached was evident in the swiftness with which official rebuke descended upon those members of the military who from time to time ventured to express opinions at variance with policy.

The principle of civilian supremacy continued to be built firmly into the institutions by which defence policy was made. The Cabinet, the ultimate forum for decision, experimented with the wartime device of an Associate Minister of National Defence (a portfolio allowed to lapse with the coming of peace) when in 1953 Mr. Ralph Campney was appointed to that post. His division of labour with the Minister of National Defence, Brooke Claxton, in keeping with the post-war ideal of service unification, was along functional rather than service lines, the Associate Minister attending mainly to administrative matters throughout the military establishment as a whole, leaving his senior colleague freer to grapple with increasingly intractable problems of policy. The line between policy and administration is notoriously difficult to draw, and this functional separation of responsibilities could only succeed, as the Prime Minister conceded when proposing it, on the basis of "an exceptional degree of harmony between the Minister and the Associate Minister, and an even greater degree of frankness and understanding than is necessary between two ministers of the government having quite separate departments."[76] The team of Campney and Claxton worked together harmoniously enough, but when the latter retired in 1954, and Mr. Campney became Minister of National Defence, no Associate Minister was appointed. The position remained unfilled until 1957, when Mr. Paul Hellyer assumed it, only to lose it in the General Election some weeks later. The incoming Diefenbaker administration did not choose to appoint an Associate Minister of National Defence until 1959. Its appointee, Mr. Pierre Sévigny, strengthened

French Canada's representation in the Cabinet without noticeably easing the heavy burdens falling upon General G. R. Pearkes, Minister of National Defence from June 1957 to his resignation in October 1960.

While the Defence Committee of the Cabinet (described above in chapter I) is normally attended by the Chiefs of Staff and the chairman of the Chiefs of Staff Committee, its personnel and tradition are such that the dominant voice is the voice of the civilian. The principal military advisers of the government are members of the Chiefs of Staff Committee, but even this committee, contrary to what its name may suggest, is not a wholly military group. It includes, in addition to the Chief of Staff of each of the three services, the chairman of the Defence Research Board, who is a civilian,* and (since 1951) a permanent chairman who, while a distinguished officer of the highest rank (General Charles Foulkes was the first incumbent, succeeded in 1959 by Air Marshal F. R. Miller, formerly Deputy Minister of the Department of National Defence), was clearly intended to infuse the Committee with a supra-service point of view. Additional civilian chaperonage is provided by the regular attendance at its meetings of the Under Secretary of State for External Affairs and the Deputy Minister of National Defence, when other than purely military matters are under discussion—as, indeed, they usually are. The presence of these influential non-military figures in the Chiefs of Staff Committee has given rise to the charge by a former Chief of the General Staff (noted above in chapter II) that it is " 'packed' to protect the government against the receipt of unpalatable advice. . . ."[77] Whether valid or not, this grave accusation is as applicable to the two key committees that serve the Chiefs of Staff Committee, for the Joint Intelligence Committee and the Joint Planning Committee are also customarily attended by officials from one of the defence liaison divisions of the Department of External Affairs.

The restraining hand of the civilian bureaucracy is found as well upon the Permanent Joint Board on Defence which, while less important than during the Second World War, retains some responsibility for planning for continental defence. To at least one highly placed military observer this arrangement has appeared less than advantageous. "The Permanent Joint Board on Defence," Lieutenant-General G. G. Simonds

---

*Whether the Defence Research Board was to be under military or civilian control was strenuously debated at the time of its creation in 1945–6, but the principle of civilian supremacy in matters of defence research prevailed over the views of the Army ordnance and the R.C.A.F. An unusually informative account of this debate is to be found in Capt. D. J. Goodspeed, *A History of the Defence Research Board of Canada* (Ottawa, 1958), pp. 28–44.

has written, "acts as a barrier to direct contact between the Canadian and U.S. Chiefs of Staff except on a person-to-person basis within individual services. The predilection of Canadian members of this joint board to experiment in the field of gadgetry has engineered decisions of doubtful military value, but very expensive in money."[78]

A further example of how the soldier is overshadowed by the civilian in planning for national security is provided by the Panel on Economic Aspects of Defence. Created in 1948-9 to consider the problems of Canadian military and economic assistance programmes in relation to the Marshall Plan and Mutual Aid, it had become by 1955 the key interdepartmental committee on all aspects of defence policy. Its only regular military participant, however, was the chairman of the Chiefs of Staff Committee, who might or might not invite other military members of his own committee to attend. Its other regular members were all from the civilian bureaucracy, and included the secretary of the Cabinet, who acted as chairman, two or three officers of the Department of External Affairs, the deputy ministers of Defence and Defence Production, and representatives of the Department of Finance and the Bank of Canada.

The classical liberal doctrine for regulating relations between soldiers and governments is offered in Lord Salisbury's famous aphorism: "If you believe the doctors, nothing is wholesome; if you believe the theologians, nothing is innocent; if you believe the soldiers, nothing is safe. They all require to have their strong wine diluted by a very large admixture of insipid common sense."[79] There are two assumptions here: first, that the corrective of common sense is supplied by the civilian politician or public servant; second, that defence policy should properly be the result of a dialectical interplay of the civilian and the military mind, the latter untroubled by political implications. The making of national security policy in nearly all of the liberal democracies since the Second World War has, however, tended to neglect the second, and corollary, assumption. The traditional process whereby objective military advice is tempered by civilians mindful of the political environment has been replaced by one in which the military mind, now trained to recognize non-military aspects of strategy, tenders advice which has already taken them into account. In its American setting the new process quickly acquired doctrinal legitimation as "the theory of political-military fusion"; it has been lucidly described by Professor Huntington:

This theory started from the undeniable fact that military policy and political policy were much more closely inter-related in the postwar world than they had been previously. It went on, however, to assert that it had become impossible to maintain the distinction at the highest level of government. . . . It was argued that new developments had rendered the old categories of "political" and "military" sterile, obsolete and meaningless. . . . In part it reflected the inherent constitutional difficulties of maintaining a clearcut delimitation of military responsibilities, and in part it derived from the feeling that because war had become total, so also had the sphere of military affairs. To a greater extent, however, it simply reflected liberal fear that the increased power of military leadership would mean increased acceptance of the professional military viewpoint. Consequently, it attempted to weaken and subordinate the professional military approach and to reconcile increased military power with liberal values by positing the inevitable transmutation of military leadership. In effect, the fusionist theory attempts to solve the post-war problem of civil-military relations by denying its existence.[80]

In Canada no less than the United States this fusionist conception has displaced since 1945 the traditional relationship between the civilian and military servants of government. If there is any difference between Canadian and American experience in this regard, it has been in the greater emphasis given in Canada to achieving fusion by bringing the civilian bureaucracy into more intimate contact with military problems, rather than by extending the domain of service officers to include political matters. But the latter development has been by no means unknown. It may be discerned in the creation of the permanent chairman of the Chiefs of Staff Committee, in the type of officer promoted to senior rank, and, above all, in the attention paid to the non-military side of senior officer training.

In 1948 the National Defence College offered the first of a continuing series of annual courses for what its handbook for participants describes as

the training of senior officers of the Armed Services and civil department of government in the principles of higher governmental administration and staff work, both in peace and war, so that they may be thoroughly versed in inter-service and inter-departmental planning, including the political and economic aspects and the organization for the central direction of war and the system of higher command, and so become qualified to take their places on the staff and inter-departmental committees which are an essential part of the machinery for planning and directing the national effort.

The thirty or so officers and civilians enrolled were accordingly instructed in "(a) historical, economic, social and political factors affecting Canadian defence; (b) international affairs and Canada's foreign policy; (c) influence of scientific development on war; (d) relationship of armed services with one another and other departments of government; (e) principles of higher command and of joint service planning on the strategic level." Many, if not the majority, of influential staff officers of the three services had by 1961 been exposed to this training. It is of some interest that the first commandant of the National Defence College became after his retirement from active service the most outspoken critic of the fusionist philosophy of which its curriculum was so clear a manifestation. "On the subject of defense," Lt.-Gen. Simonds has written, "the problem is not one of attempting to devise ways of enabling the military to encroach upon political prerogatives, but of getting politicians to face the unpleasant duty of making realistic decisions."[81]

Chapter Four

THE LEGISLATURE

FOREIGN POLICY, LEGISLATIVE-
EXECUTIVE RELATIONS, AND THE
PARLIAMENTARY SYSTEM

Control of foreign policy in a parliamentary system is the responsibility of the Executive. This is not merely a corollary of the familiar paradox that parliamentary government, in which the Cabinet is theoretically responsible to the House of Commons, has in practice undergone "a strange and alarming inversion" so that "the Commons has become instead responsible to the Cabinet."[1] Law and convention both prescribe that crucial steps in the foreign policy process are to be taken only by ministers of the Crown. Collectively those ministers set the course of external affairs. A foreign policy decision is a Cabinet decision. If a treaty is needed, Parliament may be summoned; but it does not have to be summoned, for ratification may be accomplished without its aid. If money or legislation are needed to give effect to a foreign policy decision, Parliament must approve; but the Government's majority in the House of Commons ensures that approval is rarely if ever withheld.

If Parliament is to set its mark upon foreign policy, it must therefore do so by influence. Its methods are interrogation and discussion. How effectively these are used depends partly upon the ability and drive of the Opposition, but just as much upon the readiness of the Government to allow the Opposition to play its dialectical role as the parliamentary system requires. A member may ask questions; a minister need not answer. The Opposition may demand discussion; the Government may refuse time for debate.

Safeguards against Cabinet dictatorship in external, as in other, affairs are of two kinds. Too flagrant disregard of parliamentary opinion may disaffect a Government's following in the House to the point of threatening its defeat. In practice this sanction is not severe. The member, not the Prime Minister, ordinarily fears the cost and bother of seeking re-election, and in fact the weapon of dissolution is one way a Government may keep its majority from becoming maverick. The other, and more important, safeguard lies outside Parliament. Too flagrant disregard of public opinion may disaffect an electorate to the point where it votes the Opposition into power. A Government mistaking voters' silence for indifference may discover at the next general election that it is the Government no longer. This sanction naturally operates more effectively towards the end of an administration than at the beginning.

But to discuss parliamentary government in terms of sanctions and safeguards is to disregard its central assumption. The system, if it is to work well, presupposes a degree of political maturity and restraint on the part of those who work it that is somewhat at variance with Lord Acton's dictum about the tendency of power to corrupt. It assumes that both Government and Opposition are so convinced of its advantages and so attached to its traditions as to refrain from abuses which may irreparably damage the system.

To determine legislative influence on foreign policy within a given parliamentary system, it therefore becomes necessary to inquire into two facets of political behaviour. One is the extent to which the Cabinet allows legislators time and opportunity for constructive criticism. The other is the quality of such parliamentary discussion as may result.

"PARLIAMENT WILL DECIDE"

On August 14, 1914, the Canadian Government announced that the Dominion was at war with Germany. Members of the House of Commons and the Senate, meeting two weeks later to vote funds for the prosecution of the war effort, took no part in the most momentous decision of external policy since Confederation. In 1919 Parliament, which had not been consulted about going to war, was summoned to approve the terms of peace. Its new association with the foreign policy process was due partly to the Prime Minister's emphasis on national status; but this was not Sir Robert Borden's only motive. In Canada, as in Great Britain, public opinion blamed "secret diplomacy" for the calamities of the past five years, and looked to parliamentary scrutiny of the Executive as the principal means of preventing their recurrence. The Canadian Government had not, of course, initiated any of the clandestine diplomatic arrangements of the pre-war years or during the war itself, nor was it widely understood that at the Imperial War Cabinet it had become aware of their existence. The public's desire for increased parliamentary influence was due mainly to its fear that a Canadian government, at some future imperial gathering or at the League of Nations, might commit the nation to war, or to some course of action leading to war, without its knowledge or approval.

The outcry in the United Kingdom against secret diplomacy was heard mostly on the political left, such movements as the Union for Democratic Control drawing support principally among the Labour party. In Canada the left was preaching to the converted. Not that the Government valued parliamentary control over foreign policy for its own sake; later on, in the 1930's Mackenzie King was to shield external affairs from legislative scrutiny as no other Prime Minister before or since. But the political situation of the early 1920's led him to profess attachment to the principle. Upon it, and it alone, his minority Government found some measure of agreement with the sixty-five members of the Progressive party on whose support it depended for continuation in office.

These were the circumstances giving rise to the famous formula "Parliament will decide." It was first pressed into service during the Chanak crisis of 1922. Within hours of receiving the British Government's "invitation" to send troops to help hold the line at the Neutral Zone, Mackenzie King was overwhelmed with advice not to commit any Canadian forces until Parliament had authorized him to do so, and he accordingly informed Lloyd George on September 17 that "public opinion in Canada would demand authorization on the part of Parliament as a necessary preliminary to the despatch of a contingent."[2] The Progressives rallied with gratifying enthusiasm to this position; over the tariff, over freight rates, there might be disagreement and even conflict between them and the Liberal Cabinet, but on the issue of parliamentary control of foreign policy a distinct harmony of interest was disclosed for the first time. "I believe we have found the basis," Mackenzie King wrote soon afterwards, "on which the Progressives of Western Canada may be brought into real accord with the Liberals of the Province of Quebec and other parts of the Dominion."[3] In his statement to the House of Commons, the expedient became a principle: "It is for Parliament to decide," the Prime Minister stated on February 1, 1923, "whether or not we should participate in wars in different parts of the world, and it is neither right nor proper for any individual nor for any groups of individuals to take any step which in any way might limit the rights of Parliament in a matter which is of such great concern to all the people of our country."[4]

A few months later, Mackenzie King carried this doctrine to the Imperial Conference. "The decision of Canada on any important issue, domestic or foreign, we believe should be made by the people of Canada," he told his fellow prime ministers, "their representatives in Parliament, and the Government responsible to that Parliament."[5] After much persistent effort, it was accepted by the Conference and found its way into its published report, which included the statement that "it is for each government to decide whether parliamentary approval or legislation is required before desire for, or concurrence in, ratification [of imperial treaties] is intimated by that government."* In 1926 Mackenzie King placed before a receptive House of Commons a resolution asking it to approve the procedure agreed upon at London in 1923, explaining that the Government would in future submit for parliamentary approval, prior to, and as a condition of, ratification by the Executive, "important treaties such as involve military and economic sanctions."6 These categories were further broadened in 1928. "The day has passed," Mackenzie King then told the House of Commons,

when any government or executive should feel that they should take it upon themselves, without the approval of Parliament, to commit a country to obligations involving any considerable financial outlays or active undertakings.

In all cases where obligations of such a character are being assumed internationally, Parliament itself should be assured of having the full right of approving what is done before binding commitments are made. I would not confine parliamentary approval only to those matters which involve military sanctions and the like. I feel parliamentary approval should apply where there are involved matters of large expenditure or political considerations of a far-reaching character.7

In 1950, an amendment of the National Defence Act required that whenever the Governor-in-Council places Canadian forces on active service, Parliament shall meet within ten days if it is not already in session.

It is one thing to make provision, by resolution or by law, for legislative control; it is another to put it into effect. Some reluctance on the

---

*Imperial Conference (1923), *Summary of Proceedings*, p. 14.

While attending the Imperial Conference of 1923, Mackenzie King met E. D. Morel, the leading spirit of the Union for Democratic Control. In a letter to J. S. Woodsworth, the leader of the Canadian Labour party, Morel described his interview with the Canadian Prime Minister: "I had a private and confidential talk with Mackenzie King about the European situation, and also about our circular letter about foreign policy control, which he at the time acknowledged very courteously. Without in any way committing himself at all, or even committing myself, I may say that I gathered from our conversation that he was not unfavourable to the idea, and I don't see why you or others should not consult together to see whether you cannot introduce into the Canadian House at the earliest possible moment, a resolution much on the lines of the Annex attached to the letter. . . .

"A speech which I heard Mackenzie King give with regard to Dominion participation in foreign policy at the House of Commons dinner to the Prime Ministers the other day, was very much along the lines that I have always advocated, namely, that we must avoid the Imperial Foreign Office idea and ensure that decisions on foreign policy are really democratic. That we can only do by securing full parliamentary control. . . ." (E. D. Morel to J. S. Woodsworth, Nov. 16, 1923, Woodsworth Papers.)

part of Mackenzie King to abide by both letter and spirit of the formula that "Parliament will decide" was displayed as early as 1929, when an important decision on the St. Lawrence Waterway project was taken by order-in-council without prior parliamentary approval. When criticized for this procedure, the Prime Minister first took refuge in the argument that Parliament was not competent to deal with the kind of decision involved: "In negotiating an agreement with respect to water-power, water rights, and navigation, where the considerations are so largely technical in their nature, Parliament is scarcely in a position to discuss such matters in detail; it is for experts to work out these matters." He added that the principle of parliamentary control was in this case safeguarded by a provision enabling Parliament to annul the Order-in-Council if it wished to do so. This explanation did not satisfy E. J. Garland, a Progressive member from Manitoba:

I am afraid my right hon. friend is on the horns of a dilemma in this case. If because of a lack of technical knowledge Parliament is incapable of arriving at an intelligent decision in the first place, lacking that technical knowledge how is Parliament to arrive at an intelligent decision with regard to the annulment of an order in council later?

The Prime Minister then resorted to what was later to became a favourite and familiar device, pleading the undesirable consequences of parliamentary discussion upon international negotiations in progress. "The present moment," he declared, "is perhaps a critical one at which to discuss an international matter which affects our relations with our neighbour to the south. I do not wish to discourage discussion in any way . . . but in debating this matter I hope hon. gentlemen will bear in mind the fact that whatever is said in this Parliament at this time may have a very far-reaching effect upon some decisions which may be reached in the very near future with regard to matters which are of real concern to both countries. . . ."[8]

The letter of the "Parliament will decide" formula was observed in September 1939, but whether its spirit was wholly in evidence some authorities are inclined to doubt. "In the week from September 2 to September 10," Professor K. W. McNaught has observed,

despite King's telephone denial of Canada's belligerent status to President Roosevelt, the Government's actions could be defended only on the assumption that Canada was at war. The enemy was defined, all armed services were put on a full war basis, enemy nationals were arrested, and trading with the enemy was prohibited by order-in-council. On September 7, the Governor General's speech referred to "the state of war which now exists". . . . By the time Parliament met there was nothing left for it to decide. . . . The Commons was being asked to endorse a policy already implemented and to give the Government a blank cheque for the future."[9]

Wars are seldom beneficial to legislatures. During the years 1939–45 the influence of the Canadian Parliament upon policy necessarily diminished, but its prestige suffered perhaps unnecessarily because of the Government's addiction to orders-in-council as a method for taking decisions. "Any criticism based on the sheer number of the Orders-in-Council," one of its critics acknowledges,

would be both silly and unfair. . . . About 95 per cent of them were for approval of contracts and routine administrative purposes. Only about 4 or 5 per cent were "of a legislative character," and many of these were unexceptionable. . . . Mr. King's offence, constitutionally speaking, is not that he legislated by Order-in-Council, but that he did so to an altogether unnecessary and even dangerous degree; and the offence is particularly heinous because he had himself so often denounced it. He sinned against the light.[10]

THE CABINET, THE HOUSE OF COMMONS, AND DISCUSSION OF FOREIGN AFFAIRS

The formula "Parliament will decide" implied that "Parliament will discuss"; sensible decision could only follow full deliberation of foreign policy matters. This was very different, however, from what the inventor of the formula was prepared to allow, for in Mackenzie King's view the less the legislators discussed external affairs the better. It early became his custom to discourage discussion by pleading the need to avoid upsetting delicate negotiations. Such a plea may be wholly legitimate because wholly genuine; every foreign secretary has had occasion to resort to it. But for Mackenzie King its purpose was less to further the settlement of international disputes than to prevent the expression of politically embarrassing points of view. To suppose that discussion of international affairs in the Canadian House of Commons might adversely affect the course of events in Europe was nothing if not absurd, but the absurdity of the argument did not prevent the Prime Minister from making frequent use of it. In 1926, for example, when J. S. Woodsworth sought to place before the House of Commons a motion that "Canada should refuse to accept any responsibility for complications arising from the foreign policy of the United Kingdom," Mackenzie King promptly sought to stave off discussion on the ground that "remarks made in the course of debate would almost certainly be cabled to Europe where their bearing might not be understood; it would be inadvisable to incur a risk of the kind while the League of Nations in its assembly at Geneva is considering matters of British foreign policy and of great international import."[11] It must be added in fairness that R. B. Bennett displayed as Prime Minister during 1930–5 a similar antipathy to parliamentary discussion of foreign policy. Asked by J. S. Woodsworth in November 1932 to state "what, if any, is the policy of His Majesty's Government in Canada in regard to the situation in the Far East and to the Lytton Report," the Prime Minister replied: "It is not thought desirable to enter into a discussion at this time with respect to a matter of this kind, for it not only cannot serve the public interest but would be anticipating action that might be taken, and therefore is to be deprecated."[12] But it should also be noted that Mackenzie King as Leader of the Opposition accepted this evasion without protest; indeed, a year later, when a statement of the Canadian delegate at the League of Nations on the Manchurian crisis was under scrutiny in the House of Commons, he declared that he would not be responsible for provoking parliamentary discussion by commenting on the statement.[13] After 1935, Prime Minister once more, Mackenzie King steadfastly refused to be drawn into debate in Parliament on such issues as the Government's attitude to sanctions, collective security and the League of Nations. At the time of the Rhineland crisis, for example, he met a request for a statement of the Government's attitude by observing:

I question if there is anything we of this House could add which would be helpful to those who at the moment are involved in very critical and delicate negotiations on a matter of supreme concern to mankind. . . . I think it would be in every way preferable, having regard to the extremely critical nature of the negotiations and the fact that the situation keeps changing not only from day to day but sometimes from hour to hour, for hon. members of this House to forbear, if they can see their way to do so, from proferring any request which might provoke discussion in our country at this time.[14]

When J. S. Woodsworth responded to this extraordinary reply by remarking that "we cannot go indefinitely without having some indication from the Government as to what the attitude of Canada is," the Prime Minister answered:

May I say to my hon. friend that, in a word, the attitude of the Government of Canada is to do nothing itself and if possible to prevent anything occurring which will precipitate one additional factor into the all-important discussions which are now taking place in Europe. . . .[15]

This exaggerated reticence did not go uncriticized at the time. *Saturday Night*, acknowledging that "Canada has but a minor part in the chorus of the opera now being presented on the international stage," expressed its opinion that it would nevertheless "be interesting to know what part we are going to sing when we do sing"; and the *Winnipeg Tribune* inquired more bluntly: "How can we uphold the hands of those who are endeavouring to maintain the peace of the world if we simply sit like a bump on a log and have nothing to say?"[16] It was doubtless owing to such criticism that the Prime Minister decided to break his long silence in order to make a full foreign policy statement in the House of Commons. He delivered it on June 18, 1936; and as his remarks were the first he had devoted to the international situation since December 6, 1935, he prefaced them with a justification for the absence of previous statements:

It has been contended that the Government has not made clear its policy on the important problems, immediate and future, which have been raised by the outbreak and progress of the Italian-Ethiopian conflict. It is true that the Government has declined to make a statement at some critical stages when a statement would be premature, and would complicate rather than advance a solution. I believe it will be generally conceded that the course of events in Europe has more than justified the Government's attitude.

It is undoubtedly essential that in Parliament and outside of it there should be full and responsible discussion of the vital questions of Canada's relations to other states. There has not been sufficient discussion in the past. That has been due to our slow emergence from the colonial attitude of mind; our relative immunity from any serious danger of war on our own account; the real difficulties inherent in our preoccupation with the tremendous, absorbing and paramount tasks of achieving economic development and national unity, which with us take the place of the preoccupation with the fear of attack and the dreams of glory which beset older and more crowded countries; and the unparalleled complexity of our position as a member of the British Commonwealth of Nations and one of the nations of the American continent.[17]

An honest reckoning would have added that insufficient discussion of foreign policy in Parliament had also been due to the Prime Minister's determination to keep Parliament from discussing foreign policy; only a few weeks earlier, Mackenzie King had written privately that he wanted "as little discussion as possible . . . in our House of Commons with respect to the present European situation."

If these remarks stirred any hopes that for the future the Government stood ready to embark upon a fresh experiment in public education by encouraging discussion of international affairs in Parliament, they were soon disappointed. Parliament might decide; but it must not be allowed to know what it was deciding. It was a curious and unedifying chapter in the history of Canadian democracy when, as a critic remarked after the war, "at the time of one of the great world crises . . . twenty-seven minutes were devoted to external affairs in the House of Commons and over eight hours to a tariff on asparagus."[18]

During the war years, Parliament's influence through discussion and debate suffered along with its decision-making powers. "Ideas and policies no longer travelled upward from Parliament but downward from officials to the Cabinet and then to the House of Commons for cursory approval. Parliament in wartime held little more than a watching brief with a right of criticism and the final prerogative of death sentence against the Government, and that it did not intend to use except in a supreme crisis."[19] The nadir of neglect was reached on January 25, 1940, when, summoned by the Prime Minister, Parliament listened to him announce its dissolution. Of this occasion an authority has written:

The Speech from the Throne usually ends: "In inviting your consideration to the important matters which will engage your attention, I pray that Divine Providence may guide and bless your deliberations," or words to that effect. That would not do this time; there were no "important matters"; there were to be no "deliberations." Parliament had been summoned only to listen and leave. So the Speech this time wound up: "In all that pertains to the discharge of your responsible duties, may Divine Providence be your strength and guide." Divine Providence never had an easier job. There were no "responsible duties." Members had been summoned only to hear that their duties were at an end. No other Prime Minister in any British country, before or since, ever dared to offer such an affront to Parliament. . . .[20]

On several occasions during the war, Mackenzie King warded off discussion of foreign policy in the House of Commons by stating that discussion of such matters in wartime was not in the public interest. As late as 1943, he declined to make any statement about post-war policy on the ground that "the more public discussion is diverted to questions about what is going to be the attitude of this country and that country at the peace table and in the postwar period, the less the country will be impressed with the fact that this war itself is not yet won."[21] Mr. Winston Churchill, by contrast, was under no such inhibition; two days later he outlined to the House of Commons at Westminster a Four Year Plan for post-war Britain. The waning authority of the Canadian Parliament during the Second World War was recalled in later years by a member of the War Committee of the Cabinet:

Members were rarely consulted either about policy or otherwise—a far cry indeed from the old prewar days [in the 1920's] when the same Prime Minister, then leading the House of Commons as a minority government, had strenuously upheld the doctrine that the Cabinet was only a committee of the House of Commons and could have no power without the prior decision of the members of that House. In fact, members learned of decisions from their seats in the House, in many instances long after action had been taken. If they objected, they were told that there was a war on. Even their well-meant advocacy of war measures or decisions was discouraged by the ministers concerned who, rightly or wrongly, felt competent to handle their own business in the House and were anxious to get through with it in order to deal with pressing problems in the Department.

Even the most able and most eager M.P. was bound to feel a sense of his own impotence. Departmental officers, even of the most junior order, sensed this and the prestige of Parliament decreased accordingly. The public began to look to the Prime Minister and the members of the Cabinet, they—and they alone—came to be regarded as responsible for everything concerned with the war. This increased the prestige of the Cabinet and Government enormously, and correspondingly decreased that of Parliament. The truth of the matter is Parliament has not yet [1957] recovered its position.[22]

During the post-war years, discussion of foreign affairs by the House of Commons became more frequent, but improvement was neither spectacular nor rapid. In 1947 only 450 of nearly 7,000 pages of recorded debate were concerned with international problems, compared to 150 out of 5,000 in 1935. But at least this situation could no longer justly be blamed upon the Government. Mr. Lester Pearson, on becoming Secretary of State for External Affairs in 1949, determined from the first to use his high office as an instrument of public education and the House of Commons as a means of reaching the public. If his efforts were not wholly successful, the fault lay with those members of the House who continued to be apathetic during foreign policy debates. "So far as discussions in the House of Commons are concerned," Mr. Pearson remarked in May 1950, "I would like to see all the discussion we can have on external affairs. Once or twice I have pleaded for more interest in external affairs in the House of Commons to empty benches and empty press gallery seats, and the debates have tailed off. Once the debate ended so suddenly that I found myself winding up a discussion when I thought it had just begun. Possibly we ourselves, in the House of Commons, are somewhat to blame for the lack of interest."[23]

THE MEMBER OF PARLIAMENT

AND FOREIGN POLICY

If there is such a person as an average member of Parliament, it may be said of him that over the years he has not displayed much interest in or knowledge of foreign affairs. Such indifference flows naturally enough from the prevalent conception of representative democracy in Canada. "In ninety-nine cases out of one hundred, the member goes to Ottawa to speak for his own constituency and no other. That is what the member thinks he is sent to Ottawa to do; that is what the electors think he is sent to do."[24] As a consequence the member devotes no more time to foreign policy than he believes his constituents would wish him to, which in practice is very little time indeed. "Let us conciliate Quebec and Ontario," remarked a member of the House of Commons in 1923, "before we start conciliating Roumania and Ukrainia,"[25] and this general order of priority has not radically altered over the years. No one thought it inappropriate when the Leader of the Opposition, R. B. Hanson, remarked in the course of his speech on the Address in 1940: "I did intend to say something about the St. Lawrence Waterway, but I do not think I should trespass much longer on the time of the House. . . . I cannot, however, refrain from saying something about the position of truck transportation in Prince Edward Island."[26]

If one looks to the Upper House, whose members have no constituents requiring them to fix their attention exclusively upon the home front, for more informed discussion on international affairs, one looks in vain. Of the American Senate, John Hay remarked that treaties enter it as bulls the arena, never to leave alive; in the Canadian Senate this is not true of treaties but it is of senators. They are appointed by the government of the day for life, but during the years to come—and there may be many years to come for some—rarely affect the course of external policy. Such feeble influence is due partly to the Senate's waning powers in the constitution; not since 1913, when the Liberal majority in the Senate defeated Sir Robert Borden's naval bill, has the Upper House left its mark upon national policy, and there is general agreement that any Senate rash enough to repeat the experiment would bring a long-simmering movement for its abolition to the boiling point. It is due as well to the quality of senatorial appointments. With a few conspicuous exceptions, these tend to be party workhorses past their prime for whom the Senate becomes a kind of political pasture where old age may be spent in tranquil but not unfamiliar surroundings. One might suppose that the leisurely tempo of the senatorial life, its opportunities for research and reflection, the attenuation of party ties, create unusual opportunity for elder statesmanship, particularly in internal affairs, if only for the few able and willing to take advantage of it. Even here, however, the talents of the alert senator are consumed by the extraneous functions which by convention the Upper House has come to perform. Of these its role as a divorce court is by far the most distracting. "All of the evidence has to be taken down by the stenographic staff," a senator recently complained, "and it is simply impossible to run the Senate any more than three days a week and carry on a successful divorce court proceedings. . . . The result . . . is you can barely get time to deal with the specific legislation that comes through [from the House of Commons]," let alone get time for significant contribution to the making of foreign policy.[27]

Even in the Lower House, lack of opportunity to influence foreign policy has a dampening effect upon the interest of individual members in international problems. In the United States Senate, whose members may not merely influence policy but determine it, it was not so long ago that a newly elected colleague received advice "to avoid service on a fancy committee like that of foreign affairs if he wished to retain his hold upon his constituents because they cared nothing about international questions."[28] Canadian constituents care little more, but the member of the House of Commons has not even the consolation of being able to thwart the Government on a foreign policy matter to which he is opposed. Opportunities in Opposition are restricted by the Government's readiness to allow time for interrogation and debate, and, as has been shown, this until recently was very little time. It is naïve to suppose that the Government is eager to accept useful suggestions from Opposition members. "A few of these the Cabinet may be able to accept with dignity; but let this become frequent, and the electorate will naturally conclude the simpler solution would be to place in power the party which is so fertile in valuable ideas rather than acquire them in this circuitous fashion."[29] Fertility in valuable ideas has not, however, been the conspicuous characteristic of parliamentary oppositions, especially in the field of foreign policy.

It is almost as rare, perhaps even more rare, among the rank and file supporters of the Government. Too many brilliant suggestions from the back benches may cause the front benches to look foolish by comparison, and are therefore discouraged. Lights must shine under bushels, if they are to illuminate anything at all. More exactly, they must shine in the parliamentary party caucus.

What influence members may have in this private* gathering depends mainly on the inclination of their leader to let them have their say. Mackenzie King has been described as "a great believer in the value of discussion in the party caucus, though he never permitted the caucus to determine policy. He deliberately encouraged the private members to air their grievances and even to attack the Ministers and, at times, was able in this way to get departmental attitudes and procedures changed without direct intervention on his own part."[30] The vitality of the party

---

*Or nominally private. A member of the C.C.F. party has stated: "I know inside of an hour what has taken place in the Liberal and Conservative caucuses and I'm not supposed to know. . . . All the newspapermen know. . . ." Interview for the Canadian Broadcasting Corporation (hereafter cited as C.B.C. interview).

caucus tends to fluctuate with the size of the parliamentary following, particularly in the Government ranks. If a majority is small, and therefore precarious, the caucus can be extremely important; if it is large, and therefore secure, the tendency is for it to degenerate into a meaningless ritual. One member of the exceptionally large (205 seats) Conservative majority which by 1961 had been in power for three years complained that "We spend most of our time in caucus talking about secretarial service or parking space. We are never consulted about policy, and hardly ever get a chance to discuss it at all."* Members of the Senate attend meetings of the parliamentary caucus of their party where, according to one senator, they are not always welcome guests: "They talk too much in caucus. That is the complaint of the M.P.'s. They are always giving them the experience that they had, and I think the M.P.'s resent it a little."[31]

If the ordinary member, whether on the Government or the Opposition side of the House of Commons finds himself without influence upon foreign policy decisions, he has increasing opportunity to gain some experience of external affairs. He may become a member of the House of Commons Standing Committee on External Affairs. He may attend meetings of the NATO Parliamentary Association or the Commonwealth Parliamentary Association, and fraternize with his congressional counterparts in the Canada–United States Interparliamentary Group. He may be taken on guided tours of American defence installations. He may even go to Europe or the Middle East, although parliamentary "junketing" is discouraged and infrequent. Members of Parliament, mainly but not exclusively supporters of the Government, are normally included in the Canadian delegation to the General Assembly of the United Nations.

Such assignments do not bring the member much closer to the centres of decision, but they enable him to indulge in agreeable fashion his interest in foreign affairs, they flatter his sense of self-importance, and they may contribute something to his knowledge and understanding of world problems. It cannot be said, however, that they have dramatically improved the quality of foreign policy debate, either in the House of Commons or in the Senate. There is a tendency to describe at length

*Quoted in Blair Fraser, "Backstage at Ottawa," *Maclean's Magazine*, March 12, 1960, p. 2. Other members of the same party disagree, one remarking: "Caucus [is] a less courteous place [than] the House of Commons, a more raucous place. . . . Fewer holds are barred and fewer restraints are placed on the expression of an opinion. . . . The storms that blow in caucus from time to time are prodigious." Another described the caucus as "completely unfettered," and added: "There have been Government policies altered as a result of the expression of opinion in caucus." C.B.C. interview.

the kind of world the speaker would like to live in, and for such revery to pass for serious analysis. There is a tendency to appeal to the authority of the written word, without much regard for whose word it is. Finding a press clipping bearing upon the topic under discussion, a member will quote it, wave it triumphantly aloft, and run no greater risk than to be asked to cite the date of the newspaper from which it is taken or challenged to read the quotation in its entirety.* Apart from the foreign policy spokesmen of the various parties, few members trouble to keep themselves really well informed on special problems of external policy; few if any are capable of contributing much of originality and value to such subjects as defence or foreign aid, although there is a limitless fund of expertise on forest management, gold mining, freight rates and the Great Lakes lamprey.

Whatever the reasons for this, it is not for want of time for study—not, at any rate, in the case of members of the party in power. So far from being overworked, the chief problem of the ordinary backbencher in a large majority has been to find enough significant activity to keep his self-respect. The member for the important Toronto constituency of York Centre was quoted as having said soon after his election in 1957: "What am I supposed to do? Every morning I go to my office at nine o'clock, same as I do at home. By ten, I'm all through. . . . How do I spend the rest of the day?" Two years later he told a correspondent that he could "still handle all his constituency business, check Hansard, answer his mail, write five additional letters each day to total strangers in his riding to invite their views on public questions . . . and finish before the morning coffee break, with nothing to do except listen. . . . He thinks this is equally true for all private MPs who represent urban ridings on the government side, and he says most of them dislike it as much as he does."[32] Evidence from other members tends to bear out his experience. One Government supporter told an interviewer:

The average young member is not busy and there isn't sufficient work to do. That is a sad state of affairs in my opinion, and because of it you're going to get a different type of member. . . . If you called an election soon, I feel that a lot of the younger members would not be back, because there's not

*"Mr. Pearson: . . . A Washington report of last Saturday quotes an official of the Boeing aircraft company as saying that the reduced funds for all these missiles made by the Boeing aircraft company will permit no major production at all, but will be used only to continue research. Mr. Diefenbaker: From what is the hon. gentleman reading? Mr. Pearson: From a press statement from Washington attributing a report to a high official of the Boeing aircraft company. Mr. Diefenbaker: What is the newspaper? Mr. Pearson: I have not got it before me—Mr. Diefenbaker: Ah." (Canada, House of Commons Debates, March 28, 1960, p. 2502.)

enough to do. . . . Would I come back? It's a long way from home, let's put it that way. We're talking here on a Saturday morning, and I haven't got very much to do from Friday night till Monday morning or Monday afternoon at 2.30. That's a long time to wait. . . . I think up things to do. Many things. . . . I've just come back from Squaw Valley and now I'm trying to entertain the idea of having Canada host the next Olympics in 1968. . . . It's something I've dreamed out of my own mind to keep me occupied and busy. . . .[33]

Members of the Opposition, however, particularly of a small Opposition, may with every justification plead the excuse of overwork, and if they are overworked they are also understaffed. "I could keep a staff of at least two or three going full time on research alone," the Opposition foreign policy critic was quoted as saying in March 1960,[34] and it is primarily with those like him in mind that various suggestions for improving members' facilities for research have been put forward. One of these is that there should be created for the Canadian Parliament something similar to the Legislative Reference Service of the Library of Congress. Parliament has its own library, but no provision is made for assistance in preparing material for use in speeches, and it is often suggested that there should be such provision. It is just as often overlooked, however, that the Legislative Reference Service is peculiarly the product of a legislature not only independent of but frequently at loggerheads with the executive branch of the United States government; to expect it to function with similar effectiveness in the parliamentary system may be to expect too much. A library of Parliament equipped to carry out research for opposition parties might become so effective as a source of criticism of government policy as to tempt the Government to withhold funds and cramp its facilities. It is true that its facilities would be equally available to members on the Government side, and just as true that they may need them;* but, as already pointed out, the Cabinet may have understandable if ignoble motives for dimming the brilliance of its own parliamentary supporters. For these reasons the appropriate sponsor of legislators' research within a parliamentary system of government is the political party rather than the bureaucracy.[35]

The most effective method so far devised for improving the quality of parliamentary discussion of foreign policy is the use of parliamentary committees. These are discussed in the following section of this chapter.

*"I had a Government Member yesterday tell me that . . . he never clips anything. The only files he has in his drawers are correspondence files. Well, this is fantastic . . . but points up the need for research, guidance and advice." C.B.C. interview.

PARLIAMENTARY COMMITTEES

Suggestions to create for the Canadian Parliament some counterpart of the Foreign Relations and Foreign Affairs Committees of the United States Congress were first made at the end of the First World War as part of the general sentiment for a more "democratic" foreign policy. "There should be a Foreign Affairs Committee of the House here at Ottawa," wrote a member of the Press Gallery in 1920, "which should insist as the American Senate does on seeing every document that binds the British Commonwealth. It might not do much good but it would put a crimp in secret diplomacy."[36] In March 1924 a Government motion to create a Standing Committee on Industrial and International Relations was adopted by the House of Commons without debate, and thirty-three members were appointed to it. "I think the combination of industrial and international problems would be a very proper one," the Prime Minister remarked. "International questions deal in very large part with industrial matters, and certainly our industrial problems are becoming more and more international in character."* A more specific, though unstated, reason for the odd combination was the Government's intention to use the new Committee to deal with those conventions of the International Labour Organisation giving rise to problems of jurisdiction between federal and provincial governments, although the sole reference during its first few years was the I.L.O. Draft Convention on the Limitation of Hours of Work in Industrial Undertakings. In later years only two matters of external policy were discussed by the Committee: a plan to promote peace by university scholarships (referred to the Committee in 1931); and the question of employing oriental seamen on ships of Canadian registry (referred in 1935). After 1936 the Committee held no further meetings.

In September 1945, the Prime Minister, in response to suggestions from members of the Opposition, created a new House of Commons Standing Committee on External Affairs. Its thirty-five members (ten constituting a quorum) are appointed to reflect party standing in the House of Commons, so that the Committee is in respect of membership the House of Commons in miniature. There is, however, a good deal less partisan feeling and repartee. Not only have Opposition members of the Committee generally refrained from using it as a forum for political attacks upon the Government; a number of Government supporters in

---

*Canada, H. of C. Debates, March 24, 1924, p. 617. This section throughout owes much to Oleg Alec Chistoff, "The House of Commons Standing Committee on External Affairs: An Aspect of Parliamentary Control of Foreign Policy in Canada" (unpublished M.A. dissertation, University of Toronto, 1955).

the Committee have criticized Government policy to a degree unthinkable in the House of Commons. At the outset the Committee was prevented by the rules of the House from investigating matters other than those referred to it by the House; this so restricted the usefulness of the Committee that in 1946 the Prime Minister accepted an Opposition suggestion that the estimates of the Department of External Affairs be submitted to the Committee for scrutiny. This procedure, the Prime Minister explained, would "give the Committee an opportunity to discuss anything that relates to external affairs. . . . I do not believe its members will be able to think of anything relating to external affairs which it will not be possible to bring up by reference to some particular appropriation."[37] Since 1946 this practice has been consistently followed, giving to the Standing Committee on External Affairs scope enjoyed by no other committee of Parliament.

The most important functions performed by the Committee during the years since its inception are: (i) expediting the business of the House of Commons; (ii) extracting information from the Minister and officials of the Department of External Affairs; (iii) assisting the Government in the formulation of policy through discussion unimpaired by party rancour; (iv) examining proposed legislation on international affairs to improve its quality. It might be expected that the Government would emphasize the expediting and legislative-scrutinizing functions of the Committee, while the Opposition would stress its investigative and policy-making roles; and during the formative years these preferences were clearly in evidence. While the Government did not attempt to confine the Committee's discussions to administration as opposed to policy, it tried at first to restrain any tendency towards free-wheeling investigation of foreign policy in the broadest sense. "I do not think that any members of the Committee," remarked the Secretary of State for External Affairs in 1946,

want to make any determination of what future external policy is to be because . . . that is subject to almost hourly changes in view of the developments taking place. Probably the Committee would wish to have some information about what has been taking place and what has been the attitude taken by Canada in international discussions so as to form its own opinion as to whether that was proper or not, and what it seems to indicate as a general trend.[38]

After Mr. Lester Pearson became Secretary of State for External Affairs in 1949, the Government's early unfriendliness to uninhibited discussion of foreign policy by the Committee gave way to active encouragement of such discussion. It is the practice for the Secretary of State for

External Affairs to appear before the Committee at the outset of its deliberations to deliver a general policy statement, and to respond to questions and comments arising out of his statement, before officials of the Department of External Affairs are summoned for interrogation on administrative matters. "I will be happy to be as full and frank as possible when dealing with questions of policy," Mr. Pearson told the Committee in 1951;[39] and he was as good as his word.

Whether the Committee may properly assume a policy-formulating role, recommending courses of action to the Government, is a question frequently arising during its work. The Government has taken the view that it may not formulate policy. "Here we come to a pretty fundamental principle," remarked the Minister of National Defence in 1950. "It is . . . that the hon. member for York West was not elected by the people of Canada to make such decisions."[40] The Government has occasionally departed from this principle, perhaps most notably in 1947, when the Secretary of State for External Affairs attempted to seek the Committee's "frank opinion as to what it is advisable, under all circumstances, to recommend at this time" with respect to a proposal to purchase housing for the Canadian embassy in Washington. Mr. St. Laurent sought to explain his curious initiative in these words:

As long as I am Minister, I do not mind taking the responsibility for matters which I really consider vital, but when it comes to matters which are not really vital, I should not like to have a controversy over the manner in which we are conducting the external affairs. Small controversies can have disastrous effects on the larger issues. Therefore, we want to avoid, as much as possible, having any small controversies and reserve our position so that when we do have a dispute, it will be about something which is really vital. . . .[41]

It is greatly to the Committee's credit that it refused to accept this doctrine with its untenable distinctions between vital and "not really vital" matters, between small and large controversies. The Opposition foreign policy critic, Gordon Graydon, expressed the sense of the Committee when he remarked in reply:

The responsibility for this rests entirely upon the Government and not on this Committee. I think the Committee must, in all fairness, discuss the question so the Government will then have the various points of view which are brought out. In this way, the Government may, possibly, arrive at a more sensible, more appropriate decision. I do not think it is up to the Committee. I do not think we should set a precedent. . . . Such things are really within the province of the Government rather than of Parliament.[42]

This view was later reaffirmed and has prevailed. In 1949 the question arose whether the Committee ought to summon the Canadian ambassador to China, Mr. T. C. Davis, to question him about the wisdom of recognizing the Communist régime. "Nothing we can find out from Mr. Davis," a member of the Committee remarked on that occasion, "would be of any assistance in a decision of policy because we have not got to make that decision."[43] In 1954 the Committee discussed whether the Department of External Affairs ought to inform it about plans for opening diplomatic missions:

> *Mr. Howard Green:* Are you in a position yet to tell us where the new posts are going to be?
> *Witness (Mr. R. A. MacKay, Department of External Affairs):* I regret, Sir, I am not. Negotiations are not completed in this matter and I think it would be inappropriate to make any public statement.
> *Mr. Green:* The Department is still taking the position that they won't tell us until after the event.
> *Witness:* Well, Sir, I think that is a decision for the Government. . . .
> *Mr. Green:* That means that the Committee can have no voice in the decision as to whether or not certain new posts ought to be opened.
> *The Chairman (Mr. L.-P. Picard):* Well, I think we are a committee of the legislative branch and these decisions belong to the executive branch of the government.[44]

The most useful contribution of the Committee has been to elicit information from the Minister and officials of the Department of External Affairs concerning both external policy and the administration of external policy. In the opinion of its own members, such success as the Committee has had as an investigating committee has been due to its ability to question officials directly, thus circumventing the procedure in the House of Commons where only the Secretary of State for External Affairs, together with the Prime Minister and the Parliamentary Secretary, is available for questioning. The Committee has been careful not to abuse this privilege. Witnesses are treated with courtesy and respect; they are not pressed further if they plead that answers come better from the Minister than from themselves, nor are they cajoled or bullied into disclosing information if they state disclosure not to be in the public interest. Thus, in 1949, when the Committee considered whether it should interrogate the Canadian ambassador to China, a member expressed the sense of the meeting when he remarked: "I am opposed to this to the last ditch. I do not think we should create a precedent and call an ambassador and put him on the grille." Another member asked rhetorically: "Do you think it would be proper for this Committee to look into the diplomatic valise of any of our ambassadors? It is still worse to ask an ambassador to come here."[45] Not all committees of the House of Commons have shown such consideration for their witnesses and some, indeed, have shown a marked disposition towards "hatchet forays on civil servants."[46] Witnesses appearing before the External Affairs Committee are appropriately grateful, and display their gratitude by responding to the best of their ability to questioning. "Few Committees," remarked the Opposition foreign policy critic in 1951, "have found hon. members more satisfied with their work and the way in which it is carried on."[47]

In a number of the other committees of the House of Commons, both standing and *ad hoc*, foreign policy matters frequently come up for discussion. For example, during the proceedings of the Standing Committee on Mines, Forests and Water in 1959, consideration was given to "trade with Red China, the inadequacy of export credit facilities, the threat of Russian entry into world paper markets, the competition of cheap labour in the Southern U.S.A."[48] The Standing Committee on Estimates, when reviewing the proposed expenditures of such departments as National Defence or Citizenship and Immigration, unavoidably moves into the realm of external policy. However, their practice, unlike that of the Standing Committee on External Affairs, almost invariably is to refrain from questioning the broad outlines of government policy and to confine interrogation to the details of departmental administration.

The success of the Standing Committee on External Affairs in examining policy in its broadest aspects has led to the suggestion that a similar Standing Committee on National Defence should be created. There is much logic in the suggestion. In few other areas of national policy are administrative decisions relating to expenditure more intimately connected with political decisions relating to strategy. In recent years, enormous sums of money have been devoted to the acquisition of weapons whose strategic usefulness has vanished even before they came into service, or whose strategic usefulness was challenged by officials once associated with their development, speaking up only after retirement. The feeling was widespread that the country's fortune was being squandered to no purpose, and that insufficient information was being made available to Parliament and through Parliament to the public to permit an intelligent evaluation of what had been done and of what was proposed. "We get most of our information on continental defence, about changes in defence concepts and strategy, from the reports of [Congressional] committees and not through anything we get from the Government of Canada," Mr. Lester Pearson complained in 1960. "All we have is a fog of silence penetrated occasionally by a ministerial platitude."[49]

In March 1960 the Government responded to public demands by

creating a special fifteen-member Committee of the House of Commons, along the lines of a similar Special Committee on Defence Expenditure which functioned during the fifth session of the twenty-first Parliament in 1951–2. It was to examine "all expenditure of public moneys for national defence and all commitments for expenditure for national defence since April 1, 1958, as reported in public accounts, and to report from time to time their observations and opinions thereon, and in particular what, if any, economies consistent with the execution of the policy decided by the Government may be effected therein, with power to send for persons, papers and records, and to examine witnesses."[50] These terms of reference were criticized by the Opposition. They limited, it was pointed out, discussion of defence expenditure to what had been decided before the last available report of the public accounts, and as this document bore the date March 31, 1959, the Special Committee could not take up, consistent with its terms of reference, the most recent and controversial of the Government's defence decisions— the decision to proceed with the Bomarc-SAGE weapons system. The terms of reference also specifically confined the Committee to discussion within the framework of established policy. "We visualize a very different committee," declared the Leader of the Opposition on March 17, 1960,

one that would discuss defence policy, one that would make recommendations on defence policy. . . . We visualize a committee which would question the Minister on defence policy matters, a committee which when necessary for security reasons—and it would not be necessary very often—would meet in camera; a committee which would not examine serving officers because that is contrary to our parliamentary traditions and I do not think it would be wise . . . , but a committee which could examine experts in the field of defence in this country and outside this country and get their views. . . .[51]

Such a committee did not materialize. The Special Committee, in defiance of its terms of reference and despite the attempt of its chairman to stop it, consumed much of its time debating the wisdom of the limits the Government had placed on its freedom of inquiry. A proposal by its Opposition members that it should call witnesses other than Government officials* was defeated by a vote of the Committee (7 to 5) on the grounds that it "would be a real departure from our practice in Canada to have policy discussions by those who have no responsibility."[52]

*The Liberal defence critic, Mr. Paul Hellyer, announced his intention, if the Committee allowed, to call as witness Dr. Ormond Solandt, former chairman of the Defence Research Board; General Howard Graham, former Chief of the General Staff; and Dr. Roger Hilsman, professor at the Johns Hopkins University.

Chapter Five

INTELLIGENCE

THE ORIGINS AND DEVELOPMENT
OF INTELLIGENCE FACILITIES

The term "intelligence" is used throughout this chapter to mean "the kind of knowledge a state must possess regarding other states in order to assure itself that its cause will not suffer nor its understandings fail because its statesmen and soldiers plan and act in ignorance."* It was only slowly that Canadian governments came to appreciate the intimate connection of intelligence in this sense and the quality of their external affairs. One of the earliest occasions on which the lesson was driven home was when Sir Wilfrid Laurier summoned Joseph Pope to his office on June 22, 1899, and gave him "a job which is nothing else than to prepare the case of the Canadian Govt. in the matter of the Alaska boundary."[1] The search thus begun for materials to support the Canadian contention as to where the frontier should run revealed, perhaps for the first time, the lack of even the most basic data by which Canadian vital interests might be safeguarded. It did not take Pope many days to realize that the information available in Canada was wholly insufficient for his purpose, and on July 10 he wrote to a friend in the Colonial Office for assistance:

It is a case of making bricks without straw. I find the greatest difficulty in collecting the papers necessary to a proper understanding of the case. Are there any blue books published about 1888 at home containing the correspondence of that period? If there are I wish you would send me a set of them—of all the correspondence that has been published since 1886. I have nothing between the Russian Ukase of 1825 & Lord Herschell's letters but fragmentary despatches and a few Yankee "Ex docs". . . .

I dare say you may be surprised at my requests for what are elementary papers, but you must remember my office has only to do with the internal affairs within the Dominion. Alaska matters have always been referred to the Minister of the Interior, and though I say it with bated breath, never properly dealt with. . . . We sadly lack system here.[2]

---

*Sherman Kent, *Strategic Intelligence* (Princeton, 1949), p. 3. Other studies relating intelligence to foreign policy are Roger Hilsman, *Strategic Intelligence and National Decisions* (Glencoe, Ill., 1956), and Harry Howe Ransom, *Central Intelligence and National Security* (Cambridge, Mass., 1958).

The material was duly supplied but when, a few months later, Pope, his appetite whetted, wrote for more—"it is very desirable that we should have a record of this correspondence, and the Premier rather looks to me to keep it up"[3]—the reply, delayed for two years, indicated that the British authorities could not be counted on in future as regular purveyors of confidential materials:

The F.O. [Foreign Office], after much searching of heart, have agreed to let you have the accompanying volumes of the Alaska Print for your *personal* use, and on condition that when you cease to be officially seized of that question you will return them and not pass them on to your successor. They know you but they are scarcely likely to have the acquaintance of anyone who succeeds you, at any rate to such an extent as they deem requisite for the purpose.[4]

The search for information on Alaska boundary led Joseph Pope to Washington and the State Department in 1903, and there, with considerable reluctance on the part of the official with whom he was in contact (who later became apprehensive that his conduct might be treasonable), he was allowed to photograph its collection of documents concerning Russian occupation of Alaska.[5]

The inadequacy of materials available to Canadian governments for conducting their external relations was demonstrated again a few years later when the Minister of Labour, Rodolphe Lemieux, went to Japan to try to negotiate a treaty limiting the number of Japanese who would be allowed to proceed to Canada as immigrants. Allowed by the British ambassador, Sir Claude Macdonald, to read Foreign Office papers in the embassy library, Lemieux learned more in Tokyo about the background of the problem than he had been able to find out in Ottawa.

Je n'ai pu obtenir à Ottawa [he wrote from Japan] que des bribes de documents et de correspondances, qui rapportent à ce traité. Il faut voire au contraire les comme *records* du F.O. à Londres sont parfaits et comme la genèse du traité en est complète. J'ai pu mettre la main sur ces records (12 *vols.* semblables aux factums de la Cour d'Appel). *"Forewarned is forearmed."* C'est en consultant tout cela que j'ai cause, tout en évitant d'aborder ceux qui nous étaient défavorables. Il faudra que Sir W. [Laurier] réorganise dans le service public tout ce qui a trait à la correspondance officielle. Il ne faut plus qu'elle soit repartie entre les différents ministères.[6]

On returning to Canada, Lemieux wrote to the British Foreign Secretary to see if a copy of the series could be sent to Ottawa for the future use of the Canadian Government; he emphasized how valuable this material had been to him during his recent negotiations with the Japanese authorities, and promised that its confidential character would be respected. Sir Edward Grey replied that it would "not be possible to issue completed volumes of the series owing to the strict rules we are obliged to observe with regard to their distribution and to the principle involved in these rules; but if you will specify what special documents you may wish to have, I will gladly do my best to meet your wishes."[7] Lemieux sent this letter to Joseph Pope for his comments. "I return Sir E. Grey's letter," Pope replied,

which I think calls for no answer. Not merely every volume, but according to my recollections nearly every page of the Confidential Prints, contains some reference to Canada. The series is a whole, and portions of it would be of no use. What a commentary this affords on our lack of system! If my suggestion had been listened to years ago, we should not have to ask anybody for these papers today, for we should have had them ourselves.[8]

The growing need for orderly and complete sources of information to guide the Government through increasingly complicated problems of external policy was a principal factor leading to the creation of the Department of External Affairs. "We are much handicapped here," Lord Grey, the Governor General, had written in 1907, "by the want of any organized Department for the co-ordination and reproduction of information bearing on the relations between Canada and the U.S."[9] In his memorandum of the same year to the Civil Service Commission, Joseph Pope cited the nation's deficiency in what a later generation of intelligence experts have termed "basic descriptive intelligence"— "the groundwork which gives meaning to day-to-day change and the groundwork without which speculation into the future is likely to be meaningless"[10]—as requiring the attention of a special branch of government. This material, he wrote,

has been so scattered, and passed through so many hands that there is no approach to continuity in any of the departmental files. Such knowledge concerning them as is available is, for the most part, lodged in the memories of a few officials. . . . As the Dominion grows this state of things must always be getting worse. If some reform is not soon effected it will be too late. Even now, I am of opinion that it would be an extremely difficult task to construct from our official files anything approaching to a complete record of any of the international questions in which Canada has been concerned during the past fifty years. . . .
    My suggestion is, that all despatches relating to external affairs should be referred by the Privy Council to one department, whose staff should contain men trained in the study of these questions. . . . These officials should be in close touch with the other departments, from which they could draw all necessary information, the raw material, as it were, of their work; but the digesting of this information, and its presentation in diplomatic form, should rest with them.[11]

The creation of the Department of External Affairs in 1909 did not and could not of itself bring into being a stockpile of intelligence data of sufficient scope and quality as to work immediate improvement in the conduct of external policy. That had to await the exercise of the right of legation (thus ensuring sources of information independent of the Foreign Office), and, even more fundamentally, the desire to strike out on a distinctively Canadian course in foreign affairs. But it was a step, however hesitant, in that direction.

During the years immediately preceding the First World War, the Canadian Government suffered, perhaps for the first time but certainly not for the last, from a scarcity of intelligence data of the "speculative-evaluative" variety (the term later assigned by professional intelligence officers to the kind of information required for reliable prediction of probable courses of action of other states[12]). Canadian statesmen during the years 1909–14 urgently needed some such strategic assessment of the intentions of Germany under the Kaiser in order to respond appropriately to Britain's request for emergency naval assistance. The assumption underlying Laurier's naval policy was that there was no emergency. That assumption could not be so confidently held in 1911, when the Borden Government assumed office, and the new Prime Minister did what he could to obtain a realistic appraisal of the likely danger to world peace of the *Flottenpolitik* then in progress. In the absence of other authority, Borden turned to the First Lord of the Admiralty, Mr. Winston Churchill, and it was from this eloquent if not exactly impartial source that the Canadian Government received the information causing it to abandon Laurier's policy in favour of an emergency cash contribution to the Imperial Government.[13]

The coming of the First World War greatly sharpened the anxiety of the Canadian Government concerning the reliability of the intelligence sources at its disposal and the extent to which these were being properly exploited. Within a year nearly a quarter of a million soldiers had been sent from Canada to the Western front. Their casualties were both fearful and unexpected, and a visit by the Prime Minister to England and France in 1915 left him in no doubt that much of the slaughter was due to blunders and mismanagement in the strategic direction of the war. On his return to Canada Borden cabled to the Acting High Commissioner in London, Sir George Perley:

Please inform Bonar Law that we would appreciate fuller and more exact information from time to time respecting conduct of War and proposed military operations as to which little or no information vouchsafed. We thoroughly realize necessity central control of Empire armies but Govern-

ments of overseas Dominions have large responsibilities to their people for
conduct of War, and we deem ourselves entitled to fuller information and
to consultation respecting general policy in War operations. The great
difficulty of obtaining information during my recent visit to London seemed
partially occasioned by lack of proper co-ordination between several departments responsible for conduct of War. Perhaps new Council or Committee
can arrange for information and consultation.[14]

As a former Canadian, Bonar Law might have been expected to be
sympathetic to this request, and as Secretary of State for War in a
position to do something about it; but his reply to Borden, transmitted
through the Acting High Commissioner, was disappointing:

We fully realize, I need not say, the great part which your Government is
playing in this war and as Sir Robert Borden found when he was here we
were only too delighted to put him into possession of all the information
which was available to the Cabinet. It is of course much more difficult to
keep him in touch now but it is our desire to give him the fullest information
and if there is any way which occurs to him or to yourself in which this
can be done I shall be delighted to carry it out. . . . At the same time I
should like you to repeat to him what I have said to you—that if no scheme
is practicable then it is very undesirable that the question should be raised.[15]

"Mr. Bonar Law's letter is not especially illuminating," was Borden's
comment, "and leaves the matter exactly where it was before my letter
was sent." He despatched a strongly worded reply:

During the past four months since my return from Great Britain, the
Canadian Government (except for an occasional telegram from you [Perley]
or Sir Max Aitken) have had just what information could be gleaned from
the daily Press and no more. As to consultation, plans of campaign have
been made and unmade, measures adopted and apparently abandoned and
generally speaking steps of the most important and even vital character
have been taken, postponed or rejected without the slightest consultation
with the authorities of this Dominion.

  It can hardly be expected that we shall put 400,000 or 500,000 men in
the field and willingly accept the position of having no more voice and
receiving no more consideration than if we were toy automata. Any person
cherishing such an expectation harbours an unfortunate and even dangerous
delusion.[16]

This remonstrance produced "a number of the most important documents which have been circulated to the War Council," sent to the
Canadian Prime Minister with instructions that they be shown to
no one else and burned after perusal. "They came," Borden later
recalled, "in a strong canvas bag loaded heavily with lead. On the
voyage, this bag was kept on the bridge under directions to throw
it overboard in case the ship should be subject to capture."[17] It also produced a promise by Bonar Law that he would "continue to set aside the
most important [documents] and forward them to you later." At least

one further consignment of this character reached Borden, for in July 1916 Sir George Perley himself arrived in Ottawa with a bundle containing, among other items, "five appreciations of the General Staff."[18]

Lloyd George's replacement of Asquith as Prime Minister and his creation of the War Cabinet in 1916 brought some improvement in the flow of information. The Colonial Secretary in the new Government was instructed to send to the Canadian Governor General "a weekly letter for the personal and confidential information of [the Governor and his] Prime Minister."[19] By April 1917 this had given way to a fortnightly telegram of diplomatic intelligence. The Canadian Government was still unsatisfied by these arrangements. In May 1918 the Acting High Commissioner wrote to Sir Robert Borden:

You and I have talked over several times the possibility of obtaining more regularly for you confidential information and reports. I talked this over with the Colonial Secretary more than once but no systematic arrangement was ever put into force. Since Lord Beaverbrook has been appointed Minister of Information, I have discussed the question with him, and a couple of months ago he wrote me that he was anxious to furnish the Prime Ministers of the Dominions, through the High Commissioners, with the fullest confidential information in his power. He further went on to say that he was willing to send me confidentially for despatch to you periodic summaries of the whole situation in the field and in political affairs. Of course, I was very happy to accept this suggestion and make an arrangement of this kind. It has, however, taken a considerable time to put it into force, and last month they wrote me from the Department saying that they found it rather a business getting things in order and that their intelligence staff would not be complete for some weeks. However, everything seems to be now nearly in order. . . . I hope, therefore, that the first of these reports will be ready in a few days and that thereafter they may be forthcoming regularly.[20]

More important than telegraphed or written despatches from Whitehall as a means of keeping the Canadian Government informed about the strategic direction of the war was its membership in the Imperial War Cabinet. The invitation to Borden to attend "a series of special and continuous meetings of the War Cabinet in order to consider urgent questions affecting prosecution of War, the possible conditions on which in agreement with our Allies we could assent to its termination, and the problems which will then immediately arise" was received in Ottawa on Christmas Day, 1916.[21] Borden attended meetings of the Imperial War Cabinet in February and March 1917; in June, July and August 1918; and from November 1918 through May 1919, meeting first in London and then, as the British Empire Delegation to the Peace Conference, in Paris. Of the Imperial War Cabinet, Loring Christie, who, as Borden's "fides Achates, idea man, confidential envoy and general right hand man for external affairs,"[22] saw much of its deliberations at first hand, wrote afterwards: "It brought the responsible political heads of the different states of the Empire face to face . . . and it supplied them in the most convenient way with the best information going. . . . All the commitments of the Allies, secret and otherwise, were laid before them at the outset in March, 1917, so far as they had not been disclosed before. *All* the cards were put on the table."[23] Yet even in this body there were the *longueurs* inseparable from any committee however exalted, and in his diary Borden on more than one occasion vented his impatience. "Then to War Cabinet where some futile discussion took place. As bad as our Cabinet" (March 29, 1917). "Imperial War Cabinet at 11:30 until 2 and long discussion as to channels of communication. . . . Fool talk prevailed in some quarters. It is absurd that this result should have taken two days to accomplish" (July 25, 1918). And it was in the Imperial War Cabinet that the Canadian Prime Minister received misleading estimates of the economic advantage to result from participating in the Siberian intervention; these estimates, reinforced by equally misleading intelligence from officials of his own Department of Trade and Commerce,[24] brought about the Dominion's ill-timed involvement in Russian affairs in 1918–19, from which extrication was to prove so difficult.

INTELLIGENCE AND FOREIGN
POLICY: THE YEARS BETWEEN
THE WARS

The hope and expectation of Sir Robert Borden had been that the Imperial War Cabinet would provide the basis for a new imperial partnership in time of peace. At the Imperial Conference of 1921 the prime ministers cast about for the first (and as it was to prove the final) time for some way of implementing the protean Resolution IX, which in 1917 had promised them "an adequate voice in foreign policy and in foreign relations," an ambiguous formula designed to satisfy equally those whose eyes were fixed upon the promised land of unconditional autonomy and those to whom perfection in imperial affairs meant a single Empire policy formulated in Downing Street. But the Imperial Conference did not give its blessing to an Imperial Peace Cabinet. Publicly it gave its blessing to very little. But behind the scenes it was thought that the problems of empire could be solved by the panacea of improved communications. "What you want," the British Foreign Secretary told the members of the Imperial Conference, is greater knowledge and greater influence on matters which concern you as parts of the Empire, and in which you yourselves, your Parliaments, your troops, may be involved. Now, how can we bring that about? The suggestion I made to the Prime Minister [Lloyd George] was this: you want, before you are involved in action, to know what has happened, to know what is happening from day to day. I think, so far as I can ascertain, your present knowledge is inadequate. What do you get now? Once a week, I believe, there is sent out to you . . . a paper called "The British Empire Report", and another called "The Foreign Countries Report", which contains a condensed summary of the information, telegraphic and otherwise, of the preceding week. Now look at the contrast between that and what happens when you come here. As long as you are in London you get the telegrams from day to day, you get a selection of despatches and papers sent to you by me on important matters, and you get . . . the papers recording the interviews of the Foreign Minister with various Ambassadors and Ministers, and the papers he supplies to the Cabinet. Cannot we bring your position when you are away from here into closer conformity with that which exists when you are here? . . . The suggestion I made to the Prime Minister was this: that we might send out to you, to the Prime Ministers of the Dominions, once a month, or, if necessary, once a week, a selection of those extremely confidential Foreign Office Papers which are now seen only by the Cabinet and circulated to our representatives in our Embassies and Legations abroad.

At this juncture the Foreign Secretary was interrupted by the Prime Minister of Australia. "You are speaking," said William Hughes, "of sending it by post." "Yes," Curzon answered, "and a great crisis leading up to war does not develop in a week or two. A war or any great affair in which you are concerned is the result of a process that has been going on for several weeks or months."[25]

The first "great affair" in which Canada was subsequently involved brought the country to the brink of war not during "several weeks or months," as Curzon had predicted, but in a matter of hours. This was the Chanak crisis. As it happened the Canadian Prime Minister learned of Mustafa Kemal's threat to the Neutral Zone not through a despatch from the United Kingdom Government but from a local newspaper. So much might have been forgiven, even though had Mackenzie King been in Ottawa rather than in Newcastle, Ontario, he would still have been notified of the crisis through the press rather than through the regular channel of the Governor General's office. Less easily pardoned was the inadequacy of British intelligence reports during the preceding weeks. No cabled despatches from any department of the United Kingdom Government had been received in Ottawa prior to Winston Churchill's "invitation" to the Dominions to send troops. Foreign Office reports on Turkey and the Near East, travelling by sea bag, had been arriving at irregular intervals. But in no case was a report received under three weeks from the time of its despatch; in most cases well over a month elapsed between transmission and receipt; on a single day (August 28, 1922) no fewer than eight reports arrived at once, their dates of origin varying from July 17 to August 5; and no reports at all were received during the ten days (September 7 to 16) immediately preceding the crisis. Moreover, the information contained in such Foreign Office material that did arrive left much to be desired. The report of July 25 (received on August 28) suggested that the Greek Army was "never in a more healthy or efficient state." The report of August 15 (received on September 6 and the last to reach Ottawa before the Churchill "invitation") consisted of a copy of a memorandum from the Italian ambassador in London containing the assurance that "the Turks are beginning to consider with increased inclination the necessity of terminating the war."[26] In the light of these facts a later accusation by *The Times* that the reason the Dominions remained in ignorance of the crisis until it burst upon them was that their governments failed to read the despatches sent to them by the Foreign Office was rendered more galling by its further observation that reading despatches "is no doubt a laborious task, and if there is no excuse for Ministers shirking it in London, it is clearly harder for Ministers in Ottawa or Pretoria to give their time to matters which lie so far away."[27]

Had the Canadian Government of that day been anxious to develop its own effective foreign policy, the only logical response to the failure of the British Government to provide it with some advance notice of the likelihood of war in the Middle East was to press strongly for improved methods of communication, and to exercise the right of legation granted to Canada in 1920. No effort was made to move in either of these directions. An active and independent role in world affairs was about the last thing the Canadian people wanted at this time. "There is a curious tiredness over 'foreign affairs'," the editor of a Toronto newspaper wrote privately in 1920. "We have heard so much of War Cabinets and Leagues of Nations and Ambassadors to Washington . . . that many people begin to ask if we have any questions of our own and whether or not our statesmen have any interest in the problems of Canada."[28] The Canadian Prime Minister was quick to sense this mood and eager to cater to it. To improve the quality of information might sharpen the obligation to take initiatives, and to avoid this unpalatable situation Mackenzie King deliberately shielded himself and his colleagues from intelligence which might make isolation less defensible. Thus he repeatedly turned down suggestions that his High Commissioner in London should meet regularly with the Secretary of State for Dominion Affairs or with the Foreign Secretary, in the company of his Dominion colleagues, to be furnished with background information.* Nor was he in a hurry to create a diplomatic mission at Washington. While his delay was partly due to the opposition of his Minister of Finance and to the difficulty of finding a suitable appointee, the desire to improve his Government's information about American affairs was not a strongly countervailing factor. Indeed when Merchant Mahoney, the agent of the Department of External Affairs who looked after such Canadian interests as the British embassy in Washington left unattended, offered to send to Ottawa a daily summary of the activities of the Congress when in session, the Prime Minister's office replied that a daily bulletin was too much and a weekly would be better.[29] A good deal of the information reaching the Canadian Government on United States affairs bearing upon Dominion interests came neither from the British embassy nor from the Department's agent in Washington but from a Canadian newspaperman, Tom King, whom the Cabinet authorized in 1922 "to

*As Secretary of State for Dominion Affairs at the time, Leopold Amery later wrote, "it was left to me to keep in touch with the High Commissioners as best I could. In the press of work this was not easy, unless some particular matter of special importance called for an interview. So I readily took up a suggestion of Mr. Peter Larkin's, the Canadian High Commissioner, that I should be 'at home' one morning every week for all the High Commissioners. This worked admirably, giving me an opportunity of telling them collectively of what was going on in 'high politics', as well as in economic or other affairs in which they were generally interested. . . . Unfortunately, when Mackenzie King heard of this at the time of the Imperial Conference [of 1926], he at once suspected a sinister design on my part of gradually working towards some sort of Imperial policy council situated in London—the great bugbear which he always dreaded. So poor Larkin had to come and tell me, very apologetically, that he was not allowed to see me except by himself." L. S. Amery, *My Political Life*, II (London, 1953), p. 377. The Foreign Secretary commented privately at the time of the disadvantage to him of having "no agent of the Canadian Government here with whom I am authorized by that Government to discuss confidentially these problems. . . . What I should like to see is a body of High Commissioners possessing the political confidence of their Governments, chosen for their political (I do not mean party) qualifications, and authorized to meet me regularly as a body to discuss the urgent questions of the day and the development of events as they occur. . . . If these men knew the minds of their Governments, 'devilled' the Foreign Office papers for them, and were in close touch with them, they would at least know what points in our policy most affected their respective Dominions, would call the attention of their Governments to whatever might particularly concern them, and could elicit any further explanations or information which they were instructed by their Governments to seek." Sir Austen Chamberlain to Sir Robert Borden, Feb. 27, 1926, Christie Papers.

furnish us with confidential reports from time to time."* For the next few years Tom King wrote his "despatches" in the form of personal letters to the Prime Minister; they were read, and frequently answered, and the quality of their information was such that Mackenzie King continued to use this unusual source even after the opening of the Canadian legation in 1927.

Of the three world capitals where aggressions leading to the Second World War were spawned and hatched, only one by 1939 was the site of a Canadian diplomatic mission. The legation at Tokyo neither fore-warned the Government of the danger of Japanese militarism nor offered wise counsel when the danger became obvious. Canada's first minister to Japan, appointed in 1928 and remaining throughout the Manchurian crisis, was Herbert Marler. Like the Minister to the United States, Mr. Vincent Massey, Marler had been a member of the Mackenzie King administration whose diplomatic posting followed soon after the dis-appointment of being unable to secure election to the House of Com-mons. His background in business and finance, together with the diplomatist's traditional sympathy for the country of his mission, pre-disposed him to the cause of Japan and rendered him susceptible to

*The Prime Minister officially recommended this appointment in a letter to the Governor-in-Council dated October 25, 1922: "The undersigned has the honour to represent that Your Excellency's advisers have for some time past been im-pressed with the desirability of having a resident correspondent connected with the press at Washington, who would be in a position to ascertain and report confidentially from time to time what it might be of interest for the Canadian Government to know touching legislative, administrative and judicial proceedings in that capital.

"The undersigned understands that foreign governments very generally employ in such capacity American newspapermen, who can talk with Senators, Con-gressmen, and executive officials with the object of finding out and reporting what it may be useful for their principals to know. Many things are happening in Washington from day to day of importance to the Canadian Government. During the coming session there will no doubt come up for consideration questions of special interest to the Dominion, such, for example, as the regulation of naval strength on the Great Lakes; the re-writing of the Transportation Act, especially those sections dealing with labour and labour disputes; the Borah Bill, which has already passed the Senate, exempting American coastal vessels from the payment of tolls on the Panama Canal; tariff legislation; the Ship Subsidy Bill, and others. The most important work in connection with these subjects will be done in committee, the proceedings of which are often not reported at all. It is particularly desirable, having regard to these and other questions, that we should have a trustworthy agent on the spot closely to watch this committee work and to furnish us with confidential reports from time to time.

"The undersigned accordingly recommends that he be authorized to engage in that capacity the services of Mr. T. W. King, formerly connected with the Canadian Press, Limited, and now doing journalistic work at Washington, and to pay him therefor, out of the Vote for Canadian representation in the United States. . . ."

propaganda that its soldiers were bringing law and order to a disordered China. His despatches to the Bennett Government doubtless reflected the pro-Japanese bias to be found in his private correspondence of the period with the Leader of the Opposition,[30] although his Prime Minister's declaration at the height of the crisis that he was unable to offer an opinion on events in the Far East because of "the slight knowledge that we possess"[31] suggests that the intelligence they contained was neither extensive nor important.

The lack of a legation at Rome may have deprived the Canadian Government of information without placing its policies at a disadvantage, for the more that was known about fascism in its Mediterranean setting the better disposed a significant group of Canadians became towards it. The lofty sentiments of doctrine elaborated by Mussolini's publicists, with their apotheosis of order, discipline, family, nation, their pseudo-syndicalist remedies for industrial unrest, their shrill assault upon the liberal values, gained powerful support among the élite of French Canada which a Canadian government disregarded at its peril. National Socialism was something else again. But diagnosis of the Nazi movement was hindered by the severity of economic depression at home and by the isolationist tradition.* Events in Germany were consistently misconstrued as a nationalist revival of the traditional type, distinguished, perhaps, by the odd fanaticism of its leaders, by the strut and swagger of its rank and file, but for all that a movement which might be comprehended in traditional terms, appeased and contained by traditional methods. The intelligence which might have put to flight such wishful thoughts was lacking. The Canadian Government, having no mission at Berlin, necessarily relied on whatever Whitehall might select for its instruction from the despatches of Sir Nevile Henderson, and these conveyed a sadly erroneous interpretation of Nazi policy and motives.† This unhelpful source was supplemented by the assessment of the Canadian Minister in Paris, Philippe Roy, who informed his Government on September 9, 1938, that Hitler, being "an intelligent man," would not "take the risk of spoiling his wonderful achievements in Germany." There remained that of the High Commissioner in London. Mr. Vincent Massey, whose most enduring work in a lifetime of

*This view is elaborated in my essay " 'A Low Dishonest Decade': Aspects of Canadian External Policy, 1931–1939" in H. L. Keenleyside *et al.*, *The Growth of Canadian Policies in External Affairs* (Durham, N.C., 1960), pp. 59–80.

†During the Munich crisis Henderson wrote of "Hitler's own love for peace, dislike of dead Germans and hesitation of risking his regime on a gambler's throw." Quoted in Felix Gilbert, "Two British Ambassadors: Perth and Henderson" in Gordon A. Craig and Felix Gilbert, eds., *The Diplomats: 1919–1939* (Princeton, 1953), p. 543.

public service still lay ahead, was then a gifted and experienced diplomatist; but his closest associates in Britain were of the group which moved with disastrous effect between Cliveden, Printing House Square and Downing Street, and nothing he learned from them seems likely to have provided a useful corrective to the misleading despatches passed on by the Dominions Office.[32]

The most misleading information was derived at first hand. In 1937 Mackenzie King decided to go from the Imperial Conference to Germany. There he met and talked with Hitler and other leading personalities of the Third Reich. Like so many others, the Canadian Prime Minister fell victim to the Führer's remarkable capacity for mesmerizing his visitors. "There is no doubt that Hitler had a power of fascinating men," Mr. Churchill wrote in his memoirs; and added the sage advice: "Unless the terms are equal, it is better to keep away."[33] As between the Prime Minister of Canada and the perpetrator of the Nazi *Schrechlichkeit* the terms were far from equal, and the extent of Hitler's advantage may be measured in the opinions with which Mackenzie King returned to Canada and which he shared with its public over the national radio: "Of this I am certain. . . . Neither the governments nor the peoples of any countries I have visited desire war, or view the possibility of war between each other, as other than likely to end in self-destruction, and the destruction of European civilization itself."[34] That the destruction of European civilization was precisely the Nazi objective was "speculative-evaluative intelligence" which the Canadian Prime Minister did not have at his disposal; for, as was remarked of him in a different connection, "Mr. King never quite got it into his head during his economic studies at Toronto and Harvard that our civilization is dominated by carnivorous animals."[35]

INTELLIGENCE AND FOREIGN
POLICY: THE SECOND
WORLD WAR

The Second World War helped to dispel some (but not all) of that "anti-Downing Street complex" from which Mackenzie King had suffered in the 1930's and of which the British Commonwealth of Nations was so nearly the victim.* One inhibition soon to disappear was the edict against meetings of the Canadian High Commissioner in the company

---

*A justification of this statement is contained in my essay, " 'A Low Dishonest Decade,' " pp. 72–5.

of his Dominion colleagues with the Foreign Secretary or the Secretary of State for Dominion Affairs to receive background information supplementing the daily despatches. This stern prohibition was in force as late as 1939, and was relaxed only when the High Commissioner pleaded that the pressure of business on members of the British Government was making it difficult for him continually to be requesting special audiences. Only after the war began did meetings take place on a regular rather than on a sporadic basis. "Their immediate practical purpose," an authority has noted, "was the conveying of up-to-date and accurate information about wartime developments to the Dominion representatives for transmission when they deemed it desirable to their governments, but they served equally as a channel by which the views or the representations of dominion governments could be conveyed by their High Commissioners to the Secretary of State or to the Foreign Secretary."[36]

The war gave great impetus as well to the flow of information in the despatches which daily went out from London to the Dominion capitals—"sheaves of telegrams," as the Secretary of State for Dominion Affairs described them, "on all and every subject of mutual interest—foreign affairs, economic development, military co-operation, even domestic issues here which are likely to interest our partners. We tell them everything we can."[37] In the view of Mr. Winston Churchill too much was communicated to the Dominion governments in this fashion; in December 1940 he enjoined the Dominions Office "not to scatter so much deadly and secret information over this very large circle" or to "get into the habit of running a kind of newspaper full of deadly secrets."[38]

Of greater significance than the quantity of material thus received was its quality; it is at least arguable that the Dominion governments would have been served better had they received nothing at all rather than the distorted views relayed to them in the later 1930's. The quality of information sent out by the Churchill Government, however, was of a different, and better, grade, the more valuable for being trusted by its recipients. (Marshal Stalin, it will be recalled, paid no heed to the warning of Mr. Churchill in February 1941 that British intelligence sources had information leading them to believe that a German invasion of Russia would take place some time in June of that year.) "The cool and careful appreciation of the military situation prepared by the Chiefs of Staff and sent out on 4 May 1940," writes Professor Mansergh, "was a model of its kind."[39] Hardly a model (for it will stand alone), but no less valuable, was the document composed by Mr. Churchill himself on June 16, 1940, to lesson the shock of the fall of France for the prime ministers and peoples of the Dominions. "In it he explained that Britain's resolve to continue the struggle alone was 'not based upon mere obstinacy or desperation' but upon an assessment of 'the real strength of our position', which he then proceeded to examine in some detail." As he observed later, "all came true."[40]

Lapses were inevitable. On September 19, 1941, there went out from the Dominions Office a woefully inadequate appraisal of the situation in the Far East, detecting "signs of a certain weakening in attitude of Japan towards United States and ourselves," reporting an improvement in the defences of Malaya, urging the reinforcement of the garrison at Hong Kong, and requesting Canadian troops for that purpose.* There were also errors of omission. The offer of union to France in June 1940, the ultimatum to the French fleet and its bombardment at Oran, the text of the Atlantic Charter, the unconditional surrender formula—these were some of the matters of moment to the Canadian Government about which it was not consulted and which consequently provoked in Mackenzie King reactions ranging from irritation to outrage. But notwithstanding the occasional breakdown, the Canadian Prime Minister was highly satisfied both with the machinery for transmitting intelligence between members of the Commonwealth and with the quality of the information thus transmitted. Mackenzie King's fervent defence of the system delivered to the Canadian House of Commons on February 17, 1941, and later that year in London is in striking contrast to Sir Robert Borden's dissatisfaction at a comparable stage of the preceding war.

One of the considerations in his rejection of the proposal to reconstitute the Imperial War Cabinet, mentioned in his speeches on the subject in 1941 but not there given the prominence it assumed in

---

*The text of this fateful telegram is given in full in Col. C. P. Stacey, *Six Years of War: The Army in Canada, Britain and the Pacific* (Ottawa, 1955), pp. 440–1. The Minister of National Defence at the time later admitted that "the considerations set out in the telegram were very largely the factors which influenced me" in recommending to the Canadian Government that troops be sent to Hong Kong. (Quoted in *ibid.*, p. 442).

Canada was not the only Dominion to suffer as the result of poor intelligence from the United Kingdom Government. In its despatches to Australia and New Zealand urging the use of their troops in Greece in 1941, "the hope that Turkey and Yugoslavia might act was mentioned after Eden and others had said explicitly that no such hope was reasonable. . . . Moreover, one of Eden's last cables [to London] was not repeated to New Zealand. It reported, among other things, that Longmore, for the Air Force, was not confident that he could give adequate air support to the operations. . . ." F. L. W. Wood, *The New Zealand People at War: Political and External Affairs* (Wellington, 1958), pp. 183–4.

his own mind, was the need for the Prime Minister of Canada to stay within close call of the President of the United States. The association of Franklin Roosevelt and Mackenzie King had not begun in student days at Harvard University (King's graduate work there was done in 1897–9, whereas Roosevelt entered Harvard as an undergraduate in 1900), but that Mackenzie King allowed a popular belief to the contrary to persist suggests the infinite satisfaction he derived from a relationship he was later wont to describe in somewhat extravagant terms. Their meetings as President and Prime Minister had begun in March 1937; they reached the summit of achievement in the rendezvous at Ogdensburg in August 1940.

Such meetings were of value chiefly for the policy decisions which were their outcome, but their importance as a source of information is not to be overlooked. Indeed the cables sent by the Prime Minister of Canada to the Prime Minister of the United Kingdom in the summer of 1940 conveyed the contents of the President's mind with more fidelity than did those reaching Mr. Churchill from Lord Lothian, his ambassador in Washington; for a few fleeting weeks the Canadian Government fully justified its subsequently inflated reputation as the Anglo-American "interpreter." Thereafter, as Mr. Churchill and Franklin Roosevelt forged their own friendship, and as Anglo-American co-operation grew more intimate in every aspect of the common cause, the United Kingdom and the United States had steadily less need of an interpreter's services. The Canadian Government, no longer sole confidant of each, became increasingly preoccupied with the vexing task of trying to keep itself informed of what the strategists of the Grand Alliance were up to. In November 1941, the United States government consulted representatives of the United Kingdom, China, the Netherlands and Australia concerning negotiations that had been in progress between American and Japanese officials since September; but despite what an American historian has described as "the clear Canadian interest in the political and security problems of the Pacific," the Canadian Government was at no time consulted or informed.* This was only the first of a number of similar episodes in the months to follow.

The appointment in 1942 of Major General Maurice Pope as the War Committee's representative in Washington, and the creation during

*Col. Stanley W. Dziuban, *Military Relations between the United States and Canada, 1939–1945* (Washington, D.C., 1959), p. 70. "The failure to include Canada among the powers invited to discuss the Pacific problems in late November," Sumner Welles noted after a conversation with the Canadian chargé d'affaires in Washington, "continued, despite all explanations, to rankle." *Ibid.*, p. 71.

the same year of the Canadian Joint Staff Mission (see above, chapter
II), added two potentially useful channels of communication. Intelli-
gence, however, continued to move sluggishly and intermittently.
"Looking back on those days," General Pope has written,

my recollection is that while our British friends told us all they felt they
reasonably could, the attitude of the Americans was as mute as that of their
highly-prized little-neck clams. Even so, if we were precluded from asking
direct questions, what with a word here and a phrase there, added to an
eloquent reticence on another occasion, not only could a fair picture of the
situation at the moment be assembled, but also an intelligent forecast could
be made of things that were to come. I think it is fair to say that not only
was the C.J.S.M. able to keep Ottawa abreast of C.C.O.S. thinking, but
also to indicate the strategic trend for the next months to come.[41]

In addition to Commonwealth and American sources, the Canadian
Government had its own listening posts abroad. The importance of its
French legation was much enhanced after the fall of France by the
decision not to break off diplomatic relations with the Vichy régime but
to allow its representative in Canada to continue his duties in exchange
for what Mr. Churchill was to describe as "a window through which
they could look at what was happening in France."[42] A member of
the Department of External Affairs, Mr. Pierre Dupuy, chargé d'affaires
at the mission which, after the fall of France, had moved to London,
made three visits to unoccupied France in 1940 and 1941, ostensibly
to discuss the interests of Canadians in that area with the Vichy authorities, actually to gather political information. The considerable sympathy
in French Canada for Marshal Pétain would in any case have made it
difficult for the Canadian Government to have broken off relations
during the first few months of his régime, but during 1941 and 1942,
and particularly after the Dieppe raid in August 1942 (when Pétain
sent a message of congratulation to the German defenders for inflicting
great losses on the Canadian forces) nothing could have been more
popular than severance, and it was only because Mr. Churchill insisted
on the value of Mr. Dupuy's contacts that diplomatic relations were
preserved until November 1942.*

Two other potentially important observation posts were created by the
Canadian Government during the Second World War. As Minister to the

*From London in August 1941 Mackenzie King had cabled an explanation to
Ernest Lapointe: "In conversation today Mr. Churchill was quite emphatic in
his desire to have Dupuy continue as chargé d'affaires. He said that Dupuy was
the only means of contact that he, Churchill, had with Vichy, and that while
Dupuy might be optimistic himself in reporting things told him which have to
be verified, nevertheless he gave much information which is most helpful."

Soviet Union, Mr. Dana Wilgress went to the wartime capital at Kuiby-shev. Mr. Wilgress was at the time of this appointment Deputy Minister of Trade and Commerce; he had long experience of Russian affairs, having been a member of the Canadian Economic Mission to Siberia in 1918–19 and returning to the Soviet Union on a number of later occasions; he spoke the Russian language, enjoying in this respect an advantage over his American colleagues. Major General Victor Odlum who went to open Canada's legation at Chungking had no special knowledge of Far Eastern affairs and spoke no Chinese, but his despatches, in so far as they may be presumed to have furnished his Prime Minister's knowledge of the country, might conceivably have shaped the course of post-war policy. At the Quebec Conference of 1943, when Franklin Roosevelt and Mr. Churchill disagreed about the place of China in future international organization, Mackenzie King expressed the view that "the new generation of Chinese were quite different from the old. There was a new China, a youthful China that had to be reckoned with and must not be underestimated."[43]

THE CONTEMPORARY

INTELLIGENCE COMMUNITY

By "the contemporary intelligence community" is meant the resources now at the disposal of the Canadian Government for collecting and evaluating information useful in shaping its external policies. They include the following: (1) Canadian representation abroad; (2) representatives of other Commonwealth countries; (3) agencies of the United States government; (4) certain undefined "intelligence exchanges"; (5) the repository of information and experience of government personnel at home.

(1) In 1953 the then Secretary of State for External Affairs, Mr. Lester Pearson, addressed the following remarks to the House of Commons Standing Committee on External Affairs:

In our concentration of interests over new methods of consultation, over new international agencies to be set up, we sometimes forget that we have an old and tried method of consultation through the regular diplomatic services. . . . Our best sources of information are usually the messages which we get from our representatives abroad. . . .

I do not, for instance, have to rely only on this weekly [international] committee in Washington to find out what is likely to happen in Korea. We have our Canadian Ambassador [to the United States] in touch with the State Department every day. . . . Similarly from our European missions we knew within a matter of hours what Mr. Dulles was talking about on his recent visits to Paris, Bonn and London. We did not have to apply to any central agency. Mr. Davis for instance is a pretty active person at Bonn and he found out what was said there and the reports were on my desk almost within twenty-four hours; and the same is true in respect of our heads of mission in Paris and London.[44]

The quality of the information received in this way depends, first, on the strategic location of Canadian missions abroad and, second, on the abilities of the members of those missions.

By 1961 Canada had its own diplomatic representation in roughly fifty countries in all the major regions of the globe, as well as representation through permanent delegations in the United Nations, the North Atlantic Council, the Organization for European Economic Co-operation, and commissioners on the international supervisory commissions for Cambodia and Vietnam.* This was a far-flung network by any standard, especially when fortified by the wider commercial contacts of the Department of Trade and Commerce. Its expansion had been exceedingly rapid since 1939, or even since 1945 when Canada was represented in less than a quarter of the countries in which missions had been established fifteen years later.

Even so, there were deficiencies. The head of mission in more than one key capital divided his time and energy between his mission there and another in some other country. As recently as 1961 the High Commissioner in Malaya was also responsible for Canadian representation in Burma; the ambassador to Norway was also ambassador to Iceland; the ambassador to Belgium was also ambassador to Luxembourg; the ambassador to Costa Rica had to find time for ambassadorial duties in Managua, Tegucigalpa and Panama City. Then there were a number of countries where Canada had no diplomatic representation of any kind, including (in 1961) Afghanistan, the Republic of China, the Republic of Korea, Hungary, Iraq, and Jordan. Its absence, it is fair

---

*Canadian *embassies* were located in Argentina, Austria, Belgium, Brazil, Burma, Chile, Colombia, Costa Rica, Cuba, Denmark, the Dominican Republic, Ecuador, Finland, France, the Federal Republic of Germany, Greece, Haiti, Honduras, Iceland, Indonesia, Ireland, Israel, Italy, Japan, the Lebanon, Luxembourg, Mexico, the Netherlands, Nicaragua, Norway, Panama, Peru, Poland, Portugal, Spain, Sweden, Switzerland, Turkey, the Union of Soviet Socialist Republics, the United Arab Republic, the United States of America, Uruguay, Venezuela, and Yugoslavia; *high commissioners' offices* in Australia, Ceylon, Ghana, India, Malaya, New Zealand, Nigeria, Pakistan, the Union of South Africa, and the United Kingdom; *legations* in Czechoslovakia and Iran. A commissioner's office had been opened in the Federation of the West Indies, not yet a Commonwealth member; consular offices in the Philippines; and there was a military mission in Berlin.

to add, was often as much due to the Department of Finance as to the Department of External Affairs (see chapter I); in the case of the People's Republic of China it was due to a continuing policy of non-recognition, denying to Canada as to the United States a listening post however hampered by inhospitable authorities.

In 1948 the Department of External Affairs at Ottawa received from its missions overseas no fewer than 22,500 despatches and letters, and 22,000 telegrams and teletype messages, figures which in the absence of more recent data must be presumed to be very much exceeded by those of the present day. The quality of these intelligence sources is less easily estimated. By 1961 the great embassies in London, Paris and Washington, and the Permanent Mission to the United Nations in New York, each the size of a small foreign office, were operating at peak efficiency under the direction of members of that select group of senior officials at the summit of the public service. Information received from such sources may be presumed to be as full and as accurate as any in the world, and no less perceptively interpreted.

Removed to more exotic posts, however, the Canadian diplomatist operates with less assurance as a purveyor of intelligence. He will be less experienced than the senior and exceptionally gifted public servants presiding over the historic embassies; a Heeney, a Robertson or a Léger could not be spared for Djakarta or Beirut (though it should be noted that Mr. Escott Reid was spared for New Delhi). That is neither unusual nor decisive for, as has been wisely remarked, "no government service can be made up entirely of first-class men; . . . efficiency is finally determined not by the stars but by the average second class."[45] Appraisal of the average second class in the Department of External Affairs comes best, perhaps, from outside observers; an Australian finds its members "articulate, worldly-wise yet earnest, seeking few favours but determined to be active."[46] If they are handicapped in the intelligence aspect of their work (as opposed to its negotiating and propagandist aspects), it is less by their personal qualities than by the long-standing (if diminishing) departmental prejudice against specialization, and the assumption that it is not only possible but desirable for an official to serve just as effectively under palm as under pine. The practical consequence of this generalist approach is the shifting of personnel every two or three years between mission and mission and between home and abroad; and as the most intelligent or ambitious of foreign service officers can hardly acquire real expertise during so short a sojourn, there is accordingly a shortage of experts and an impairment of the quality of intelligence. It should be stressed that this defect is being overcome by longer postings (especially on country and regional desks in the Department at Ottawa) and by a more rational allocation of postings; an Arabic-speaking officer will rarely any longer find his special knowledge diminishing through disuse in some Latin-American capital, and area specialists are now retained at the East Block for five years or even longer.

(2) Supplementing, and in some areas substituting for, Canadian sources of information are those of other Commonwealth nations. Before the emergence of the Commonwealth in Afro-Asia, the United Kingdom was by far the most important source. "Through our mission in London, Canada House, as well as through our embassy in Washington and at other posts where we are both established," the Under Secretary of State for External Affairs commented in 1952, "we do have the advantage of a great deal of information which comes to the United Kingdom through their much wider network of posts."[47] But even by 1952 other Commonwealth capitals were assuming greater importance along the communications system. New Delhi had already demonstrated its importance during the Korean War, its embassy in Peking furnishing the Canadian Government with valuable data about the People's Republic of China. Whereas much of the information received from the United Kingdom came from the Commonwealth Relations Office, information from Indian sources was usually conveyed in conversation with the High Commissioner in New Delhi, a mark of the especial confidence reposed in Mr. Escott Reid as Canada's representative, and passed on in his despatches.*

*Since some Canadians tend to exaggerate the value and significance of the "Ottawa-New Delhi axis," opinions of qualified Indian observers on this matter are of particular interest. One Indian scholar comments: "With Canada, for various reasons, India came to have an unusually warm friendship which was next only to that with the United Kingdom; indeed, it would be no exaggeration to say that at the end of 1956, India and Canada were closer to each other in some respects than was India even with the United Kingdom." M. S. Rajan, "India and the Commonwealth, 1954–56," *India Quarterly*, vol. XVI, no. 1, Jan.–March, 1960, p. 31. The Indian contributor to the *Round Table*'s Jubilee issue remarks: "Till India became independent, Canada was to most Indians no more than a name on a map. All interest in America was directed towards the United States. Once freedom was attained, however, relations with Canada expanded rapidly. The considerable economic assistance received, and the fact that the two countries saw eye to eye on many issues of foreign policy, helped greatly in this. But the primary cause was that India found Mr. St. Laurent, Mr. Pearson and Mr. Diefenbaker (all of whom have visited the country) sympathetic personalities. Party politics in Canada have had no influence on Indo-Canadian relations." "An Indian View," *Round Table*, no. 200, Sept. 1960, p. 373.

A potentially important source of political information was the prime ministers' meeting, where the leaders of an expanding Commonwealth more or less triennially indulged in what their sparse communiqués described as "frank and friendly exchanges of views." A number of member governments, however, including Canada's, were disinclined to use this forum to ventilate intra-Commonwealth grievances, thus striking off their agenda (although not off the agenda of bilateral discussion to which a number of delegates reverted when in London) such important matters as the Kashmir dispute, the neutralist response to communist aggression, and the political implications of *apartheid*.* Whether any real unburdening of mind and heart could take place under such circumstances might well be doubted. A further barrier to communication was concern over security. Older members could not help but feel some misgiving at sharing sensitive information with new and untried colleagues of such exotic political complexion that the assassination in 1959 of the trotskyite Prime Minister of Ceylon, S. W. R. D. Bandaranaike, was thought to have deprived the Commonwealth of one of its trusted senior statesmen. It has thus come about that not much of interest flows indiscriminately throughout the entire Commonwealth communications network, each member instead deciding for itself which, if any, of the others are to be favoured recipients of political secrets. If this works, as it must, to the disadvantage of the "second class members," it does preserve the quality of information for the favoured few.†

(3) In paying tribute to the value of United Kingdom intelligence sources for Canadian foreign policy, the Under Secretary of State for External Affairs observed in 1952 that "we are also indebted to the United States in much the same way for the information and assistance that we get from Washington . . . which it would be very difficult to do without."[48] From the various parts of the United States policy machine, information of all kinds pours into the Canadian capital, impelled mainly by fear of surprise attack upon the common continent.

*Even at the prime ministers' meeting of March 1961, which resulted in South Africa withdrawing its application to remain in the Commonwealth as a republic, discussion of *apartheid* took place only with the permission of the South African Prime Minister; had Dr. Verwoerd refused to give permission, the issue could not with propriety have been discussed. See Canada, *H. of C. Debates*, March 17, 1961, p. 3085.

†Such a practice, however subversive to Commonwealth ideals, is not new. At the Imperial Conference of 1923 "very confidential matters were discussed not at the Conference but at a meeting of 'Prime Ministers,' a device to exclude the Irish Free State and India." R. MacGregor Dawson, *William Lyon Mackenzie King: A Political Biography*, I, *1874–1923* (Toronto, 1958), p. 461 n.

Political personages shuttle back and forth, sometimes alone, sometimes in committee. The two embassies continuously engage in transmitting political intelligence. Military intelligence is gathered principally by the Canadian Joint Staff at Washington, with its contacts at the Defense Department and the Office of International Security Affairs, while "some 60 Canadian officers of the army, the navy and the air force" (the Minister of National Defence disclosed in March 1960), "sitting in daily on various committees at the Pentagon," keep "the Chiefs of Staff here in Ottawa advised by letter, telegram and telephone."[49] Scientific and technological intelligence, relating mainly to weapons development, is the responsibility of the Defence Research Board, and gathered at its liaison posts at the United States Air Research and Development Command at Baltimore, and at the United States Air Force Cambridge (Mass.) Research Center and Lincoln Laboratory; the historian of the Board has written that it probably "obtained a relatively better return for the money which it has spent on liaison than for any other type of expenditure."[50] Intelligence on subversive activity is exchanged by the Royal Canadian Mounted Police and the Federal Bureau of Investigation, an arrangement that became widely known in 1957 when the Canadian Government threatened to end it to prevent the improper use of information by United States authorities beyond the control of the administration.[51]

The proximity of the United States has one other important if overlooked advantage for the Canadian intelligence community. The *New York Times*, an intelligence source not to be despised for being unclassified,* may be read in Ottawa twelve hours after publication at a cost of $16 a year.

(4) Government officials have made very occasional and very guarded references to "the intelligence exchanges." From their cryptic comments it is impossible to tell whether these constitute special sources of information, or special kinds of information. "The intelligence exchanges,"

---

*"The truth is," wrote Philip Kerr when private secretary to Lloyd George in 1917, "that one derives far more news from the press than from any other source, and every day in the club [The Travellers] one sees long rows of high Foreign Office officials, including Balfour, going eagerly to the notice board to find out what is really happening." Quoted in J. R. M. Butler, *Lord Lothian* (London, 1960), p. 66. Forty years later a former Canadian foreign secretary expressed the view that "there are foreign correspondents of newspapers whose despatches can be as full, shrewd, and useful as any diplomat's. Sometimes they are based on an even greater knowledge and broader experience of the country —and its people—about which they are both writing." Lester B. Pearson, *Diplomacy in the Nuclear Age* (Toronto, 1959), p. 16.

remarked the Under Secretary of State for External Affairs to members of the Senate Standing Committee in 1958, "have to remain secret. . . . This is a field in which I hope you will not press me."[52] And no one did. Governments do not ordinarily disclose the existence, let alone the details, of any espionage or clandestine intelligence activity in which they may be engaged, and the Canadian Government is no exception. Having some if not complete access to the product of the Anglo-American espionage systems, it has little incentive to embark itself on such a dangerous and disreputable enterprise. There has been no public discussion of the propriety of Canadian participation in clandestine intelligence work, but most officials, if asked for their opinion, would probably subscribe to the view expressed in 1946 by the Royal Commission investigating Soviet espionage in Canada: "The transplanting of a conspiratorial technique, which was first developed in less fortunate countries to promote an underground struggle against tyranny, to a democratic society . . . is singularly inappropriate."[53]

(5) The most important sector of any intelligence community is to be found at home rather than abroad, for the most accurate and elaborate information can have little beneficial effect upon foreign policy if ignored by its recipient. The problem of the responsiveness of political leaders to information supplied by experts has been discussed briefly in chapter II. The problem to be considered here is that of collating, evaluating and transmitting to the makers of national policy the information received from governmental contacts throughout the world.

The most striking feature of the machinery by which these tasks are performed is the absence of anything resembling the Central Intelligence Agency of the United States government. The much smaller scale of intelligence operations in Canada, together with more efficient procedures for sharing and co-ordinating information—procedures resulting both from the parliamentary system and the intimacy of the Ottawa environment—make an autonomous intelligence sector less urgent if not altogether unneccessary.

The centre of foreign policy intelligence is within the Department of External Affairs, where three aspects of intelligence work may be distinguished. There is, first of all, the important function of bringing information to the attention of those responsible for foreign policy decisions. This presupposes a good deal of knowledge and indeed of wisdom. The volume of incoming despatches is so great that only a select few can be brought before the senior officials of the Department, and fewer still before the Secretary of State for External Affairs. Mr. Howard

Green, commenting in 1959 on "the number and the quality of the dispatches which come in to the minister of the Department every day from all over the world," confessed that he did "not think that perhaps more than 10 per cent of the total volume would be passed on to me."[54] In 1946 the procedure for disposing of incoming despatches was described by the Associate Under Secretary of State for External Affairs. Asked by a member of the House of Commons Standing Committee, "How does the information get to the top policy men in the Department?," Hume Wrong replied:

It depends on the nature and urgency of the subject how an incoming document is treated in the Department. Routine communications go to the division concerned with the matter in the Department and they can dispose of them. Matters affecting policy go straight to the top and may then go down, and they may be brought up by the Under Secretary to the Prime Minister. You cannot lay down a general rule for dealing with business of that sort. We have varying correspondence covering a large range of subjects.

Q. It comes down to the old source of the mail and to whom it is directed; whether it is marked private and confidential or just confidential.

A. No, it is not nearly as automatic as that. I wish sometimes it could be made automatic, but it is impossible to do it. A large element of human discretion and intelligence must be allowed for.

Q. As long as the stream of communication is small and the Department is small it can act in one way, but after a while as volume grows you have to have a system?

A. You have to have a system, and it is not something you can reduce to a simple formula because there must be a residual element of judgment as to what treatment this deserves if it is obviously an important question. Usually it will go to the chief of the division concerned and he will take it up with the Under Secretary or myself who, if the matter requires it, will see that it is brought to the attention of the Prime Minister [and Secretary of State for External Affairs]. On the other hand, sometimes it might be obviously a matter which need not be brought to the Prime Minister's attention or require the personal attention of the Under Secretary or myself. I do not know any large organization except possibly a mail order house which can reduce to an absolute formula how to treat incoming communications.[55]

By the early 1950's the increased volume of incoming communications had led to the formation within the Department of a Political Co-ordination Section having among its duties "providing a number of political information services for Cabinet Ministers" and preparing regular reports "on the background and current aspects of major international developments" for the general use of members of the Department.[56] (In a later reorganization the Political Co-ordination Section, stripped of the second of these functions, was renamed the Liaison Service.) An officer of the Department visits the Prime Minister each day to bring to his attention important information received during the previous twenty-four hours. The foreign service officer performing this task for the administration headed by Mr. John Diefenbaker is, unlike his predecessors, a senior member of the Department, and his rank is a measure of his importance in the policy process when relations between the professional foreign service and its political masters are less intimate than in the past.

A second function of intelligence work performed within the Department of External Affairs is that of collating the returns of the various agencies of government, such as the Defence Research Board and each of the three services, which maintain their own systems for gathering information. The integration of political, scientific and military intelligence is the primary task of one of the two defence liaison divisions of the Department of External Affairs. The Department also provides the chairman of the Joint Intelligence Committee which, with its representatives from the three services, brings intelligence data to the attention of the Chiefs of Staff Committee and other senior interdepartmental bodies concerned with problems of national defence.

Finally, the Department of External Affairs may itself contribute to intelligence sources by bringing its own experience and judgment to bear upon information received. This function, passing imperceptibly into the realm of policy planning (discussed in chapter VI), consists primarily of forecasting foreign policy, anticipating political and strategic contingencies and attempting to devise ways and means for coping with them. Only in recent years has the intelligence community in Canada consciously addressed itself to this important aspect of its work; during the Second World War, the historian of the Canadian Army has observed, the country had "no intelligence organization . . . capable of making a fully adequate estimate of the situation in the Far East."[57] Today the Joint Planning Committee, composed of representatives of the three services and officers of the two defence liaison divisions of the Department of External Affairs, "co-operate[s] closely with the intelligence and planning agencies of the armed forces in the preparation of papers for consideration by the Chiefs of Staff."[58]

For a small (or, if it be preferred, a middle) power, Canada is unusually and perhaps uniquely well endowed with diversified sources of foreign policy intelligence. Its own fact-gathering apparatus is now located in over fifty countries; it has access to much of the product of the immense intelligence community of the United States; and as a senior member of the Commonwealth of Nations it occupies a central position in the far-flung communications network linking thirteen countries together in one of the most remarkable if unpublicized intelligence systems in the world. If, therefore, in spite of these tremendous assets, the foreign policy decisions of a Canadian government seem ill-suited to their objectives, responsibility rests to an unusual degree upon those ministers who fail to exploit the exceptional intelligence facilities at their disposal.

Chapter Six

PLANNING

PLAN OR NO PLAN?

"There is no such thing as originality in foreign policy," Mussolini once remarked in a moment of clarity. The possibility, let alone the wisdom, of planning for a future as inscrutable as that awaiting a member of the modern states system remains in doubt. Geography sets a hard if not an iron law for foreign ministers of all nations, and it is remarkable how even the most powerful dictatorships, freer than most to manœuvre and sacrifice with a minimum regard for life and happiness, stray so slightly from the old established ways. Governments of open societies, planning for foreign policy in the sense of mapping a detailed course for the longer run, have been restrained by more than the inertia and fickleness of their electorates. They have encountered and to some extent shared a liberal democratic tradition that is hostile to policy planning on the grand scale. If (paraphrasing Dicey) all were planners fifty years ago, planning as a panacea later lost much of its allure. "In political activity men sail a boundless and bottomless sea," Harold Laski's successor at the London School of Economics affirmed in a famous lecture: "There is neither harbour nor shelter nor floor for anchorage, neither starting place nor appointed destination."[1] This reaction was more than a philosophical movement; it was the outcome of hard and tragic experience. Planners allowed to indulge their fearful logic had led much of mankind not to utopia but through the valley of a totalitarian ordeal to the unspeakable horrors of "the final solution."

But as the surviving liberal democracies moved defensively into the second half of the twentieth century, planning for national policies began to appear in a new and seductive guise. For this the external challenge of Soviet (and increasingly of Chinese) communism was more than anything responsible. That challenge was not new. Since 1917 (perhaps earlier) Western liberalism had been startled by a rival claim to interpret the democratic tradition, and the interpretation provided by Lenin was as different from that of liberal democracy as *State and Revolution* from Mill's *On Liberty*. But by 1950 a more threatening aspect was apparent. Communism was no longer a rival theory; it had become a rival example, offering glittering prizes of productivity and prestige to those looking to Moscow for models and methods. Planning in its most doctrinaire form was held to be the key to these triumphs. "The high vocation of Soviet diplomacy," writes a Bolshevik court historian, "is made easier by the fact that it wields a weapon possessed by none of its rivals or opponents. Soviet diplomacy is fortified with the scientific theory of Marxism-Leninism . . . [which gives] it a special position in international life and explains its outstanding successes."[2]

Couched in these terms, it might appear to its Afro-Asian audiences that this greatest of all "great debates" was no more (if no less) than the old argument about "plan or no plan." But to the extent that this interpretation prevailed, the case of liberal democracies already identified in Afro-Asian minds as the unreconstructed exemplars of planlessness was bound to be lost by default. It therefore became urgently necessary to recast its terms, to make clear beyond doubt that its protagonists were not planners on the one hand and non-planners on the other, but totalitarian planners on the one hand and libertarian planners on the other. The rehabilitation of the policy planner had begun, even if his appeal stemmed not from inner conviction, or not yet, but from external necessity.

What made his triumph certain was the growing conviction of Western publics that the achievements of Soviet technology had resulted in spite of—perhaps even because of—the rigours of Soviet planning. During the months following the launching of the *sputnik*— the first of many subsequent Russian intrusions into space—less and less was heard of the doctrinal incubus supposedly hindering communist technological breakthroughs. The fashionable contrast was now between the aimlessness and drift of liberal democracies and the stern and purposive mission of Soviet society. With mounting frequency and bluntness the point was made that it would be necesary for the West to emulate the Soviet example to survive. The democracies (so a growing number of their leading citizens were saying) needed something of the sense of mission and direction of the communist world, some doctrinal underpinning for decisions hitherto pragmatic, to challenge as much as to respond, and, above all, foreign policies continuously relating to a long-term assessment of national goals and of the methods by which these might be attained. The planner was back on his throne.

FOREIGN POLICY PLANNING
AND THE NATIONAL STYLE

Of all the liberal democracies, the United States has most ardently reassessed planning as a technique and indeed as a condition of national survival. Such was the natural response of the leader of the nations that were standing together in conscious opposition to the spread of communist influence. But it was also a response wholly in keeping with what W. W. Rostow has called "the American national style," discerned a century or more ago by de Tocqueville: "Americans have a great deal of curiosity and little leisure; their life is so practical, so confused, so excited, so active, that but little time remains to them for thought. Such men are prone to general ideas because they are thereby spared the trouble of studying particulars."[3] Thus emerged the paradox of "a nation of individualistic empiricists . . . powerfully drawn to a particular use of highly abstract concepts,"[4] an attraction at once a cause and a condition of the planning approach to foreign as to other national affairs. For the assumption of the foreign policy planner must necessarily be that there is order and rhythm in the movement of events, a pattern, even a grand design, which wise reflection will disclose and careful analysis exploit to the nation's advantage. For if history were otherwise, one crisis succeeding another at random, devoid of reason and regularity, impervious to understanding and so incapable of prediction, wherein lay the planner's task? Did he have a task at all? The American national style discourages such questions, just as the British style, empirical, pragmatic, expediential, shying away from abstract principle, distrustful of doctrine, assumes their answers to be negative. "An eminent British economist," a Canadian colleague once recalled, "who was in the public service used to say that he rejoiced when some civil servant or minister referred to him as academic. He then knew that he had been guilty of thinking as much as six months ahead."[5]

The Canadian style, despite the influence of the French-Canadian tradition (itself very different from the rationalist, Cartesian tradition of modern France), resembles the British in its inhospitality to basic assumptions about planning for foreign policy. There is a strong disposition to deal with external affairs in a workaday manner, eschewing doctrine and the long view, taking one thing at a time and being prepared to take much time over that one thing. Cautious, patient, compromising, flexible, are the words by which Canadian foreign ministers of recent years have described their endeavours; such words, while not unknown to the vocabulary of planning, are there used more often as pejoratives than as praise.*

For this attitude a number of circumstances have been responsible. Perhaps most basic have been the circumstances of Canadian history

---

*Professor Harry Johnson calls them "weasel-adjectives." See his "Canada's Foreign Trade Problems," *International Journal*, vol. XV, no. 3, Summer 1960, p. 235.

and the absence from that history of a revolutionary tradition comparable to that in the United States.* If revolutions breed philosophers and heroes they also beget doctrinaires, and that stern sense of self-righteousness which, if it sustains the weak, is not an unmixed blessing for the strong. From the American revolutionary tradition derives that characteristically American belief that some swift and spectacular stroke may permanently solve problems which in their nature admit only of amelioration. The Canadian style knows no comparable addiction to the "one-shot solution," to the "crash program," to "doctrines" whether they bear the name of Monroe or Stimson, Truman or Eisenhower. There has been little in Canadian experience to encourage the expectation that injuries to society may be healed in the same fashion and with the same hope of success as a machine is repaired or an appendix removed. It is the Canadian style to try to garden in the field of politics, not to dam or dredge.

The pragmatic approach to foreign policy is natural in a country which, like Canada, has few if any opportunities for exercising important and sustained assaults upon major international problems. Lacking both resources and occasions for bold and independent approaches, its initiatives are limited to those rare occasions when (as during the Suez crisis in November 1956) an inspired mediation may save the great powers from their own miscalculations. Its policy must nearly always be one of response to the moves of others. This, to some, has seemed to mean that Canada can have no foreign policy of its own, implying that a policy of response is not a foreign policy at all. "As if the Canadian Government could have a foreign or external policy like the governments of other countries," wrote a member of the Department of External Affairs in 1938. "To assert that your government can form a policy is to assert that it has a choice of action and a capacity to give the choice effect."[6] "Over the years," a senior Canadian diplomatist, now retired, has written,

I have heard a number of earnest souls (some of whom were noticeably long-haired), glibly talk of Canadian foreign policy, and this to my no little puzzlement. And after a spell of over a decade in posts abroad my mind is still unreceptive in this regard. That, over the centuries, the United Kingdom should have striven to prevent a first-class European power from occupying the Low Countries; that, as long as she was able to do so, she did everything in her power to ensure the security of the Suez Canal; that neither Germany nor Russia should succeed in establishing themselves on the northern shores of the Indian Ocean; that France has ever been watchful over her north-

*I have drawn here from my essay, "From Canada" in Franz M. Joseph, ed., *As Others See Us: The United States in Foreign Eyes* (Princeton, 1959), pp. 280–1.

eastern frontier; and that the Italians, since the earliest times, have resisted the southward thrust of the Teutonic races—these are objects of foreign policy that I find it easy enough to understand. But when I turn my mind to our so fortunately placed country, I am at a loss to know if it is possible for us rationally to assert that there is such a thing as a Canadian foreign policy.[7]

However this may be, it is true that the incentive to plan policies in external affairs is greatly reduced by the comparative unimportance of Canada in the general configuration of power politics. A former Cabinet Minister, experienced in diplomacy, has made this plain:

It would, of course, be idle to pretend that Canada, like other countries in the free world, has succeeded in constantly keeping the initiative in planning much of its foreign policy during these disturbing years since the Second World War ended. . . . We have, as you know, rarely been in a position to take the initiative, and we have, throughout these years, been very largely on the defensive. In consequence, our foreign policy has been what I might call responsive; just as when, in playing hockey, with two or three of the Canadian team in the penalty box—a phenomenon which does, on occasion, arise—we are constrained to play a purely defensive role rather than an aggressive one in which we can use our full forces of strength and initiative. . . . This makes it difficult to discuss accurately and realistically the manner in which our foreign policies are planned since so frequently they have been shaped to deal with aggression or the menace of it against ourselves and our friends.[8]

Another factor accounting for the pragmatic approach to foreign affairs has been the manner and method of the Prime Minister and Secretary of State for External Affairs throughout much of the formative period of Canadian foreign policy. "Upon many matters of external policy," a close associate has written of Mackenzie King, "he took decisions as all in the day's work; that is, except for the advice and knowledgeability of his principal advisers in the public service, they were decisions based not upon profound personal study of issues, but upon the apparent needs of the moment."[9] It is unlikely that the subject of this appraisal would have taken serious issue with it, and more than once he confided to his diary, as on April 20, 1941 (the "grand Sunday" on which he and Franklin Roosevelt worked out the Hyde Park Agreement together): "I recall what Lord Morley said about not planning too far ahead in politics. That events determine what is possible."[10]

Such a style might not be expected to survive a change in government and minister, but only if it is not deeply ingrained in the bureaucracy as well. In February 1960 the Secretary of State for External Affairs, Mr. Howard Green, suggested in his first major review of foreign affairs in the House of Commons that the time had come "to drop the idea that Canada's role in world affairs is to be an 'honest broker' between the nations. We must decide instead that our role is to be to determine the right stand to take on problems, keeping in mind the Canadian background and, above all, using Canadian common sense. In effect, the time has come to take an independent approach."[11] This statement was on the whole well received throughout the country, with one curious exception. Members of the Department of External Affairs were disturbed at the implications of their Minister's remarks, and even relatively junior foreign service officers (who one would have thought might respond enthusiastically to such a call to greatness) privately expressed misgivings about his "magnificent obsession" and his "*politique de grandeur*."*

So cautious a response reflected, of course, the traditional bias of their calling. The attitude of the professional diplomatist to foreign policy planning is essentially negative, scornful of the bold initiative, distrustful of the grand design. Mr. George Kennan has well described "the weary skepticism that characterizes the more experienced ranges of the diplomatic profession. . . . The professional . . . sees the task of diplomacy as essentially a menial one, consisting of hovering around the fringes of a process one is powerless to control, tidying up the messes other people have made, attempting to keep small disasters from turning into big ones, moderating the passions of governments and of opinionated individuals. . . ."[12] It would be hard to describe more exactly the *Weltanschauung* of the Department of External Affairs.

Reinforcing it is the operational code of the foreign service officer, traditionally hostile to blueprints and the forward look. A senior official of the Department of External Affairs once remarked to a small group of academic social scientists that in his view foreign policy "is the result of a continuing series of *ad hoc* decisions, which frequently have to be made with inadequate study and inadequate data. . . . It is always a case of realizing as fully as you can the implications of what you propose to do, and of doing it according to the best judgment you can make in a single circumstance at the moment of time."* In this classic

---

*One such officer, freed from reticence by recent resignation from the Department, gathered together in a widely circulated magazine article several of his former Minister's utterances in this vein, describing them as his collection of "Greenery." "To be influential with modest means," the article concluded, "one needs to be modest in demeanour." Peyton V. Lyon, "Canada Is Becoming a Mouse That Roars," *Maclean's Magazine*, June 18, 1960.

statement of the pragmatic approach to foreign politics a measure of rationalization may be detected. For if an aversion to planning is the occupational prejudice of the foreign service officer, the plea of over-work, of the steady unrelenting stream of detail and crisis said to make reflection difficult if not impossible, is his occupational disease, espe-cially in the senior ranks. Does he exaggerate, does he welcome, the pressures and the daily strain as an escape from the planner's hard creative tasks? To such a question it would be presumptuous to return a final answer; but one may recall, in leaving it, Walter Bagehot's view that if the head of a large enterprise spends his life at his desk, there is likely something wrong with the organization.[13]

MACHINERY FOR FOREIGN
POLICY PLANNING

The general scepticism in which the planning of Canadian foreign policy has been held by governments and bureaucracy alike is reflected in the dearth of special machinery. There has never been within the Department of External Affairs the equivalent of the State Depart-ment's Policy Planning Staff established in 1947, or the Permanent Under-Secretary's Committee of the United Kingdom Foreign Office established in 1949;† and no Minister or senior official has publicly suggested it would be desirable to have one. Special planning bodies are perhaps less essential in the parliamentary system, where the Cabinet is responsible for policy decisions, than in the presidential. But conscious

*Quoted in B. S. Keirstead, *Canada in World Affairs: September 1951 to October 1953* (Toronto, 1956), p. 37. The U.S. State Department has a similar operational preference for "making policy on the cables." "Despite uncounted high-level directives stressing the need for prevision and an adequate operational plan," writes an American authority, "the Department retains much of its pre-1941 disinclination to plan in advance. Agencies exist within the Department whose function it is to plan, acting under the general direction of the Assistant Secretary for Policy Planning; much effort is expended in devising blueprints for the future. The objective observer, however, is still impressed by the extent to which the usual desk officer refuses to 'deal with hypothetical questions' and seems to get considerable satisfaction out of making the 'brush fire' approach a normal operating procedure." Charles O. Lerche, Jr., *Foreign Policy of the American People* (Englewood Cliffs, N.J., 1958), p. 43.

†The work of the Policy Planning Staff is well known; that of the Permanent Under-Secretary's Committee much less so, for its existence has only recently been disclosed by its sometime chairman, Lord Strang: "The duty of this com-mittee was to try to identify the longer term trends in international affairs and to prepare studies on the possible bearings of these trends upon the future formulation of British policy." Lord Strang, "Inside the Foreign Office," *International Relations*, vol. XI, no. 1, April 1960, pp. 19–20.

aversion to planning may be detected in the fact that there is not now, nor has there ever been, an External Affairs committee of the Cabinet, matching its committees on defence and economic policy, where the minds of four or five ministers together with those of senior civil servants and high military officers might grapple collectively with questions of foreign policy in a more reflective fashion than the day-to-day operations of a busy foreign office allow.

If any institutions concern themselves mainly with foreign policy planning, these are the interdepartmental committees of senior civil servants drawn from various departments of government. On such committees the Department of External Affairs traditionally occupies a commanding position, frequently supplying their chairmen. Their use for the consideration of foreign policy problems dates from the first Mackenzie King administration of 1921–5. When the Prime Minister of that day was urged to expand the Department of External Affairs, he replied to the suggestion:

We are not confined, so far as permanent officials are concerned, to the staff of the Department, in the consideration of foreign affairs. I am a strong believer in the policy of inter-departmental co-ordination, and the present government, I think, has made a distinct progress in applying this policy. The waterways questions outstanding with the United States, which in my opinion constitute the most difficult and most momentous issue of Canadian foreign policy, have been studied for two years by a strong inter-departmental committee, which is making a more thorough analysis of the situation than to my knowledge has ever been made by a Canadian government. When the Geneva Protocol was under consideration, a similar committee was appointed, and at the present time questions of Oriental Immigration are being considered jointly by the Immigration and External Affairs Departments.*

During the later 1930's the device fell into disuse, but came back into its own during the Second World War, particularly during the last two years when post-war problems began to be systematically considered. One of the more important interdepartmental committees thus constituted was the Post-Hostilities Planning Committee created in February 1943, dealing, among other matters, with possible Cana-

*Mackenzie King to N. W. Rowell, Dec. 7, 1925, Rowell Papers. The interdepartmental committee examining the Geneva Protocol was composed of the following: O. D. Skelton and W. H. Walker of the Department of External Affairs; L. C. Moyer and R. O. Campney of the Prime Minister's office; Major General J. H. MacBrien and Commodore W. Hose of the Department of National Defence; W. S. Edwards of the Department of Justice; Thomas Mulvey of the Department of the Secretary of State; O. M. Biggar, Chief Electoral Officer; and R. H. Coats, Dominion Statistician.

dian approaches to international organization for the coming peace. In 1943 the War Committee of the Cabinet created an interdepartmental committee to consider international monetary problems, and in June of that year the Interdepartmental Committee on International Civil Aviation (replacing the Interdepartmental Committee on Air Transport Policy set up in May 1942). On these and other such committees, perhaps ten or twelve in all, were to be found the same key members of the bureaucratic élite to whom the Government was learning to turn with increasing frequency and confidence for guidance on a broadening range of domestic and foreign policy problems (see above, chapter II). Many of these key officials, their ranks depleted by the death of some and the entry into non-governmental occupations of others, have continued since 1945 to exercise their important influence on policy planning through such committees as the Interdepartmental Committee on External Trade Policy and the Panel on the Economic Aspects of Defence Policy.

Chapter Seven

NEGOTIATION

THE NEGOTIATOR AND HIS
CHANGING WORLD

Much has been made in recent years of the decay of the method of conducting foreign policy by negotiation. The lament proceeds characteristically from negotiators themselves, usually, indeed, from retired negotiators. Their memoirs deplore the passing of "the old diplomacy," the diplomacy of which they had the good fortune to be the last exponents, diplomacy in its rightful sense and proper meaning. Lord Vansittart wrote of "The Decline of Diplomacy"; Sir Victor Wellesley of "Diplomacy in Fetters." Sir Nevile Bland notes "a growing tendency . . . to substitute for the discreet exchange of notes tendentious press conferences and abuse over the air," and resolutely refuses to sully his edition of Satow's *Guide to Diplomatic Practice* by offering neophytes hints for their effective exploitation. "What we have come to call diplomacy in the course of the past twenty years," observed Hugh Gibson, "has failed to achieve results and has led into all sorts of disasters. But it wasn't really diplomacy. It was the usurpation of diplomatic functions by politicians and inept amateurs."[1]

The eclipse of the negotiator in foreign policy has been caused, paradoxically enough, by an expansion of his functions. No longer is it sufficient for him to explain his government's policy, or a version of that policy, to the government to which he is accredited; he has to an increasing extent to explain it to its people. He has, that is to say, a propagandist function, and more than ever the effectiveness of the modern diplomatist depends upon the shrewdness and imagination he brings to its performance. Whereas the negotiating function stands at the origin of his art, the propagandist function is comparatively new, generated by spectacular improvements in the technology of communications. Millions of people previously isolated from world events might now be appealed to, and the negotiator has accordingly had thrust upon him the unaccustomed role of public persuader. He must address himself not only to officials but to mass publics both at home and abroad.

So far, then, from contracting, the universe of modern diplomacy has been infinitely expanding. But this expansion has rarely been regarded with much favour. More often than not the negotiator has looked upon the propagandist aspect of his work as a threat to his position rather than a means to further triumphs. Temperament has been in part responsible for this fearful response. The old-style diplomatists, Mr. George Kennan has observed,

tended everywhere to view propaganda with distaste and skepticism. The profession of diplomacy induced a weary detachment, foreign to all political enthusiasms and *ex parte* pleas. Propaganda smacked of overt interference in the domestic affairs of other countries—something that went strongly against the grain of diplomatic tradition. Most diplomatists were instinctively convinced that government was everywhere in some degree a conspiracy and that, whatever the outward trappings of democracy, it was always more important to influence a few select individuals than to appeal to the broad electorate. The professional diplomatist thus tended to shy off, temperamentally, from the very thought of distributing propaganda. And he was generally held, then as now, by the enthusiasts of the propagandistic approach, to be quite unqualified for this sort of work.[2]

In one respect these enthusiasts, the new apostles of mass enlightenment and mass bewilderment, were absolutely correct, for the professional diplomatist did lack one of the most important qualifications of the successful public persuader. He was, as a rule, unknown to the public. And, being unknown, he had little influence with it. It was easier, it was surely safer (so it was argued) for governments to entrust the propagandist function to a celebrity. The head of government or, if unavailable, the foreign minister, being the most celebrated, were best equipped for the job. Failing these potentates, it could be given to generals and admirals, to press lords, to captains of industry, even to stars from the firmament of entertainment (for who shone more brightly than they?)—to almost anyone, it must have seemed to those who made diplomacy their career, but themselves.

The professional negotiator might have borne these intruders with more composure had they concerned themselves solely with that aspect of diplomacy for which their reputations were thought to qualify them. Such hopes were quickly dashed. "The art of diplomacy," Harold Nicolson has observed, "as that of watercolours, has suffered much from the fascination which it exercises upon the amateur."[3] Few of those imported to help with diplomatic public relations have been content with that alone. Nearly all have yielded to the temptation of believing themselves, precisely because of their extra-diplomatic status, better qualified than the professional to perform his traditional assignments. Sometimes the belief was justified; more often not; but always it reduced his effectiveness. Few career negotiators can read without sympathy the *cri de cœur* of the United States ambassador in London in 1941, John G. Winant: "The increasing number of people who negotiate with the British Government, often without definite assignment to the Embassy . . . seriously interfere with the work of the Embassy. I want very much to have our relations with the British both friendly and orderly so that we can build confidence that permits continuing trust and co-operation. Please help me."[4] But no help came. The plight of his colleague in Moscow was no less pitiable. "For long months," writes Admiral William H. Standley in his memoirs, "I saw Special Representative after Big Dignatory come to Russia, leapfrog over my top-hatted head. . . . I also watched the situation deteriorate."[5]

The more grandiose ambitions of the amateur diplomatist have been sustained by a variety of forces, not least by a prejudiced public which, when things go wrong, so quickly makes a scapegoat of the professional:

> Some diplomat no doubt
> Will launch a heedless word,
> And lurking war leap out.

But this hostility, powerful as it was and is, could not of itself have propelled the interlopers to their present dizzy heights of power and influence. Technology has been more than anything responsible for that. An ambassador in foreign parts used to be very much on his own. He would have instructions, of course, but these were necessarily phrased in general terms, leaving him free to fill in important details, frequently to make policy in his own right. In 1898 Sir Julian Pauncefote, the British ambassador at Washington, urged upon the Foreign Office that certain concessions be granted to Spain in negotiations then proceeding in the American capital. "If Pauncefote had not associated himself with this policy," the Acting Foreign Secretary minuted, "I confess I should have rejected it at once; but he knows our views, he is on the spot, and he is a man of solid judgment. It seems a strong order to reject his advice."[6] Today, nothing is more easily, or readily, done. Autonomy to the modern negotiator is almost unknown. His discretionary powers have been steadily weakened by the telegraph, the telephone, and the four-engine aircraft.

Whatever nation he represents, whatever form of government he serves, the diplomatist experiences a predicament common to his profession. Yet diplomatists of different countries are confronted with special problems, and their common predicament is presented in different ways. The Canadian negotiator is no exception. His experience illustrates at once the pressures and tensions to which the diplomatist of every nation is prey, and the peculiar historical environment from which, as a Canadian diplomatist, he comes and attempts to defend.

THE DEVELOPMENT OF
NEGOTIATING MACHINERY

Much the greater part of Canada's negotiations with other countries has been, as it remains, with the United States. Before the appointment of a Canadian Minister to Washington in 1926–7, the Dominion's interests were formally the responsibility of the British ambassador to the United States. The development of distinctively Canadian negotiating machinery was largely a response to a well-founded feeling on the part of successive governments at Ottawa that these interests could not be adequately cared for in this way.

Criticism attached partly, and by no means improperly, to the representatives of the British Government themselves. Thus in the aftermath of the negotiations at Washington in 1871 there was widespread and adverse comment in Canadian newspapers upon the less than helpful attitude of Sir Edward Thornton (whom with his wife even the Secretary of the British delegation had described as "a dreadfully dreary pair, looking as if the life had faded out of them in South America and the spirit was evaporating in Washington"[7]). Thornton's successor, Sir Lionel Sackville-West, was recalled in the memory of an aide of Joseph Chamberlain as "a man of extremely reticent nature, who seldom spoke unless someone spoke to him. So retiring, indeed, was he, that, if I remember aright, his only oral contribution to the 30 meetings of the Conference [dealing with a fisheries dispute of great importance to Canada] was the expression of a wish that a certain window might be closed."[8] It was Sackville-West (best known for the naïve intervention in an American presidental campaign resulting in his recall) who in 1888 failed to transmit to the United States authorities the terms of a Canadian protest against American occupation of part of the disputed territory along the Alaska frontier; when, a decade later, the Canadian Government came to prepare its case, there was nothing in the record, as Joseph Pope wrote in some disgust to Laurier, "to indicate *what part* of H.M. Dominions was being encroached on, and consequently the protest, as such, is worthless. This is the more aggravating when we consider that Canada's cause was all that it should be. We were specific . . . but old West botched it."[9]

But the more fundamental grievance was not that Canadian interests suffered from being "botched" by British negotiators. It was rather that on many matters the interests of Britain and Canada were not only different but diametrically opposed, so that a British ambassador, charged with responsibility for both, could uphold one only by sacrificing the other. It became the settled and, once again, well-founded conviction of successive Canadian governments that, faced with this dilemma, the British ambassador would pursue his imperial mandate at the expense of the Canadian. To have Canada negotiate with the United States authorities where Canadian interests were involved seemed essential if sacrifices were not to become a ritual.

The remedy took two main forms. For the occasional but (from the Canadian standpoint) crucial conferences in which British and American representatives met, sometimes for months on end, in an effort to clean the slate, nothing less than the personal intervention of the Prime Minister himself was thought sufficient protection. Thus Sir John A. Macdonald took part as a member of the British delegation at the High Commission in Washington in 1870-1,* while Sir Wilfrid Laurier, his position as Canada's representative more clearly defined than Macdonald's, similarly negotiated for the Dominion at the Joint High Commission of 1898-9.

On the more frequent occasions when specific topics were under negotiation, the Canadian Government would send its own negotiator to Washington to see that the Dominion's point of view was receiving sufficient attention. This practice implied a lack of confidence in the capacity of the British ambassador, as well as eroding (the imperial authorities often charged) the then sacred principle of the diplomatic unity of the Empire; it was therefore neither highly publicized nor very often used. But it was indispensable on occasion. In 1907, George C. Gibbons, a civil service member of the Canadian section of the International Waterways Commission, went at Laurier's behest to Washington to see how the British ambassador was making out in negotiations intended to result in a permanent Boundary Waters Commission between Canada and the United States. "My visit to Washington was not satisfactory," he reported to the Prime Minister. "I got little from Mr. Bryce except talk, nine-tenths of it quite outside the issue. His courtesy and personal kindness make it awkward to tell the truth, but I have had an opportunity as I have never had before of sizing the situation up and the truth demands that I should tell you that Mr. Bryce is of no assistance but, in my opinion, an obstruction to obtaining what ought to be insisted upon, a permanent Commission."[10] A few days later Gibbons wrote: "I think if you would make it clear to Mr. Bryce that you want me to join in the negotiations at Washington with Mr. Root and the American authorities, we will have a chance of accomplishing something. I do not see how they can refuse our proposals, if properly presented. The

*Macdonald's negotiations are brilliantly described in Donald Creighton, *John A. Macdonald: The Old Chieftain* (Toronto, 1955), pp. 82-102.

matter will fiddle along, month after month, if left to the British Ambassador, and I very much doubt even then of his being able to accomplish anything. I am not at all clear that I can, but, if I fail, it will not be for want of effort."[11] Laurier accepted this suggestion and Bryce, to his credit, did not object. Nor did Gibbons fail. Two years later the Governor General of Canada wrote to the Colonial Secretary:

I have despatched a cable to you, with the greatest satisfaction, begging you in the name of the Dominion Govt. to instruct Bryce to sign the Gibbons Draft Treaty re International Waters. This Treaty is a great triumph for Gibbons, Sir Wilfrid Laurier and Canadian diplomacy. In saying this I do not wish to imply any disparagement of Bryce, who has in many respects proved an admirable British Ambassador to the U.S., but it is impossible to deny that the direct, outspoken and rather choleric manner of our Canadian Amateur Diplomatist has been more successful than the deferential attitude towards Root of the British Ambassador.[12]

This was not the only occasion on which Canadian negotiators were to find fault with James Bryce as a protector of Dominion interests. Even one so devoted to the British connection as Joseph Pope privately expressed dismay at Bryce's readiness to turn against Canada for the sake of British foreign policy. In 1911, sent to Washington to help in the negotiations over pelagic sealing, Pope noted in his diary:

Called upon Mr. Bryce. Fear we are going to have trouble to get him to sustain our view, i.e., that we should receive compensation from Russia and Japan, in return for abstaining from Pelagic Sealing in the Western half of the Pacific Ocean . . . [May 10].
. . . Mr. Bryce made me stay behind, and spoke to me at length saying the U.S. consider our position *quoad* Russia and Japan as a piece of sharp practice. That we were partners and should work together. The charge of sharp practice brought by the authors of the scheme to tax our case is rich. Mr. Bryce who seems wholly on their side in this business urged me to withdraw my statement which I can't do . . . [May 19].

A year later, dealing then with fish rather than with seals, Pope's impression was unchanged. "Mr. Bryce," he wrote, "is of course all for yielding to the U.S. . . . It's a shame."[13] Repeated incidents of this kind made the eventual creation of a separate Canadian mission in Washington inevitable, although it was not until six years after the right of legation had been established in 1920 that Mr. Vincent Massey received his credentials as Canada's first Minister to Washington.

The new legation was soon immersed in the minutiae of negotiation which form a normal and necessary feature of Canadian-American diplomacy. In less than the first year of its existence it despatched over a thousand messages to the Department of External Affairs at Ottawa and over three hundred messages to the United States Secretary of State, in addition to countless other less formal communications with various agencies of the American government, dealing with such matters as boundary waters, immigration, allocation of radio broadcasting channels, suppression of smuggling, extradition, fisheries. Thus even at this early stage there was little to justify the charge of W. S. Fielding, the Minister of Finance whose opposition delayed the creation of the mission for several years, that "a Canadian representative at Washington . . . would have an almost entirely ornamental position" as "there is really no diplomatic work he could do."[14]

The Canadian legation (which in 1943 became the Canadian embassy) in Washington was the normal but not the only means of negotiating with the United States. The mission of George Gibbons resulted in 1909 in the creation of the International Joint Commission, a standing tribunal of six commissioners in each of its Canadian and American sections, authorized by the Treaty bringing it into being to settle disputes submitted by the two governments over the systems of waterways which follow and traverse the frontier. To observe that the celebrated Article IX of this Treaty, providing for referral of "any other matters of difference arising . . . along the common frontier," has yet to be invoked is not to suggest that by confining itself to disputes over waterways the Commission has devoted itself to trivia: where water is scarce, the welfare of people and the rate of economic growth are at stake, and there can be no more vital national interests than these. The Commission has failed to produce a mutually satisfying solution in only one of the thirty odd cases of which it has been seized; it eventually resolved, despite many setbacks and uncertainties, the future of the immense hydro-electric resources of the Columbia River system.

There has been some tendency for Canadian leaders mistakenly to attribute this record of achievement to the nature of the institution, rather than to the exceptional relations of the two North American neighbours which alone have made it possible; and therefore to urge the institution upon other countries. "I am convinced," Mackenzie King wrote in 1923, "that [the International Joint Commission] contains the new world answer to old world queries as to the most effective methods of adjusting international differences and avoiding the wars to which they give rise";[15] in 1942 he expressed to President Roosevelt the view that it might serve as the basis for post-war international organization.[16] But as a prescription for the ills of others, this new world remedy was wholly inappropriate, arising as it did from a wholly different situation:

> The toad beneath the harrow knows
> Exactly where each tooth-point goes.
> The butterfly upon the road
> Preaches contentment to that toad.

The butterfly is wiser now. But more than once in recent years Canadian spokesmen have commended the International Joint Commission to audiences in Asia, as thirty years previously they had done to audiences in Europe. It may be presumed that the Asians, if more polite in their response, have been no less sceptical of the suggestion.

The Permanent Joint Board on Defence, like the International Joint Commission a forum for functional negotiation with the United States, is discussed above in chapter III.

Canadian interests in the United Kingdom were attended to by a High Commissioner many years before his diplomatic status was formally signified. (The special nature of the office of High Commissioner in London is referred to above in chapter II.) In 1928 the British Government for the first time sent its own High Commissioner to Ottawa. Thereafter two instruments for negotiation with the British Government were available to Canadian ministers. Mackenzie King preferred to negotiate through the British High Commissioner in Ottawa rather than through the Canadian High Commissioner in London because he could then conduct negotiations himself. "To see from my office window on an adjoining side of Parliament Square a building which I know to be that of the representative of the Government of the United Kingdom," he remarked in 1928, "with whom, at a moment's notice I can confer, or who, at a moment's notice can confer with me . . . is, I assure you, deeply comforting to one in my position."[17]

Canadian interests in countries other than the United States and the United Kingdom were fewer, and the need for negotiation less urgent. In France an agent of the Dominion government had in fact if not in law represented Canada since 1882 when Hector Fabre, originally appointed by the government of the province of Quebec, was commisioned by Ottawa to follow instructions from the High Commissioner in London so as to improve relations between the two countries; in 1911 he was succeeded by Philippe Roy, who assumed the new title of Commissioner General of Canada in France and, although without official recognition or diplomatic standing, attended to a variety of diplomatic duties before his appointment in 1928 as Canada's first Minister to France.

The presence in Ottawa of a number of consular representatives of foreign countries provided the government with a method of negotiation prior to the opening up of Canadian diplomatic missions abroad; these, while lacking diplomatic accreditation and formally responsible only for commercial affairs, were resorted to on occasion as if members of a regular *corps diplomatique*. At the turn of the century, Laurier, wishing to sound the French Government on the question of the compensation it might be prepared to accept in exchange for relinquishing fishing and other rights on a section of the Newfoundland shore, entered into negotiation with the French consul general in Montreal, A. Kleczkowski, notwithstanding the doubts of the Colonial Secretary whether "the French consul would be in any case able to speak for his government or . . . do anything more than express his own personal opinions."* Similar approaches were made to the Japanese consul in Vancouver, S. Shimizu, and the consul general in Ottawa, Tatsgoro Nossé, on the subject of Japanese immigration during the period 1899–1909.

But the more usual method of negotiating with foreign governments before the creation of Canadian missions abroad was to exploit the facilities of the British government. The conflict of interests confronting a British ambassador charged with the protection of Canadian interests in some foreign country was usually not so acute as in the case of the British ambassador in Washington, but on occasion it could be; and as in matters of trade and commerce his knowledge of Canadian conditions and requirements was likely to be slight and his interest in driving a hard Canadian bargain even slighter, the practice developed of sending to the ambassador's side a Canadian negotiator, usually of Cabinet rank, to fortify the Dominion's case. The fledgling Canadian diplomatist was often tempted on such occasions to dispense entirely with the ambassador's services. But there usually supervened the recollection that the credentials of a Canadian negotiator were likely to be greeted with suspicion by a foreign government, if recognized at all; the presence of the ambassador, if only to hover ceremoniously in the background, was therefore essential. Sometimes his expertise was as helpful as his status, and a visiting Canadian mission, working in close co-operation with the resident British authority, could achieve results not possible if either worked without the other. In 1907 Rodolphe Lemieux was able

*Joseph Chamberlain to the Earl of Minto, Jan. 18, 1899, Laurier Papers. Chamberlain was in error, for the negotiations continued for over two years. In 1901 Laurier informed the Governor General that he had recently seen Kleczkowski in Montreal and that the latter had "advised his Minister—M. Delcassé—to throw up the claims of the French in Newfoundland entirely. He considered they were of little use to France and that the Minister would probably be inclined to come to terms except for the strong anti-English feeling in France which had been stirred up by the Fashoda question." Memorandum of interview with Laurier, Jan. 19, 1901, Minto Papers.

to persuade the Japanese government to undertake to limit future emigration to Canada largely because of the assistance of the British ambassador in Tokyo, which the Canadian generously acknowledged. "Whatever may be the outcome of the negotiations," Lemieux wrote from Japan, "Canada owes a debt of gratitude to the British Ambassador. After having presented my credentials to the Foreign Office in Tokio, he took, from the beginning, a deep interest in the question itself. He not only obtained for Canada the full support of His Majesty's Government—but he personally attended each and every meeting at the Foreign Office. He thus gave Canada the prestige of Great Britain . . . and besides, we had the benefit of his vast experience as a diplomat."[18]

The relationship between Canadian and British authorities in such a situation was not always so untroubled. Israel Tarte, Minister of Public Works in the Laurier Government, while in Europe in 1900 to arrange for Canadian participation in an international exhibition, succeeded in irritating the Colonial Secretary. "I have seen something of Mr. Tarte's manners & temper since he has been over here," Joseph Chamberlain wrote to the Governor General of Canada, "and I am sorry that he has so much influence in the Dominion Government. His idea evidently is that Canada should practically be regarded in France as almost an independent French Republic. He has been very fussy and irritable, and the Commissioners of the Exhibition have found it almost impossible to satisfy his requirements."[19] Some years later, when W. S. Fielding, the Minister of Finance, went to Berlin to negotiate a trade agreement with the German government, similar tension arose. "I do not doubt his sincerity in wishing to maintain and in a general way strengthen the Imperial tie," wrote a member of the editorial staff of *The Times* to its Toronto correspondent, "but [Fielding] seems to me to have acquired a taste for large negotiations and the sense of wielding plenipotentiary powers, and I think he may indulge that passion from day to day without quite realizing how far it is carrying him. The way in which negotiations were undertaken in Berlin has caused some regret here."[20] These isolated incidents became less and less frequent as the British Empire transformed itself into the Commonwealth of Nations and as the doctrine of diplomatic unity was replaced by the concept of a like-minded community of independent states. The reliance of successive Canadian governments upon British negotiation of their day-to-day interests in foreign countries was however to continue for some time; apart from legations at Washington, Paris and Tokyo no more missions were opened until the eve of the Second World

War. Even today, with more than fifty diplomatic establishments of its own, the Canadian Government relies in some countries upon the British embassy for negotiating with their governments on its behalf.

POLICY-MAKING AND

NEGOTIATION:

AT HOME AND ABROAD

The discretionary powers of Canadian negotiators, as those of other countries, were from an early date severely curtailed by improvements in communication which made home governments reluctant to delegate authority to their representatives abroad. Rodolphe Lemieux, Minister of Labour and Postmaster General in the Laurier Government, was one of the first to experience their effect. After weeks of intensive and difficult negotiation with the Japanese authorities in Tokyo on the question of limiting further emigration to Canada, Lemieux felt he had reached a satisfactory agreement and on December 5, 1907, he cabled to Laurier a synopsis of the proposals and advised their acceptance. "Enfin," he wrote elatedly but, as it was to prove, prematurely, "tout sera fini lundi à 3 p.m. le 9 décembre. Les négociations, grâce à Sir Claude Macdonald, ont pu terminer plut tôt que je ne crois. Bien que le traité reste ce qu'il est dans son intégralité, il se trouve désormais profondement modifié par l'accord conclu."[21] This mood of triumph was rudely jarred four days later by the arrival of a telegram from Laurier stating that the terms of the arrangement were unacceptable to the Canadian Government. In some exasperation Lemieux wrote to Sir Louis Jetté, the Lieutenant-Governor of Quebec and a relative having some influence with the Prime Minister, in an attempt to clear up what he regarded to be no more than a misunderstanding:

Il est impossible à cette distance, d'expliquer par cablegramme tous les détails de l'accord que je suis en mesure de conclure si—comme je l'espère —je reçois mes instructions dans ce sens. Je comprends le désir de Sir Wilfrid d'obtenir tout ce que Nossé a promis, mais si, *indirectement* et *en fait*, j'arrive *au même résultat*, il n'y a pas à hésiter. Dix minutes de conversation avec Sir Wilfrid mettraient les choses à point, mais je suis à l'autre bout du monde![22]

To Laurier Lemieux wrote a lengthy letter of explanation, concluding with the remark that he, Joseph Pope and the British ambassador had "spent many hours and many days to reach this stage of the negotiations" and that all felt that "although not perfect, the arrangement under present circumstances is the best obtainable."[23] But this entreaty, and others (including a plea from the British ambassador to the Governor General), were of no avail. Lemieux was instructed not to conclude any agreement with the Japanese government and to return to Ottawa to explain his proposals to the Cabinet. This confrontation took place on January 11, 1908.

My explanation of the whole scheme [Lemieux wrote] and the recital of negotiations occupied the whole day. The proposed arrangement is not only accepted, but everyone admits that I have obtained more than could have been expected. The reasons why settlement was deferred are (1) because they did not fully understand the terms of the proposals. (2) Because the British Columbia members wanted to see me before any acceptance could be made. (3) Because this being the great issue during the present session, they felt a little nervous about saying "yes" from such a distance. My explanations, however, have been fully accepted, and after I had read my report (70 pages), everybody congratulated me very warmly.[24]

An even less happy outcome awaited another Canadian negotiator in later years who attempted to exercise discretionary authority without precise instructions from his home Government. This was Dr. W. A. Riddell, the Canadian Permanent Advisory Officer at the League of Nations, whose repudiation by the Canadian Government at the time of the controversy over oil sanctions against Italy provides an important footnote to the diplomatic history of the 1930's.

During the last days of the Bennett administration, the Canadian delegation at Geneva, acting with the support of the Prime Minister, had taken certain initiatives concerning sanctions against the Mussolini régime, which had begun to win favourable response from the advocates of collective security. The change of Government at the General Election on October 14, 1935, left Dr. Riddell, now in charge of the delegation, in some uncertainty about how to proceed. Pressed by events and lacking replies to his cabled requests for specific instructions, he fatefully decided to speak in favour of imposing oil sanctions. "It seemed a moment," he wrote afterwards, "when an immediate decision had to be taken if sanctions were to become really effective and if I were to safeguard Canada's interests."[25] History has confirmed this verdict, if not the propriety of a career diplomatist setting his country's policy on a course its government was not prepared to follow. Dr. Riddell's initiative was dogged by ill fortune for, barely an hour after his requests for instructions arrived at Ottawa, replies were sent telling him specifically to avoid the action he had already taken by the time they reached him. Word of what he had done brought an immediate and sharp reprimand to the effect that requests for instructions should arrive sufficiently in advance to permit full consideration of the situation by the Canadian Government, and that he was on no account to act in an important matter in the absence of instructions. Dr. Riddell's telegraphed reply to this message pleaded "the difficulty of my position: with meagre instructions and no basic statement of policy to co-operate fully to secure effective application of economic sanctions while safeguarding Canada's interests. I regret exceedingly if I have caused the Government any embarrassment."[26] The Prime Minister remained unmoved, and cabled coldly that the position taken by Dr. Riddell was neither sound policy nor within the scope of his authority. The Cabinet considered carefully whether to repudiate immediately the statement of the Permanent Advisory Officer, but only when mounting publicity had drawn world-wide attention to "the Canadian proposal" did it do so. A press statement was issued on November 29, the final paragraph of which was as follows:

The suggestion which has appeared in the press from time to time, that the Canadian Government has taken the initiative in the extension of the embargo upon exportation of key commodities to Italy, and particularly in the placing of a ban upon shipments of coal, oil, iron and steel, is due to a misunderstanding. The Canadian Government has not and does not propose to take the initiative in any such action; and the opinion which was expressed by the Canadian member of the Committee—and which has led to the reference to the proposal as a Canadian proposal—represented only his personal opinion, and his views as a member of the Committee, and not the views of the Canadian Government.[27]

It remained Dr. Riddell's belief that his repudiation was due to the circumstance that the Prime Minister and the Under Secretary of State for External Affairs were both out of the country at the time the press statement was given out and the Department left in charge of "two French Canadians," Ernest Lapointe, as Acting Secretary of State for External Affairs, and Laurent Beaudry, as Acting Under Secretary.[28] In this he was in error. An exchange of telegrams between Skelton and Beaudry on November 28 and November 29 makes clear the proposal to disavow Dr. Riddell originated not in Ottawa but at Sea Island, Georgia, where the Prime Minister and his Under Secretary had withdrawn for a brief but in the event unattainable respite from the pressure of world events. Had Dr. Riddell followed more closely the course of the election campaign he would have had some forewarning of the probable response of the future Prime Minister to any untoward initiatives from permanent diplomatic officials; in a speech at St. John, New Brunswick, Mackenzie King had criticized the Bennett administration for leaving the conduct of Canadian policy during the Ethiopian crisis "in the hands of three who have never been returned to responsible positions in the institutions of the country."[29]

The "Riddell incident" has come to exert an important, if unremarked, influence upon the foreign policy process in Canada. It engraved indelibly upon the minds of his colleagues (most of whom later rose to high positions in the Department of External Affairs) the unwisdom of exercising important diplomatic initiatives without explicit political direction from the East Block. In 1959 the Under Secretary of State for External Affairs was asked by a member of the House of Commons Standing Committee to comment on the degree of discretion customarily allowed a Canadian representative abroad. The reply suggests that Dr. Riddell's experience cast a long shadow:

I would say that consultation on any question of policy between a representative abroad and the government at home would be complete and continuous. . . .

Nowadays with communications as prompt and secure as they are, any representative abroad . . . can get in touch with Ottawa within a day and consult, or get instructions as to the action he should take. That is one result—and I think that is true of all the diplomatic services—of the enormous speeding up, not only of telegraphic but telephonic communications, [and] of the provision for automatic cyphering which they have between a good many of the important offices.

A situation in which the representative is isolated for a while and has to use his own judgment without being able to inform his government does not happen very much now; it is very rare.[30]

The role of the Canadian representative at the United Nations provides even less opportunity for independent initiatives, for the proximity of New York City to Ottawa allows virtually continuous consultation. In periods of crisis the foreign minister himself may, at short notice, arrive to take charge of negotiations, as Mr. Lester Pearson did at the time of the Suez crisis in November 1956. Instructions prepared by the Cabinet for Security Council delegates in 1948 enjoined them specifically to seek authority from the Government before making any commitment, or, if time did not permit, to abstain from voting.[31]

Delegates to the General Assembly have been allowed even less room for manœuvre, and the frequency with which as a consequence they have resorted to withholding their vote has caused them to be known to the pundits of the delegates' lounge as "the total abstainers." While a number of abstentions have been due to government policy rather than to the lack of it, the testimony of a parliamentary member of the delegation (the more impressive as coming from a supporter of the Government) is that Ottawa keeps a close and almost distrustful watch upon its activities at all times. Mr. Arthur Smith complained to the Under Secretary of State for External Affairs in 1960 that the delegation found itself "consistently in a position of having to refer to your office and you, in turn, to your advisers, on questions of procedure and policy," and he wondered whether it was not leaving itself "somewhat inflexible realizing how quickly events take place." Mr. Norman Robertson replied:

Basically, it is very important to see that any statements made in the name of Canada are consistent, that they are in line with Cabinet policy; and whenever you can, you want to check and confirm before a decision is taken. A good many quick decisions have to be taken in the course of the Assembly, but some of them have quite important consequences. Now that we have a pretty good and very fast system of communication with our office, I think there is a great deal to be said for encouraging [the delegation] to consult frequently and quickly with the Government in Ottawa, when they can. But there are situations when a snap decision has to be made and the man in charge has to use his best judgment, which may not always coincide with the judgment here. I do not think any Government can delegate responsibility to, let us say, a delegation at a conference, or more particularly the United Nations.

This was especially the case, he added, with social and economic questions, for these required more extensive interdepartmental consultation in Ottawa than purely political questions.[32] His reply did not altogether satisfy Mr. Arthur Smith, who observed that if the Under Secretary's argument were carried to its logical extreme, "it would mean there would be little point in having the delegation there at all—rather just a spokesman who is responsible for repeating views that may have come out of the office of a civil servant in Ottawa." As it was, he concluded, "before you go to have a cup of coffee you have to receive instructions."*

The style of Canadian negotiation has thus come to be characterized by a reluctance on the part of professional diplomatists to commit their governments in the absence of instructions, by an exaggerated

*Canada, H. of C. Standing Committee on External Affairs, *Minutes of Proceedings and Evidence*, no. 12, April 6, 1960, pp. 302–3. The testimony of an American congressional member of the United States delegation during the same Assembly offers an instructive comparison. "Once the broad limits of national policy were established on any issue," Mr. Harold Riegelman recalled, "there remained a wide area for negotiation within which the delegate in charge had a very real and challenging discretion." Letter to *New York Times*, March 14, 1960.

circumspection in making public statements,* and by a readiness, not shared by the profession at large, to acquiesce without complaint in that general demotion of their place in the scheme of government brought about by twentieth-century politics and technology. Such a style is not without its advantages. "Quiet diplomacy" has come into favour as the result of repeated indiscretions by less inhibited representatives. And yet it has its price, exacted chiefly in the form of opportunities for constructive interventions missed or neglected by diplomatists abroad for fear of the consequences to come from home.

POLICY-MAKING AND
NEGOTIATION:
ABOVE AND BELOW

Among the forces assailing the traditional position of the professional diplomatist is the growing popularity of what has come to be known as "summit diplomacy," a process of negotiation wherein by a kind of inverted Gresham's law senior statesmen drive out junior, and politicians, preferably heads of government, take over direct responsibility for what was once the ordinary work of career ambassadors. This trend was particularly striking in the United Kingdom during the years between the two world wars when an unusually brilliant corps of professional diplomatists found itself increasingly displaced by "a succession of politician-diplomats with such striking and memorable characteristics as plus-fours, Scots brogues, shaggy coiffures, white linen neckties, underslung pipes, and various kinds of umbrellas."[33] The eclipse of diplomatists by politicians has been less obvious in Canada, partly because prior to 1945 few career ambassadors served as alternative channels for negotiation; but it has taken place.

Negotiating at the summit has always been to Canadian governments a natural way of dealing with disputes with the United States, for the Prime Minister and other members of his Cabinet were never more than a day's journey from Washington to which they could and often did

*In 1946 the Associate Under Secretary of State for External Affairs remarked in reply to a question whether an American State Department practice of the time requiring overseas representatives to clear public statements with Washington before delivery was followed in Canada: "We trust to the good sense of our representatives abroad not to say things which are embarrassing, and if they do we reserve the right to criticize, which we exercize without stint in the case of a lapse." Canada, House of Commons Standing Committee on External Affairs, *Minutes of Proceedings and Evidence*, no. 4, June 4, 1946, p. 67.

directly repair to take up matters with the President and his administration. It thrived as never before or since during the early months of the Second World War when Mackenzie King and Franklin Roosevelt met several times to dispose of issues large and small. The role of the Canadian legation was necessarily diminished by this practice. On one occasion, when the Canadian Minister, Loring Christie, was present at their discussion, the President "turned to Christie and said: 'You will not mind if [in future] I go over your head and talk straight across the phone to Mr. King'. Christie said no; on the contrary he would be very much relieved."[34] In 1943 the House of Commons was informed that in regard to certain negotiations ordinarily the concern of the legation the Canadian Minister (then Leighton McCarthy) had played no part whatsoever, which drew from an opposition critic the comment: "If agreements of this sort, involving Canada and the United States, are not matters for discussion by our legation at Washington, what is the legation for?"[35] The answer to this criticism, which the Prime Minister did not give at that time, was that so long as matters might more expeditiously be taken up by the two heads of government there was no point in involving the legation. "It is indeed fortunate," Mackenzie King wrote on the eve of one of his visits to Franklin Roosevelt, "that we so completely share each other's confidence and sympathies. There is absolutely nothing that we do not feel able to discuss with each other."[36]

No Canadian Prime Minister and American President have since come close to approximating this camaraderie, which owed much to the extraordinary circumstances of war. President Truman's relations with both Mackenzie King and Mr. St. Laurent, while cordial enough, seemed somehow lacking in warmth; the presidency of General Eisenhower brought a temporary revival of personal diplomacy in Canadian-American relations. In December 1956, Mr. St. Laurent was easily persuaded to join the President in his favourite pastime. "I was very happy," the Prime Minister told the House of Commons soon afterwards,

when, towards the end of my short holiday in Florida, I received a telephone call from the White House that the President would be glad if I would drop off at Augusta, Georgia, on my way back, have lunch with him and have a game of golf. Well I found in fact, you know, that a game of golf with one of those electric go-carts was about the best way to have an international conference because you are getting off the go-cart quite frequently for only a couple of minutes but for time enough to reflect on what has been said up to the then present moment and to reflect on what is going to be said when you get back on the seat of the go-cart. . . . I came away with the impression that the golf game had been very enjoyable but that there had been other aspects on the half day I spent with him that were quite more important than the golf score.[37]

Thirty years previously Lloyd George had discovered the dangers of doing diplomatic business on the golf links,[38] while half a century previously Sir Wilfred Laurier had reacted, a little too violently perhaps, against the flattery of London duchesses. Mr. St. Laurent's excursion into go-cart diplomacy, however gratifying to Canadian self-esteem, ran the double risk of misunderstanding and neglect when the mood of mateship passed.

Canada's introduction to summit diplomacy on the larger world scene may perhaps be dated from the Colonial Conference at the end of the nineteenth century; its distinctively twentieth-century quality was first savoured when Mackenzie King allowed himself to be bundled into a Liberator bomber and flown to London in 1941 for conferences with Mr. Churchill and other British war leaders. In recent years Canadians, while professing scorn for the airborne diplomacy that John Foster Dulles carried to such remarkable lengths and heights, have been profoundly satisfied to watch their own leaders circle and re-circle the globe in a swift succession of good-will tours. These, it should be added, have ordinarily ceremonial rather than political significance; the Canadian diplomatist abroad has rather less often than his American colleague suffered the mortification of having his foreign minister drop from the sky to assume personal charge of negotiations becoming really interesting for the first time in years of painful preparation. Mr. Lester Pearson, when Canadian foreign minister, went so far as to counsel against this method. "We might well be advised to leave more of diplomacy to the diplomats," he wrote. "They are trained for the job and they are usually happy to conduct a negotiation without broadcasting the score after each inning. . . . But when foreign ministers, or, even more, when heads of government meet, with their inevitable retinue of press, radio, and television companions, with experts, advisers, and advisers to advisers, with clever men to work behind the scenes and even cleverer men to supply the scenes behind which to work, then things tend to become difficult."* Well aware of the temptation, Mr. Pearson was not

*Lester B. Pearson, *Democracy in World Politics* (Toronto, 1955), p. 62. This view of negotiation, it has been pointed out, "that one should pick good negotiators to represent him and then give them complete flexibility and authority—a principle commonly voiced by negotiators themselves—is by no means as self-evident as its proponents suggest; the power of a negotiator often rests on a manifest inability to make concessions and to meet demands." Thomas C. Schelling, *The Strategy of Conflict* (Cambridge, Mass., 1960), p. 19. Soviet negotiators have demonstrated this more obviously than most; see Philip E. Mosely, ed., *Negotiating with the Russians* (Boston, 1947), *passim*.

always able to resist; his successors, lacking his background in professional diplomacy, were at times eager to succumb.

POLICY-MAKING AND
NEGOTIATION:
OPEN AND CLOSED

In Canada, as elsewhere, the tragedy of the First World War was widely attributed to the evil machinations of diplomatists allowed to hatch nefarious plots hidden from a watchful public. Closed diplomacy had been the virus, open diplomacy was to be the cure. There was no surer way of discrediting external policy than to shout "secrecy" at those responsible. Mackenzie King as Leader of the Opposition, lacking argument to attack the Government for announcing in 1920 the negotiation with the British Government of the right of legation at Washington, took up the familiar cry: "Well, Sir, all I can say is, it is a mighty bad beginning in a new departure if our foreign policy . . . is to be bound up with a secrecy from the start. We are driving right into the very vortex that created the whole situation in Europe, going against the very thing which the allied nations have been urging so strongly, namely, that diplomacy should not be secret but that it should be open and above board."[39] After becoming Prime Minister, Mackenzie King paid lip-service to the principle of open diplomacy, not least because of its strong appeal to those sixty-five representatives of the Progressive party on whose continuing parliamentary support the life of his Government depended.

It was also useful in imperial relations. Throughout the first Mackenzie King administration a series of crises large and small arose between Ottawa and Whitehall, and a steady stream of agitated telegrams passed between the two. It was then Mackenzie King's aim to loosen the hold which the British Government sought to retain over the conduct of the Dominion's external affairs, and for this purpose it was frequently expedient to make public his correspondence with that Government. Much of it, however, in accordance with a now firmly established convention of intra-Commonwealth consultation, was secret correspondence, and to bring down the texts of secret despatches required the approval of the British Government as author or recipient (and also of any of the Dominion governments affected by their disclosure). In effect, therefore, the United Kingdom authorities possessed a power of veto over the publication of their correspondence with the Dominion

Government merely by marking it "private" or "confidential"; and even in the case of communications not so marked it was the contention of old-fashioned constitutional authorities that, addressed as they were (until 1926) to the Governor General, such messages required the Governor's approval before disclosure—approval not likely to be forthcoming if the British Government, whom the Governor as yet still represented, directed otherwise.

The dispute latent in these circumstances arose in 1923 when the Canadian Government wished to bring down its correspondence with the United Kingdom Government to clarify Canada's constitutional position in regard to the Treaty of Lausanne. To support his case—a strong one—Mackenzie King again invoked popular sentiment against secret diplomacy. In a letter to the Governor General's secretary (affording, incidentally, a fair example of his literary style in its characteristic, though not its best, form), he wrote:

With respect to correspondence between the Government of Canada and the Government of Great Britain on matters originating with the Canadian Government, and with respect to which the fullest publicity is desired, . . . unless—when the return of such correspondence is asked for by the House of Commons—the Government is free to exercise the same judgment and discretion with respect to the prompt presentation to Parliament of the correspondence requested as is exercised with respect to all other returns of correspondence, documents, etc., it will be increasingly difficult to avoid the charge that the Administration is lending itself to a species of secret diplomacy with respect to public business which is in no way warranted, and which, were the impression permitted to be fostered, would be most unfortunate for our inter-imperial and international relations.[40]

In his reply the Governor's secretary argued that correspondence addressed to the Governor General was in fact as in form the Governor-General's Correspondence and, as such, his to disclose or withhold as he saw fit. This sanctity of official correspondence, he insisted, "does not imply secret diplomacy" but was "intended to provide a safe means whereby matters of public concern may be discussed in private."[41] Mackenzie King's eventual response was to raise the whole question at the Imperial Conference later in the year where, after much argument, a resolution, largely drafted by him, settled it along the principles he desired. Its most important paragraphs were these:

The Conference gave its attention to the desire of the Parliaments of the various parts of the Empire to be afforded the fullest information possible on all matters on which negotiations were going on, or discussions taking place, between two or more Governments.

The Conference recognized that, if consultation, to which it attached great importance, was to be carried out effectively, this must involve a frank and confidential exchange of views in written or telegraphic communications, and that many of the communications exchanged between the Governments, particularly in connection with foreign policy and defence, could not be made public. At the same time the feeling of the Conference was that as many communications as possible ought to be made available for the use of the Parliaments, and it was thought desirable to discuss the circumstances in which official communications between the Governments could and could not be made public.

It was generally agreed that any official communication not marked "confidential" or "secret" or not clearly intended to be treated as such might be regarded as available for publication wtihout reference to any other government.

It was understood that, so far as each Government was concerned, and subject to the need for mutual consent in certain cases, the responsibility as to publication of correspondence with other Governments rested with the Ministers of the Crown in the Dominions as in Great Britain.[42]

Mackenzie King's disenchantment with "open covenants, openly arrived at" coincided, surely not by accident, with the strengthening of his parliamentary position in 1926, and with a lengthening experience of diplomatic negotiations fortifying a taste for secrecy acquired as early as 1908 when he undertook a mission to England at the request of President Theodore Roosevelt the real purpose of which had been deliberately concealed from the public.* In 1929 the British Prime Minister, Ramsay MacDonald, paid a visit to Ottawa. Mackenzie King invited him out to his country retreat in the Gatineau Hills, and they "had a delightful tramp together through the woods and over the moors, and tea together in my little cottage by the lake. That particular experience has convinced me more than ever of the wisdom of what I have done at Kingsmere. I believe that more and more, much of our public life is going to be carried on in the open, and that partly as a means of self-preservation from the stress, strain and pressures of the highly intensified and complex life of our day, men who have really great problems to consider are going to meet in the quiet retreats of Nature and thresh out their problems there."[43] Henceforth, this belief in the value of intimate negotiation with leaders of government, untroubled by the mischievous scrutiny of the public and the press, influenced to an increasing extent Mackenzie King's conduct of external policy. It was manifested in a distrust of multilateral conferences—"the more I

---

*"The Canadian Cabinet could not possibly announce that King was going to England at Roosevelt's request, and an ostensible reason for the trip had to be found. . . . [This was] that . . . he was being sent to England to discuss various aspects of [immigration] with the Government of the United Kingdom." R. MacGregor Dawson, *William Lyon Mackenzie King: A Political Biography*, I, *1874–1923* (Toronto, 1958), p. 160.

see of conferences the less patience I am coming to have with them," he exclaimed in an unusually frank outburst in the House of Commons in 1937—and, more positively, in a decided preference for "quiet diplomacy." His reaction to the "Atlantic Charter" meeting between Roosevelt and Churchill in the summer of 1941 was revealing in this respect. "To me, it the apotheosis of the craze for publicity and show," he wrote in his diary. "There is no need for any meeting of the kind."[44]

Mr. Lester Pearson brought to his office as Secretary of State for External Affairs from 1949 to 1957 the training and the outlook of twenty years in professional diplomacy. It is not surprising, therefore, that he shared to the full, and helped in considerable degree to formulate, the reaction against negotiating in the limelight so dominant in recent years. "The purpose of negotiation," he has written,

is the reconciliation of interests, the exploring of a situation in an effort to find some common ground, some possibility of compromise, the seeking of agreement through mutual adjustments. Such adjustments are not made easier, and may well be made impossible, when the negotiators fear that any concession or compromise will within the hour be printed, pictured, or broadcast back home as a capitulation. . . .

There are situations—and they are sometimes the most difficult and important ones—where . . . highly publicized meetings offer the least promising of all methods of negotiating. An atmosphere of drama is inevitably generated when the spotlights of the world are focussed on a single "parley at the summit". Such an atmosphere may well be a public relations officer's dream, but a negotiator's doom. . . .[45]

Negotiations conducted in public, in fact, by political personages, are simply not permitted to fail—at least for some time. This is one reason that diplomatic negotiations should normally be conducted in private. . . .

Full publicity for objectives and policies and results does not mean, or at least should not mean, that negotiation must always be conducted, step by step, in public. Certainly no private activity, not even a public relations business, could be operated by such methods. And government is today the most important and delicate activity of all. Negotiation in an agitated goldfish bowl, then, is often a serious obstacle to the reaching of agreement. . . .[46]

These reflections may appear to embody no more than the conventional wisdom of their subject, but reflection of any kind is rare enough in politicians, and of this kind rarer still.

Chapter Eight

PROPAGANDA

PROPAGANDA VERSUS "PUBLICITY"

In common with leaders of liberal democracies everywhere, the makers of Canadian foreign policy have been reluctant to develop as part of the ordinary machinery of government the instruments of what is variously described as information, propaganda, psychological or political warfare. Ready enough to exploit such devices in war, the Canadian government has regarded them as inappropriate for peacetime use. It was only gradually, and with evident distaste, that the legitimacy of propaganda as a means of implementing foreign policy in normal times was established, as it became apparent that the old dichotomies of "peace" and "war" were no longer relevant to the international scene. And even then the most experienced and knowledgable officials were inclined to approach it with great caution. "It is a very tricky business," remarked Mr. Lester Pearson in 1953, "to conduct psychological warfare in a time of cold war and through the agency of coalition of free states."[1]

Notwithstanding these inhibitions against using propaganda to influence the foreign policies of other states, Canadians have been quite ready to accept it for another and, as they conceive it, a more innocuous purpose, creating a climate of opinion abroad in which Canadian interests could blossom and prosper. Provided no attempt was made directly to intervene in matters of high policy, provided efforts were confined to what later became known as "projecting a favourable image of the Canadian community," no serious objection was raised. In this diluted version, often described as "publicity" so as to avoid a more offensive if more accurate connotation, propaganda has become an accepted form of governmental activity. Indeed, it has been suggested that such activity is more important to the Canadian government than to most others. "We are a comparatively new arrival on the international scene," Mr. Vincent Massey has written, "and less is known about Canadian life than would be the case if we had been a grown-up member of the family of nations for a longer time. . . . The paradox of enjoying at the same time the complete independence and the privilege of membership in the British Commonwealth is confusing to the foreigner. This imposes a special obligation on us to enlighten others as to how we carry on our affairs."[2] The enlightenment of foreigners has been in fact a continuing if incidental part of the work of Canadian officials, from W. T. R. Preston who in 1900 wished to destroy all lantern slides depicting Indians, ice palaces and snow slides,[3] to Mr. Lester Pearson who in 1954 remarked to an American audience that Canada was after all "far more than an enormous cold spot on the map, inhabited by Mounties, Eskimo, trappers, quintuplets and Rose Marie."[4] And if the need has lessened, it has not yet passed.

EARLY PROPAGANDA FOR

IMMIGRATION AND TRADE

Propaganda was first employed in aid of external policy to bring more people to the country. "Our immigration policy," remarked the Minister responsible for it in 1911, "is in the first instance simply an advertising policy—a means of placing the advantages of Canada before such people in other countries as we desire to come to Canada."[5] Enlisted in this cause were a variety of propagandist techniques, employed the more vigorously, if crudely, by Dominion agents unrestrained by the niceties of normal diplomatic practice. They soon ran into trouble. European countries, if they did not, like Russia, forbid emigration altogether, were not anxious to lose their labour forces, and they prohibited with varying degrees of severity and effectiveness emigration propaganda by foreign agents. Canadian propaganda became the subject of official complaint to the imperial authorities by the German ambassador in London; the *Hamburger Nachrichten* deplored "the arrogance of the Canadian [High Commissioner] Lord Strathcona, and the utter disrespect shown by him . . . in publicly conducting his emigration propaganda on German soil. . . . Apart from the weakening of the Fatherland which the success of such propaganda entails, the attempt to lure our fellow-countrymen to this desolate, sub-arctic region is, upon humane grounds alone, to be denounced as criminal."[6] In the United Kingdom, however, the High Commissioner and the agents of the provincial governments could and did give freer reign to their ingenuity. Newspaper advertisements, letters to editors, pamphlets, lectures abetted by the magic lantern, sought to depict the Dominion as a land of opportunity if not of milk and honey. "In later years two exhibit wagons were on the move in Ireland and Scotland, and two motor cars travelled through England . . . , stopping wherever a crowd could be collected and an opportunity for speaking and giving out pamphlets could be found."[7]

Propaganda was similarly pressed into the service of commercial policy. Agents already engaged in drumming up immigrants turned their attention to goods and capital. John Dyke in Liverpool was instructed in 1885 to "furnish information on . . . questions of trade . . . between Canada and Europe," and henceforth depicting the fortunes awaiting traders and investors in the new Dominion became an increasingly important aspect of the work of Canadian agents and, later, of trade commissioners. Members of the Canadian Economic Commission which visited Russia in 1918 were keenly aware of the value of propaganda in pursuing its objectives:

Before leaving Siberia your Commission urged that an illustrated pamphlet describing Canada and her resources should be prepared and translated into Russian for distribution throughout Siberia. Not having had time to accomplish this during their stay in Vladivostock, a small leaflet was prepared for distribution through the medium of the Trade Commissioner. Your Commission, however, feel that the original proposal should be carried out, and a carefully prepared pamphlet in Russian issued for wide distribution.

It was arranged before the Commission left for Siberia that certain moving picture films illustrating Canadian national life and industries should be prepared and forwarded for use throughout the country. They failed, however, to come to hand, and your Commission now recommend that a series of such films be prepared with the proper Russian titles and made available for use by the Trade Commissioner in carrying on an illustrated propaganda through the medium of the co-operative societies, the zemstvos, the schools and other suitable organizations, who would be glad to arrange for the exhibit of these films.[8]

WARTIME PROPAGANDA IN
THE UNITED STATES

The Canadian Government did not venture in the company of its more powerful Allies into the exciting experiments conducted at Crewe House and later by George Creel's Committee on Public Information (although Canadians served under Lord Beaverbrook in the British Government's Ministry of Information created in February 1918[*]). Lacking both appetite and means for psychological warfare on such a scale, the Canadian Government resorted for the first time to propaganda for the purpose of achieving a political objective of external

*Beaverbrook, according to one critic, relied on Canadians "whose experience of foreign affairs and whose knowledge of foreign languages was as limited as his own." Laurence Lyon, *The Pomp of Power* (London, 1922), quoted in Harold D. Lasswell, "The Organization of Psychological Warfare Agencies in World War I" in William E. Daugherty and M. Janowitz, eds., *A Psychological Warfare Casebook* (Baltimore, 1958), p. 123 n.

policy as distinct from commercial advantage. The objective was to
enlist American sympathy for the Allied cause. The method could
hardly have been more discreet. In January 1917 the Canadian Prime
Minister, Sir Robert Borden, asked Major Charles W. Gordon, a
Canadian author better known as Ralph Connor, if he would exploit his
considerable reputation in the United States to speak there on the
subject of the Allied, and particularly of the Canadian war effort. "It
occurred to me," Borden wrote to the Colonial Secretary,

that he might go informally to some of the cities in the United States and
deliver addresses descriptive of conditions at the front, where he had an
experience of many months, and of the work and achievements of the
British forces, and more especially of the Canadian Army Corps, to which
he was attached as a chaplain. It was suggested that incidentally he could
set forth in these addresses the causes which had compelled Canada to
throw herself heart and soul into the struggle and that in this way he might
awaken in his audiences a fuller appreciation of the purpose of the Allied
nations and of the magnitude of the issue as it concerns the whole world.[9]

No sooner had Gordon arrived in Washington than the United States
broke off diplomatic relations with Germany, and a few weeks later it
was at war. He was advised by the British ambassador to confine his
efforts "to a campaign devoid of any great publicity,"[10] and events in
any case soon made more ambitious efforts unnecessary. The Canadian
Government throughout 1918 took the view, well expressed by a
prominent Toronto business man at the time, that "to find the United
States our associate in foreign policy, even to the fighting point, is so
much beyond our wildest hopes of three years ago that we feel that
what American sentiment needs for the moment is a certain amount of
letting alone."[11]

The problem arose again between September 1939 and December
1941. When in the spring and summer of 1940 the twilight war
deepened into the black night of battle and disaster, the voices of many
influential Canadians were raised to demand that their Government
appeal to American opinion to press the Roosevelt administration into
closer co-operation with the United Kingdom. Mackenzie King, like
Borden before him, was greatly averse to propaganda of this kind. While
he did not shrink from placing privately before the President and his
officials requests for matériel and other forms of assistance, he was
intensely sympathetic to the President's difficulties in coping with
isolationist opinion in an election year and most anxious to avoid anything in the nature of a public appeal, or the kind of private appeal
which might become public. Thus he viewed with great displeasure a
speech made by the Attorney General of Ontario on April 3, 1940,
urging that Canada "bring about the active participation of the United

States in support of the Allied cause."[12] The speech was widely and adversely commented upon in the American press, and drew from the Secretary of State the extraordinarily sharp public rebuke that "no nondescript utterances of minor officials or individuals abroad . . . have anything remotely to do with the policy of this Government at home or in its international relations."[13] The Under Secretary of State for External Affairs described the spech as "the most stupid and harmful . . . made by any Canadian in years," the Canadian Minister telephoned from Washington to report that it had greatly strengthened the hand of the isolationists, and the Prime Minister thought it advisable to issue a statement declaring that "the Canadian Government particularly has no thought of attempting to intervene, directly or indirectly, in the affairs or policies of the United States."[14]

But feeling persisted that it should. The former Minister to the United States, W. D. Herridge, sought support for a mission to Washington of eminent statesmen and soldiers of the Allies to inform the American public and government of the urgency of the situation and of the need for massive and immediate assistance; he proposed that the Canadian Government should initiate this project, first by seeking the President's approval, and then by taking it up with the governments of France and the United Kingdom. Although the Under Secretary of State for External Affairs privately described the proposal as "cockeyed and dangerous" (an opinion fully shared by his Prime Minister), the Canadian legation in Washington was instructed to broach it informally with the Secretary of State who, as expected, sternly disapproved. Mackenzie King was also instrumental in deflecting a proposal of the Prime Minister of Australia that the United Kingdom and the Dominions should simultaneously appeal to the President and, through him, American opinion, for immediate aid. "Any change of policy in the United States," he cabled to Mr. Churchill on May 24, 1940, "will have to result from conviction that a change is necessary in their own interest. I feel strongly that at the present moment any public appeal by outside governments would arrest rather than assist the formation of public and Congressional opinion favourable to action."[15] Even to such modest proposals as public lectures by pro-Allied speakers he was distinctly cool. "With respect to what you have in mind as to lecturing in the United States," he wrote to a correspondent offering her services as a public speaker to American audiences, "I must tell you that from the beginning of the war our Government has rigidly refrained from identifying itself in any way with propaganda in that country. We have not even sought to divide responsibility with the United Kingdom.

We have had to inform the British Government that its ministry must use its own judgment and take responsibility for such work in the nature of propaganda in the United States as it deems advisable."[16] There can be no doubt that this policy of restraint was the right policy, and wholly justified by events. Later in the war the Prime Minister referred to the matter in the House of Commons:

There was in the United States a strong feeling against any attempt on the part of Canada to influence the people in a way which might be held to be political, namely, to make from Canada by way of propaganda an effort to bring the United States into the war. It was held the reactions might be serious. I am justified in saying that I was asked by the highest authority in the United States to see that great care was taken to avoid making any move by which it could be said that the government of Canada was trying to influence public opinion in the United States with a view to having the United States brought into the war against its will.[17]

By 1941 the case for restraint had less to commend it. Franklin Roosevelt had been triumphantly returned for a third term, isolationist sentiment was on the wane, Anglo-American co-operation was assuming the more tangible form of an easterly flow of munitions and supply if only, as yet, for "cash on the barrel-head." This rush of events had tended to obscure the nature and extent of Canada's own contribution to the war effort, and Mackenzie King became increasingly responsive to the great pressure on the Government to step up its informational activities in the United States. By May 1941, even the Washington legation urged this course:

We . . . respectfully suggest that you should at an early date deliver a speech somewhere in the United States to be carried on a national hook-up, publicizing the war-effort of Canada, and urging the American nation and government to see that the tools which they are so splendidly manufacturing, and asked for by Mr. Churchill, reach the source where they are desperately required and not sunk in the Atlantic Ocean.

Further, we respectfully suggest that Ernest Lapointe [the Minister of Justice] should at the earliest possible moment deliver a similar speech in the United States which should be broadcast throughout the country, replying to the article in *Life* whereby the Province of Quebec is classed as "Fifth Columnist", as well as urging delivery of the tools under protection which will prevent their being sunk.[18]

While these suggestions were not acted upon, it is clear that the Prime Minister's thoughts were moving in the same direction. A few weeks earlier he had himself spoken with Cordell Hull about the inadequacy of information about Canada in the United States. "I told him of my having wanted to avoid any interference when the Lend-Lease Bill was on. Said I had been asking myself whether it might not be well

to give a radio broadcast to the U.S. setting forth Canada's position."[19]
By mid-summer he was considering new machinery for a sustained programme of information in the United States. "There is, as you know,"
he wrote to the Minister in Washington in September,

a very strong feeling throughout the country, and more particularly on the
part of the Press, that Canada should have, in New York, an office somewhat similar to that over which Sir Gerald Campbell presides [the United
Kingdom Information Office]. I doubt if those who have to do with the
creating of public opinion and *public prejudice* in Canada will ever be
satisfied that the Government is doing its duty unless some additional
agency of the kind is established. I might say I think the same would be
more or less true of the Members of Parliament.

As matters now stand, the Legation is coming in for wholly unwarranted
as well as unnecessary criticism on the score of inadequate publicity being
given in the United States to Canada's war effort. Indeed the criticism is, as
you will know, aimed not less at myself than the Legation. . . .

I am sure that something can be worked out which will prevent any
conflict of jurisdictions or of services.[20]

The Minister, not unnaturally, was less sure, and took unkindly to the
creation in the neighbouring American city of an agency bound to
become to some extent a rival of his own. "There is need for us to
continue and expand the quiet work that is being done in this country,"
he conceded in a letter to the Prime Minister. "There is need perhaps for
a more dramatic presentation from Ottawa of our war effort. But this is
not the moment to establish, with the attendant publicity required to
meet the Canadian criticisms to which you refer, a registered bureau in
the United States, which would naturally have to justify its existence by
attracting and retaining the public eye."[21] For the moment this view
prevailed. But Pearl Harbor disposed of any remaining objections, and
in 1942 the Wartime Information Board came into being.

The considerations leading the Government to take this important
step were described by the Prime Minister to the House of Commons on
July 13, 1943:

The success of the combined efforts of the allied powers depends largely
upon mutual good-will. Good-will in turn demands accurate, full and constant information. It is the acknowledged aim of the enemy's propaganda to
sow discord among the United Nations by spreading lies and half-truths in
each of the allied nations about its partners. So important do the Nazis
consider this warfare of words, or political warfare, that they have spent and
continue to spend staggering sums on propaganda. The germs of false propaganda can only do their evil work in the darkness of ignorance. They can
be destroyed only with the light of truth. But it is still more satisfactory if
accurate information can be supplied before the false propaganda is spread
abroad. That is why every free country at war has given so much attention
to disseminating information outside its own borders.

Before the present war, Canada had little or no experience of this important side of wartime activity. The government approached it with caution and hesitation. For obvious reasons, it was more important for Canada to see that accurate information was available in the United States than in any other country. Before the United States entered the war that was a matter of extreme delicacy. After the entry of the United States, the technical difficulties were not so great, but the American people became increasingly absorbed in their own war effort, and consequently relatively less interested in the activities of another country. This situation increased the danger of misunderstandings. There was a growing concern in Canada to find some means of preventing possible misunderstanding by the provision of accurate information to the United States. Several hon. members gave expression to that concern. The concern was fully shared by the Government, and it was out of that concern that the Wartime Information Board was established.[22]

The Wartime Information Board (W.I.B.) was from its inception placed under the ministerial direction of the President of the Privy Council (a portfolio then and normally held by the Prime Minister) "in order," as Mackenzie King later explained, "that interdepartmental co-operation might be more effectively obtained. This was not likely to be the case to the same degree if the Board remained under any one other particular minister."* Its first chairman was Charles Vining, a public relations counsellor not previously in government service, who had prepared for the Government a report on the need for informational activity and on the machinery by which it might be provided. One recommendation of the Vining Report was that external and domestic information services should be combined under a single administration, and accordingly the new W.I.B. took over the work and personnel of the small Bureau of Public Information which since July 1940, under the Department of National War Services, had concerned itself solely with information on the home front. When Charles Vining resigned for reasons of health, the W.I.B. chairmanship was made an advisory rather than administrative position and a new post, that of general manager, created. To it was appointed Mr. John Grierson, the director of the National Film Board. Mr. Grierson fully agreed with the recommendation in the Vining Report that "there should be nothing in the nature of a publicity campaign, that there should be a minimum of commotion, that the offices of the Board should be small and efficient,

*This same consideration had led to a number of other wartime agencies and functions being placed under the President of the Privy Council, with the result that the Prime Minister was greatly overburdened. To meet this situation, the post of Parliamentary Assistant to the President of the Privy Council was created in 1943, and first occupied by Brooke Claxton. Upon him devolved the duty of administering and dealing in the House of Commons with the Wartime Information Board.

that they should largely work through the press and other instruments, and not in any way seek to take the place of the press."[23] Early in the war he had written to members of the Prime Minister's staff about the dangers of too large and too noisy propaganda machinery:

I must say, I don't like the idea of a big Ministry of Information with large personnel, on the lines of the English one. It became, as you know, a disaster of heavy-weight officialdom. . . .

The alternative method—and one which I think would admirably suit Canadian conditions . . . —is to have a Bureau of Information which travels as light as possible. . . . All you require is a small group of liaison officers or secretaries of information—one for each medium which the Government wishes to use—with a principal Secretary of Information who would report directly to the Prime Minister and convey policy decisively to the others. . . .

Your information service would therefore be something in the nature of a flying squad, proceeding from specific job to specific job and co-operating with people only in respect of specific jobs; but doing so with the authority of the P.M. in the background and a considered and single policy regarding the various problems involved, e.g., national unity, presentation of Canadian views to the United States, advising the British Information Service on Canadian realities, etc. . . .

One of the principal problems will be to keep the lunatics in leash. I have already heard them talk of working the people up to fever pitch, forcing the U.S. into the war by preventive tactics. . . .[24]

There is considerable danger for Canada if it is exploited as a base for the cruder forms of propaganda. . . . There is no question but that American opinion is super-sensitive to exploitation by the cruder forms of propaganda, and that ill-will may be created by it. . . . In other words, while the voice of Canada must inevitably develop great importance in the United States at the present time, it may be wise to determine with great care and foresight the nature of that voice. I have advised the [British] Embassy at Washington to concentrate for the time being on an intensive development of cultural relations between England and the United States. . . . The same policy might be adopted by Canada with a judicious introduction of information concerning Canada's war activities, its views on the war, and, particularly, its national interpretation of the democratic issues at stake.[25]

These views could not have more exactly coincided with the Prime Minister's own opinions, and they were no doubt recalled by him when he appointed their author as general manager of the W.I.B. At the same time they were easier to express than to carry into effect. The W.I.B. was frequently and heatedly criticized, partly on the ground that it had become an instrument for political party propaganda, but also, and perhaps more fairly, that it had not remained as modest in size and in demeanour as it set out to be. These charges were naturally rejected by the Government. "It is modest, it is not aggressive in any improper sense, it has an admirable personnel, and is doing a good job," declared Brooke Claxton to the House of Commons in 1943. He described its work in these words:

The men in charge of the Washington and New York offices receive an advance upon a story coming through over the Canadian Press or the British United Press from Canada. They at once get into contact with the heads of the American services and the editors of the leading American papers, pointing out that this story is of the type which would interest them. . . . The members of the Board have assisted in the preparation of articles, have provided facilities and materials for writers and for journalists having to do with the war effort. . . . The Board replies to inquiries—and they are pouring in all the time—and it furnishes still photographs and other materials. . . . The Board has co-operated in the closest possible way and has the friendliest relations with both the British Ministry of Information officials in the United States and the Office of War Information of the United States. The latter organization has helped in the dissemination of Canadian news all over the world because of arrangements made by the Wartime Information Board.

He was asked why, in the course of his exposition, he had implied that the W.I.B. was not a propaganda organization:

Mr. Hanson (York-Sunbury): . . . Is not the whole thing propaganda, to make the people of the United States understand what Canada is doing?

Mr. Claxton: If my hon. friend uses the word "propaganda" in that sense, which is its true literal sense, I agree with him. But propaganda has in addition certain unfavourable connotations, and I do not use the word for that reason.[26]

PROPAGANDA AND FOREIGN
POLICY SINCE 1945

In 1943, answering a question whether the Wartime Information Board would be continued as a peacetime instrument of government, Brooke Claxton replied for the Prime Minister that "it is absolutely certain that [its] work will not go on after the war in its present form. . . . If the work now done by the Board is carried on, it will be totally changed in character and certainly changed in name and form."[27] The future of W.I.B., and, more generally, of post-war government information policy, were considered by the Mackenzie King administration soon after the end of hostilities against Japan. A memorandum prepared by the general manager of the Board in August 1945 argued strongly for the continuation of its external activities with the object of conveying factual information about Canadian life to the people of other countries, particularly in the United States. For this purpose a new agency was proposed outside the Department of External Affairs though working closely with that Department, having its own information officers who, like the officers of the Departments of Trade and Commerce and National Defence, would be under the general supervision of heads of diplomatic missions while reporting independently to the agency's Ottawa headquarters. These recommendations were largely accepted. In September 1945 the W.I.B. was disbanded. In its place emerged a new Canadian Information Service (C.I.S.), under the guidance of an interdepartmental committee on which were represented those departments and agencies having an interest in external informational activity—External Affairs, Trade and Commerce, the Canadian Broadcasting Corporation and the National Film Board. The chairman of this guiding committee was the Clerk of the Privy Council, then Mr. A. D. P. Heeney. The C.I.S. had its own director, Mr. Geoffrey C. Andrew, who, prior to this appointment, had been assistant director of the W.I.B. (The director of W.I.B. at the end of the war, Mr. A. D. Dunton, became chairman of the Canadian Broadcasting Corporation.)

Operating with some of the staff and a much smaller part of the budget of the W.I.B., the C.I.S. was neither charged with nor equipped for the major responsibility of conducting political warfare on any scale. It confined itself to the task of providing more or less factual information about Canada for overseas governments and publics. In this modest function, performed on a modest scale, it acted in close conjunction with the Department of External Affairs. In addition to the Under Secretary of the Department, who represented it on the guiding committee, a less senior official was a member of the C.I.S. working committee which met once or twice a week to review and direct operations. Daily contact between the personnel of C.I.S. and of the Department was assured if only because the two were housed in the same building. Its overseas officers in London, Paris and Canberra (the C.I.S. had succeeded to the W.I.B. offices in those capitals) were members of the Canadian diplomatic missions there and responsible to their heads, while in New York City and Washington they worked very closely with the consul general and the ambassador. Liaison between the two was in fact so intimate and their functions so similar that it quickly became evident that there was little point in maintaining the C.I.S. as a separate institution. By order-in-council, the C.I.S. on February 5, 1947, was integrated into the Department of External Affairs.

Since 1946 the Department of External Affairs had been experimenting with a small information division of its own. Its name, the Associate Under Secretary of the Department conceded, was "possibly a little misleading. We debated for some time before the name was agreed on. The name used for corresponding activities in the Department of State at Washington is the Cultural Relations Division, which strikes me as being rather high-sounding and not a particularly significant title. So we adopted perhaps the most nondescript title to indicate the portion of the Department which was concerned with a collection of duties connected with providing data and answering queries."[28] When the C.I.S. was disbanded in 1947, its director became the head of the Department's information division, and most of its staff was taken into the Department to augment the personnel of the division. The process of integration, reported the Department's chief administrative officer in 1947, "was not an easy job at first."[29] He did not elaborate this cryptic statement, perhaps implying a more than routine administrative difficulty in absorbing additional personnel from a disbanded agency. The established foreign service officers looked upon the new arrivals with something of the diplomatist's traditional contempt for the manipulators of mass media, while the ex-information officers, sensing their inferior status, sought to leave it behind by striving after appointment to political divisions of the Department. It was a marriage of convenience but it was not a happy marriage, and the former director of the C.I.S. left the Department soon afterwards.

The information division had really very little to do with propaganda as an instrument of foreign policy. It acted as the Department's press office, furnishing texts of official statements to the diplomatic corps and the Parliamentary Press Gallery. It shared with other divisions the job of circulating within the Department information derived from incoming despatches, and of preparing "general reports for the background information of missions on economic and political developments in the various countries in which our missions are located, or on trends of thought and policy in the Department."[30] It prepared the Department's publications and reference materials. In short, it was doing what it was supposed to do if it pooled information among the members of the Department, conveyed to the home public something of the direction and detail of Canadian foreign policy, and projected to peoples abroad a favourable impression of Canadian life. There was little if any conscious attempt to influence the policies of other governments.

This more frankly propagandist task was the responsibility of the International Service of the Canadian Broadcasting Corporation.

The creation of a government-owned short-wave broadcasting station had been urged by the C.B.C. as early as 1937, although without any suggestion that it should be used for transmitting propaganda. Indeed, when the United Kingdom Ministry of Information revived the proposal in 1941, one of the opposing arguments brought forward by an official of the Department of External Affairs was "the danger of indulging in 'propaganda' abroad."[31] The term was evidently not thought to embrace the more innocuous if no less constructive function of projecting "the major issues at stake in the present war, which would be a positive factor in strengthening the resistance within the occupied countries of Europe, . . . exchanging views and information with other parts of the Commonwealth, and . . . reaching the countries of South America," for these were cited as favourable consequences of the proposal. On September 27, 1941, the Prime Minister minuted: "I favour the short wave station & intended to recommend its establishment at last meeting of War Committee had principal members been present." Three years were to pass, however, before the short-wave facilities were used by the Government for the transmission of propaganda. During the interval, the Wartime Information Board used the transmitters of the British Ministry of Information and United States Office of War Information to carry some of its material abroad. But the extent to which these facilities could be exploited was limited, for the principal theme of the W.I.B. propaganda was the distinct and on occasion the superior achievement of the Canadian war effort vis-à-vis those of the United States and the United Kingdom. Such a message was more fittingly carried over Canadian than Anglo-American facilities, and in 1944, the year of the invasion, the Cabinet authorized the creation of the International Service of the Canadian Broadcasting Corporation. Its transmitter was located at Sackville, New Brunswick, and its operating headquarters, mainly for technical reasons, in Montreal, the nearest large city.

C.B.C.–I.S. began its broadcasts in February 1945. These consisted principally of short-wave transmission of programmes to the peoples of Germany and of occupied Europe, and their objectives were to disrupt the Axis cause and to sustain the morale and vigour of the resistance. But the coming of peace brought a sudden end to this work so recently begun; in Ottawa (as in all other Allied capitals save Moscow) there was no disposition to continue propaganda as a conventional instrument of foreign policy. Foreign language broadcasting was continued, and indeed expanded, but the emphasis was solely upon projecting "a picture of Canadian life with special reference to social, cultural, and economic development."[32]

The communist seizure of power in Czechoslovakia radically altered the character of C.B.C.–I.S. broadcasting. Prior to 1948 there had been built up in Czechoslovakia what the director of the International Service later described as "one of our largest and most responsive European audiences."[33] Rather than abandon it to the raucous monopoly of Radio Prague and Radio Moscow, the Canadian Government fatefully decided to continue to broadcast programmes in Czech and Slovak but to alter their content so as to achieve two wholly new purposes: "(1) to expound and develop the aims and policies of the Western democratic powers and particularly of Canada; (2) to combat communist ideology and Soviet imperialism."[34] Other areas of Eastern Europe were soon added as targets of transmission. Short-wave broadcasting in Russian to the Soviet Union was begun in February 1951, and a Ukrainian service, also directed at the Soviet Union, was inaugurated in July 1952. Transmission in Polish to Poland was started in 1953 and, following the revolution in Hungary in 1956, programmes in Magyar were beamed to the people of that unhappy land.

The value of these efforts was attested to by the assiduity of Soviet jamming, although (so small was the proportion of programming reaching its intended audience) it might be, and was, asked whether the game was worth the candle. To this question the director of the International Service in 1953 returned the following answer:

The main arguments in favour of maintaining these programmes [to Eastern Europe] are reasons of prestige, since it would appear to be indispensable to stress in people's minds the independence of Canada as an entity distinct from Great Britain and the United States, and reasons of strategy, since it is important to secure channels of communication which may become useful in time of emergency. In the course of conversations with senior officials of the Voice of America and the B.B.C., I was told that the Voice of Canada is rendering a good service to both these broadcasting organizations by keeping a middle course between the aggressive Voice of America and the dispassionate Voice of Britain.[35]

No formal apparatus of liaison kept the International Service in touch with the political broadcasting instrumentalities of Canada's allies, notably the Voice of America and the B.B.C., but the Service was kept closely informed of both long-range policies and day-to-day programming. "There is a constant flow of information, of material," the Service's director remarked in 1953. "It is a sort of Niagara of teletypes."[36]

The process by which propaganda, so obviously an instrument of foreign policy and as such the prerogative of foreign offices, became in Canada as in the United Kingdom (and later on as in the United States) the responsibility of a separate instrument outside the Department of External Affairs, did not reflect settled convictions about the inability of diplomatists to become propagandists. There were no inhibitions on that score in Ottawa. "Every Canadian official is an information officer," commented the Under Secretary of State for External Affairs in 1947, "or should be."[37] It was due, rather, to a tradition of public broadcasting over a state-owned radio system, and to the location of the system's short-wave facilities in Montreal, over a hundred miles from the capital. To have moved those facilities to Ottawa would not have been impossible but it would have been costly. So, for better or worse, the decision was taken to entrust the preparation as well as the transmission of propaganda to the International Service in Montreal. It may be assumed that it was taken with some awareness of the difficulties that might follow as a consequence, for by that time there was available the experience of the British Government which had attempted with indifferent results to divide the propaganda function between the B.B.C. and the Foreign Office.* With the inauguration of broadcasting to Eastern Europe three years later, the International Service embarked on a more obviously propagandist tack, and the increasingly important problem of effective liaison between the Service and the Department of External Affairs became the subject of searching inquiry by the House of Commons Standing Committee on External Affairs.

The earliest statement of arrangements for liaison was given by the Secretary of State for External Affairs to the Standing Committee in May 1951. Mr. Lester Pearson conceded that "in the earlier days of the Service . . . consultation was not as effective as might have been desired." To improve it, a foreign service officer was appointed for liaison duties with the International Service, and the Department undertook to supply it with "policy guidance memoranda which are supposed to govern the policy side of their broadcasting to foreign countries."

*"When war broke out . . . the B.B.C., whilst maintaining their independence, entered into a gentlemen's agreement with the Government to accept official guidance in their treatment of public affairs. That is to say they undertook to conform to official policy, whilst reserving the right to execute it in their own way by the free selection of speakers, arrangement of programmes, and so forth. The Ministry responsible for giving guidance was to be the Ministry of Information. . . . It is perhaps not surprising that this arrangement did not work well. In the first place, the B.B.C. had no access to secret information regarding the conduct of the war, a circumstance which led to a number of discreditable mishaps. Secondly, too many people in the Ministry of Information and in other Government departments tried to influence and guide the B.B.C. in their day-to-day handling of affairs. Since interests of Government departments or even sections of the Ministry of Information were apt to conflict, guidance from different official sources was often contradictory. The result was friction, resentment on both sides and a mounting sense of unmerited dissatisfaction with the performance of the B.B.C." *The Inner Circle: Memoirs of Ivone Kirkpatrick* (London, 1959), p. 156.

But, Mr. Pearson insisted, "we do not . . . tell them how they will carry out that policy. We do not write their scripts, and I think I am right in saying that we do not censor their scripts, but we examine all their scripts afterwards and if, in our opinion, they depart from the policy laid down, we bring it to their attention."[38] Two years later he reported: "Every month I get a great stack of texts of broadcasts to countries behind the iron curtain . . . and I try to see the line being followed and to satisfy myself it is the right line."[39] The texts were also furnished to the Canadian diplomatic missions in the target countries for their comments and criticisms.[40]

In 1952 an attempt was made to secure a still closer relation between the Department of External Affairs and the International Service by appointing to the Service as its director general a senior Canadian diplomatist, the late Jean Désy, at that time ambassador to Italy. Désy did not resign from the Department to take on his new position, and as a continuing member of it he enjoyed what his predecessors and successors could not enjoy—the right of access to all departmental files. He informed the Standing Committee in 1953 of this privilege and its consequences: "I am entitled to read all the secret memoranda, secret telegrams, secret documents coming from all over the world, from our missions, and these documents enable me to form an opinion as to what is good [propaganda] and what is bad."[41] In practice, however, the director's resort to departmental files appears to have been limited to what the Department's officials themselves decided to send for his guidance. A foreign service officer, Mr. Yvon Beaulne (who had served under Désy in Rome), travelled once or twice a week between Montreal and Ottawa to acquire confidential documents for the Director's perusal. Within the Department itself a political co-ordination section was created on March 1, 1953, primarily for the purpose of "keeping the C.B.C. informed of developments which should be reflected in their broadcasts,"[42] and it was to this section that Mr. Beaulne (or Désy when in Ottawa) turned for information and direction on policy.

Further alterations in the liaison apparatus occured between 1953 and 1959. With the appointment late in 1953 of an International Service official (Mr. Charles Delafield) as Désy's successor, the Department of External Affairs withdrew Mr. Beaulne from his courier duties. Its political co-ordination section continued to act as a channel of communication to the International Service, but the Service itself assumed greater responsibility for keeping in touch with Ottawa. It had for this purpose its own policy co-ordinating unit, whose head was responsible for liaison with the Department both by daily telephone conversations and by personal visits to Ottawa. The head of the policy co-ordinating unit also transmitted the Department's views on policy to the chiefs of the various language sections within the Service.

Such machinery might work well enough when there was agreement all round on the purpose and content of political broadcasting abroad. But enough was already known of what had happened elsewhere to suggest the wisdom of anticipating a certain tension between a separate propaganda agency and the regular foreign office, and of doing what could be done to ensure that what might ideally be a healthy blending of experience did not degenerate into a crippling rivalry. To some critics an obvious weakness lay in the physical separation of the two. "Why in the world," demanded the Opposition foreign policy critic, Gordon Graydon, in 1953,

should we separate the CBC International Service by putting Jean Désy in Montreal and then having a commuter service where a man commutes back and forth once or twice a week to tell him what the Department of External Affairs wants beamed to other countries? . . . I think what we should have is a CBC International Service right here in Ottawa, and Jean Désy or whoever is responsible for the material that goes out should be right here on the spot where consultations can continually go on instead of a . . . remote control of policy.[43]

Following this blunt criticism, Jean Désy was asked whether "he would think advisable, as was suggested, that being the big boss . . . of the CBC–I.S., he should station himself in Ottawa instead of Montreal." He replied: "I do believe that it is more useful for me to be near my personnel in Montreal, to work in close co-ordination with them, than to be in Ottawa."[44] The same opinion was offered by his successor, Mr. Delafield, in 1959.[45]

Some members of the House of Commons Standing Committee on External Affairs displayed a commendable curiosity about what might happen in the event of a fundamental disagreement over policy between the International Service and the Department of External Affairs. "I think the division of authority, the division of direction, and the division of approval with respect to these international broadcasts leave very much to be desired," Gordon Graydon declared in 1953. "I think the government ought to give consideration right away to making sure there is one boss and one final person who is responsible for the International Service broadcasts. As it is now it is certainly very confused."[46] Jean Désy attempted to dispel the confusion. "I am not serving two masters," he insisted. "Whereas the Minister of National Revenue [the Minister through whom the C.B.C. reported to Parliament] may be compared to my Father Superior, as they say in clerical circles, the Secretary of State for External Affairs is more like a 'directeur de conscience', a spiritual director. I am at liberty to follow the advice of my spiritual director, but should I commit any sin I have to turn to my Father Superior, either for absolution or reprimand."[47] Désy did not make it appear as if the advice of his "spiritual director" was much of a force to be reckoned with: "I receive no definite instructions from the Department of External Affairs, I receive information, and it is for me to decide as to whether I am going to say this or to say that. If I make mistakes, they are my own, because I am acting under no precise instruction. They rely on my judgment, and if my judgment should fail, then I am responsible."[48] If it should fail so drastically as to warrant the director's removal, the power to remove was that of the Minister of National Revenue, not that of the Secretary of State for External Affairs.[49] In the less improbable event of disagreement over the tone or content of broadcasting, however, the lines of responsibility appeared blurred, and it was not until the following year (1954) that the Standing Committee received a direct if reluctant answer from Désy's successor:

Q. (by Mr. Starr): Does the Department of External Affairs influence the content of the International Service broadcasts?
A. (by Mr. Delafield): We are always guided by their advice.
Q. (by Mr. MacNaughton): Who has the final veto?
A. I do not think the question has actually arisen, so I would not know.
Q. But in a case where it did arise, who would have the final say? . . . Is it the CBC or the Department of External Affairs? . . .
A. I think that perhaps External Affairs might make some comment on that point. . . .
A. (by Mr. R. M. Macdonnell, Assistant Under Secretary): I would certainly endorse what Mr. Delafield has said about there being no disputes of this sort having arisen, and I think it is very unlikely that they would arise. However, we feel quite confident that the CBC would give due weight to suggestions made in the political field. . . .
Q. It would almost be a case of "when in doubt, leave it out."
A. That might possibly be so.
Q. Where would the final responsibility lie?
A. (by Mr. Delafield): It rests with the CBC.
Q. You say: "It rests with the CBC."
A. Yes. The CBC is the agent chosen by the government for the establishment and presentation of the International Service.[50]

The assurance that no important conflict over policy had taken place between the International Service and the Department of External Affairs, conveyed to the House of Commons Standing Committee in 1954 and reaffirmed in 1959, was of course no guarantee that their future relations would continue untroubled. The principal potential source of difficulty was Eastern Europe. As the monolithic bloc of Stalin's day gave way to the more puzzling challenge of a communist "commonwealth," disagreement over the role of political broadcasting in the foreign policy process was not only likely but inevitable. And in countries where the propaganda function was vested in an agency separate from the foreign office, such disagreement could hardly take place without disputes between the two. In the United Kingdom it has been charged without convincing refutation that the B.B.C.'s Russian Service displayed "a too pro-Soviet attitude for the job in hand" and had followed a line of "moral compromise and appeasement"; the same grave accusation was later levelled at its Yugoslav Service.[51] While there is no direct evidence of Foreign Office dissatisfaction with broadcasts from Bush House, intellectuals in university and other circles free to express their views were critical of the dispassionate and restrained tone of B.B.C. comment on communist affairs. In the United States, on the other hand, the separation of propagandist agencies from the Department of State (where they had originally reposed) was designed to permit a more vigorous prosecution of cold war activities, implicit in the promise to "liberate" the Eastern European satellites, than it was felt the Foreign Service would approve or allow. The enthusiasm with which the Voice of America and other instruments of the Information Agency took up this mandate brought upon them the very different charge that their operations lent to American foreign policy a shrill and strident air the administration neither intended nor favoured. A study prepared for the Senate Foreign Relations Committee has recommended that the propaganda function be brought back under Foreign Service control, so as to guard "against the tendency of the information activities, under the press of particular events or currents of opinion at home or abroad, to generate a separate foreign policy and to express it without reference to broader policy considerations."[52]

In Canada this tendency is minimized by the parliamentary system of government, which more effectively than the presidential co-ordinates the instruments of national policy and protects them from capture by special interests. Nor has there been any strong desire to influence foreign policy in this way, for the members of interested parties are scattered and few, and the effort involved in bringing pressure to bear upon the government of a small and relatively unimportant power has hardly seemed worth while. Some, however, have persisted notwithstanding these handicaps, particularly those whose ancestors or who themselves had made their way from the nations of Eastern Europe fallen to communist rule. The most important group among them politically are the 500,000 Canadians of Ukrainian origin; their influence was demonstrated by the decision to inaugurate Ukrainian broadcasts to the Soviet Union, a policy which on the face of it appears subversive of the non-provocative approach to Eastern European affairs clearly favoured in the Department of External Affairs. Their spokesmen have expressed their desire for a still more strongly anti-Soviet line. In 1959 the director of the International Service was interrogated by a member of Parliament of Ukrainian descent among whose constituents were many with relatives in Eastern Europe:

Q. (by Dr. Kucherepa): Have you received any complaints or representations from Canadian individuals or organizations relative to your programming [to Eastern Europe]?
A. (by Mr. Delafield): . . . It is true that we do receive a certain amount of comment and suggestions as to the type of thing we should do.
Q. Do you follow any of these suggestions?
A. We assess them and, depending on the guidance and advice we receive, we adjust ourselves accordingly. . . .
Q. Have you in recent years been requested by anyone to change your policy relative to the degree, shall we say, of your psychological warfare, which you may be carrying on in your political broadcasting to this area?
A. As you know, there is a variety of Canadian opinion on this subject. . . .
Q. May I assume that most of your broadcasts behind the iron curtain are designed to counteract communist propaganda which is being disseminated in that area?
A. Yes, but we do it not by giving wider publicity to that propaganda than is necessary in replying; also, we tend to take a positive approach in this field, that is, by . . . presenting a Canadian view of Canada's position, the western position, and the virtues of the western stand on a particular issue.[53]

From this, and other, testimony it is evident that the International Service has displayed remarkably few of the characteristics usually associated with a propaganda agency lying beyond direct foreign office control. It has not struck out on its own line of policy, it has refrained from experimenting with new techniques and methods, it has appeared wholly content to accept the guidance of the Department of External Affairs on every aspect of its operations. Such deference is so different from the behaviour of propagandists elsewhere that one looks for explanation. It is to be found partly in the centripetal and co-ordinating action of the Cabinet, partly in the tradition of interdepartmental co-operation, partly in the administration of the Service. But perhaps the most potent inducement to compliance is to be found in the circumstance that the whole propaganda establishment has increasingly come to be viewed as a marginal concern, the funds for which could be applied to the solution of more urgent problems without public protest and with no damage to the national interest. Any major contretemps in which the International Service became involved would quickly bring this argument into the open, and so it has preferred the quiet life to the risk of no life at all.

Early in 1960, an interdepartmental committee was formed to consider the future role of the International Service. It was put to it that by the simple expedient of turning the Sackville transmitter in a different direction, an audience in the Canadian north could be served, and more usefully served, than audiences in foreign countries. This use of short-wave as an aid to Prime Minister Diefenbaker's celebrated "vision" of northern development provided a tempting alternative to the increasingly controversial policy of transmission to Europe, but the policy eventually agreed upon proved rather different. The Cabinet ordered a cut of $500,000 from the $1,900,000 sought by the International Service for its 1961 operations. To achieve this economy without too drastic a reduction of its propagandist role, it was decided that foreign language broadcasting to Italy, the Netherlands, Norway, Sweden and Denmark, which had continued without interruption since 1945, should be discontinued, and replaced by transmissions in English and in French to Africa south of the Sahara, with special emphasis on the Commonwealth audience in Ghana and Nigeria. No alteration was contemplated in broadcasts to Eastern Europe. The new operation began on January 29, 1961.

References

CHAPTER ONE:

THE POLITICAL EXECUTIVE

1. R. MacGregor Dawson, *The Government of Canada* (Toronto, 1949), p. 22.

2. O. D. Skelton, *Life and Letters of Sir Wilfrid Laurier* (Toronto, 1921), II, p. 163.

3. Quoted in J. W. Dafoe, *Clifford Sifton in Relation to His Times* (Toronto, 1931), p. 333.

4. Wilfrid Laurier to J. S. Willison, Oct. 14, 1899, Willison Papers.

5. James Bryce to Lord Grey, July 4, 1910, Grey Papers.

6. Quoted in Henry Borden, ed., *Robert Laird Borden: His Memoirs* (2 vols., Toronto, 1938), I, p. 245.

7. Borden Papers. See also Gaddis Smith, "Canada and the Siberian Intervention, 1918–1919," *American Historical Review*, vol. XLIV, no. 4, July 1959, pp. 866–77.

8. R. MacGregor Dawson, *William Lyon Mackenzie King: A Political Biography*, I, *1874–1923* (Toronto, 1958), pp. 341, 417.

9. Diary of Sir George Foster, June 5, 1921, Foster Papers.

10. *Ibid.*, Aug. 13, 1921.

11. W. Downie Stewart, "Viscount Bennett: Some Personal Reminiscences." (From a newspaper, the title and date of which are unavailable.)

12. J. W. Dafoe to Vincent Massey, July 22, 1932, Dafoe Papers.

13. Harry Sifton to J. W. Dafoe, July 10, 1932, Dafoe Papers.

14. See Dawson, *Mackenzie King*, I, pp. 443–6.

15. Memorandum by O. D. Skelton of telephone conversation with R. B. Bennett, Oct. 10, 1935, Department of External Affairs, Ottawa.

16. Canada, *House of Commons Debates*, Feb. 10, 1936, pp. 67–8.

17. Toronto *Star*, Sept. 16, 1922.

18. Quoted in Dawson, *Mackenzie King*, I, p. 409.

19. Quoted in *ibid.*, p. 410.

20. W. S. Fielding to Mackenzie King, Sept. 18, 1922, King Papers.

21. Ernest Lapointe to Mackenzie King, Sept. 19, 1922, King Papers.

22. W. S. Fielding, "Memorandum on Canadian Representation in the United States," April 24, 1923, Fielding Papers. See also John S. Galbraith, *The Establishment of Canadian Diplomatic Status at Washington* (Berkeley and Los Angeles, 1951), p. 86.

23. Quoted in K. W. McNaught, "Canadian Foreign Policy and the Whig Interpretation, 1936–1939," *Report of the Canadian Historical Association*, 1957, p. 48.

24. Bruce Hutchison, *The Incredible Canadian* (Toronto, 1952), pp. 236–7.

25. *The Times*, Aug. 22, 1941.

26. A. D. P. Heeney, "Cabinet Government in Canada: Some Recent Developments in the Machinery of the Central Executive," *Canadian Journal of Economics and Political Science*, vol. XII, no. 3, Aug. 1946, p. 289.

27. W. E. D. Halliday, "The Executive of the Government of Canada," *Canadian Public Administration*, vol. II, no. 4, Dec. 1959, p. 240.

28. Canada, H. of C. Special Committee on Defence Expenditures, *Minutes of Proceedings and Evidence*, no. 11, June 10, 1960, p. 266.

29. Walter Millis, ed., *The Forrestal Diaries* (New York, 1951), p. 474.

30. Canada, *H. of C. Debates*, Dec. 18, 1945, pp. 3734–5.

31. *Ibid.*, July 15, 1960, pp. 6377–8.

32. Letter to the author, Aug. 6, 1960.

33. "Canadian-American Meeting," *The Economist* (London), Sept. 10, 1955.

34. Canada, *H. of C. Debates*, March 28, 1960, p. 2509.

35. *Ibid.*, July 12, 1943, pp. 4670–1.

36. *Ibid.*, p. 4670.

37. *Ibid.*, Jan. 24, 1956, pp. 463–5.

38. Canada, H. of C. Standing Committee on External Affairs, *Minutes of Proceedings and Evidence*, no. 6, May 3, 1956, p. 154.

39. *Ibid.*, no. 1, April 4, 1952, pp. 19–20.

40. Nancy Harvison Hooker, ed., *The Moffat Papers: Selections from the Diplomatic Papers of Jay Pierrepont Moffat* (Cambridge, Mass., 1956), p. 373.

41. Diary of Sir Joseph Pope, March 4, 1909, Pope Papers.

42. 2 George V, c. 22.

43. Borden Papers.

44. Canada, *H. of C. Debates*, April 2, 1946, p. 490.

45. W. A. Riddell, *World Security by Conference* (Toronto, 1949), pp. 140–1.

46. Canada, *H. of C. Debates*, April 2, 1946, p. 490.

47. *Ibid.*, July 12, 1943, p. 4670.

48. Kenneth W. Thompson, *Political Realism and the Crisis of World Politics* (Princeton, 1960), p. 106.

49. Jacques de Bourbon-Busset, "Decision-Making in Foreign Policy" in Stephen D. Kertesz and M. A. Fitzsimmons, eds., *Diplomacy in a Changing World* (Notre Dame, 1959), pp. 79–80.

50. Canada, *H. of C. Debates*, April 2, 1946, pp. 491–2.

51. Hutchison, *The Incredible Canadian*, p. 424.

52. *Ibid.*, pp. 433–4.

53. *Globe and Mail* (Toronto), March 18, 1958.

54. *The Listener*, Jan. 10, 1957, p. 69.

55. *Round Table*, vol. XLVIII, 1957–8, p. 291.

56. Blair Fraser, "The Man Who'll Speak for Canada," *Maclean's Magazine*, Nov. 9, 1957.

57. The Earl of Ronaldshay, *The Life of Lord Curzon*, III (London, 1928), p. 149.

58. Lord Grey to James Bryce, June 2, 1909, Grey Papers.

59. Dawson, *Mackenzie King*, I, pp. 174–5.

60. James Bryce to Lord Grey, July 4, 1910, Grey Papers.

61. W. F. Sladen to Mackenzie King, Jan. 24, 1923, King Papers.

62. Lord Willingdon to Mackenzie King, May 2, 1928, King Papers.

63. Dawson, *The Government of Canada*, p. 188.

CHAPTER TWO:

THE BUREAUCRACY

1. J. E. Hodgetts, "The Civil Service and Policy Formation," *Canadian Journal of Economics and Political Science*, vol. XXIII, no. 4, Nov. 1957, p. 471.

2. R. Barry Farrell, "The Planning and Conduct of Foreign Policy in Canada" (unpublished doctoral thesis, Harvard University, 1952), p. 68.

3. *Ottawa Journal*, July 21, 1949.

4. J. J. Deutsch, "Some Thoughts on the Public Service," *Canadian Journal of Economics and Political Science*, vol. XXIII, no. 1, Feb. 1957, pp. 85–6.

5. M. W. Sharp, "Reflections of a Former Civil Servant," typescript of speech delivered on Nov. 14, 1958.

6. Canada, *House of Commons Debates*, May 24, 1960, p. 4184. The speaker was Mr. Douglas Fisher.

7. K. C. Wheare, *Government by Committee* (Oxford, 1955), pp. 23–4.

8. Sharp, "Reflections of a Former Civil Servant."

9. Lt.-Gen. G. G. Simonds, "Where We've Gone Wrong on Defense," *Maclean's Magazine*, June 23, 1956.

10. K. C. Wheare, *The Civil Service in the Constitution* (London, 1954), pp. 27–8.

11. Quoted in J. W. Pickersgill, *The Mackenzie King Record*, I, *1939–1944* (Toronto, 1960), p. 38.

12. *Globe and Mail*, April 9, 1958, "The Government and the 'Establishment.'"

13. *Financial Post*, Jan. 9, 1960, "Naming of Deputy Minister Tricky Political Question."

14. Arthur Meighen to Loring Christie, Jan. 13, 1926, Christie Papers.

15. Loring Christie to Sir Robert Borden, March 15, 1926, Christie Papers.

16. R. MacGregor Dawson, *William Lyon Mackenzie King: A Political Biography*, I, *1874–1923* (Toronto, 1958), p. 454.

17. Canada, *H. of C. Debates*, July 25, 1942, p. 4712.

18. Canada, H. of C. Standing Committee on External Affairs, *Minutes of Proceedings and Evidence*, no. 1, May 17, 1948, p. 18.

19. Lester B. Pearson, "Canadian Diplomacy," address given to the Alumni Federation, the University of Toronto, Jan. 11, 1947. Quoted in Farrell, "The Planning and Conduct of Foreign Policy in Canada," p. 157.

20. Canada, H. of C. Standing Committee on External Affairs, *Minutes of Proceedings and Evidence*, no. 6, May 6, 1954, p. 148.

21. *Ibid.*, no. 11, May 24, 1956, p. 274.

22. *Ibid.*, no. 1, Nov. 18, 1949, p. 24.

23. Victor Odlum to Mackenzie King, May 20, 1942, King Papers.

24. Canada, *H. of C. Debates*, Aug. 1, 1942, p. 5151.

25. Lester B. Pearson, "International Public Relations," address given to the Canadian Public Relations Society, Montreal, Jan. 5, 1954. Dept. of External Affairs, *Statements and Speeches* (Ottawa, 1954), no. 2.

26. Canada, H. of C. Standing Committee on External Affairs, *Minutes of Proceedings and Evidence*, no. 1, April 4, 1952, p. 24.

27. Canada, *H. of C. Debates*, May 15, 1931, p. 1651.

28. *Ibid.*, p. 1647.

29. *Ibid.*, pp. 1647, 1649.

30. Mackenzie King to P. C. Larkin, April 23, 1924, King Papers.

31. N. W. Rowell to Mackenzie King, Nov. 30, 1925, Rowell Papers.

32. O. D. Skelton to Mackenzie King, Dec. 9, 1925, King Papers.

33. Mackenzie King to N. W. Rowell, Dec. 7, 1925, Rowell Papers.

34. Canada, H. of C. Standing Committee on External Affairs, *Minutes of Proceedings and Evidence*, no. 4, June 4, 1946, p. 63.

35. *Ibid.*, p. 61.

36. *Ibid.*, p. 63.

37. *External Affairs*, vol. V, no. 7, July 1953, pp. 220–1.

38. *Towards a Stronger Foreign Service: Report of the Secretary of State's Public Committee on Personnel, June, 1954* (Washington, D.C., 1954).

39. Canada, H. of C. Standing Committee on External Affairs, *Minutes of Proceedings and Evidence*, no. 1, Feb. 23, 1953, p. 36.

40. "The Foreign Service Officer Competition," *External Affairs*, vol. X, no. 9, Sept. 1958, p. 229.

41. *Ibid.*, p. 228.

42. Marcel Cadieux, *Le Ministère des affaires extérieures* (Montréal, 1949), pp. 75–7.

43. Farrell, "The Planning and Conduct of Foreign Policy in Canada," p. 127.

44. Canada, H. of C. Standing Committee on External Affairs, *Minutes of Proceedings and Evidence*, no. 9, May 17, 1956, pp. 240–1.

45. *Ibid.*, no. 6, May 6, 1954, pp. 149–50.

46. *Ibid.*, no. 4, Aug. 6, 1958, p. 163.

47. Deutsch, "Some Thoughts on the Public Service," p. 86.

48. Canada, H. of C. Standing Committee on External Affairs, *Minutes of Proceedings and Evidence*, no. 1, May 17, 1948, p. 16.

49. *Ibid.*, no. 2, April 8, 1952, p. 34.

50. Mackenzie King to J. L. Ralston, Sept. 28, 1927, King Papers.

51. Col. C. P. Stacey, "The Canadian-American Permanent Joint Board on Defence, 1940–45," *International Journal*, vol. IX, no. 2, Spring 1954, pp. 108–9.

52. Loring Christie to O. D. Skelton, July 26, 1940, King Papers.

53. Col. Stanley W. Dziuban, *Military Relations between the United States and Canada, 1939–1945* (Washington, D.C., 1959), p. 73.

54. *Ibid.*, p. 73.

55. *Ibid.*, p. 74.

56. Diary entry of Dec. 29, 1941. Quoted in Pickersgill, *The Mackenzie King Record*, I, p. 326.

57. Nancy Harvison Hooker, ed., *The Moffat Papers: Selections from the Diplomatic Papers of Jay Pierrepont Moffat* (Cambridge, Mass., 1956), p. 374.

58. Dziuban, *Military Relations between the United States and Canada*, p. 75.

59. Memorandum of the Minister of National Defence, March 11, 1942. Quoted in Maurice Pope, unpublished manuscript.

60. *Ibid.*

61. "Memorandum for the Prime Minister," April 13, 1942, King Papers.

62. Canada, H. of C. Standing Committee on External Affairs, *Minutes of Proceedings and Evidence*, no. 4, May 26, 1948, pp. 97–8.

63. *Ibid.*, p. 98.

64. Diary entry for May 14, 1943. Quoted in Pickersgill, *The Mackenzie King Record*, I, p. 501.

65. The Brookings Institution, *The Administration of Foreign Affairs and Overseas Operations* (Washington, D.C., 1951), p. 244.

66. W. H. Walker to Joseph Pope, May 13, 1909, Under Secretary of State: Semi-Official Correspondence.

67. Canada, *H. of C. Debates*, March 4, 1909, col. 1983.

68. Pope diary, Jan. 16, 1910.

69. N. W. Rowell to Mackenzie King, Nov. 30, 1925, Rowell Papers.

70. Mackenzie King to Rowell, Dec. 7, 1925, Rowell Papers.

71. Canada, H. of C. Select Standing Committee on Industrial and International Relations, *Minutes of Proceedings and Evidence*, no. 1, March 25, 1930, p. 11.

72. Canada, H. of C. Standing Committee on External Affairs, *Minutes of Proceedings and Evidence*, no. 1, Oct. 25, 1945, pp. 7–8.

73. *Ibid.*, no. 3, May 30, 1946, p. 51.

74. *Ibid.*, no. 2, Nov. 22, 1949, p. 54.

75. *Ibid.*, no. 3, Dec. 6, 1957, p. 94.

CHAPTER THREE:

THE MILITARY ESTABLISHMENT

1. Henri Bourassa, *Great Britain and Empire* (Montreal, 1902), p. 4.

2. Quoted in O. D. Skelton, *Life and Letters of Sir Wilfrid Laurier* (Toronto, 1921), II, p. 293.

3. League of Nations, *Records of the First Assembly* (1920), p. 379.

4. Henry Borden, ed., *Robert Laird Borden: His Memoirs* (2 vols., Toronto, 1938), II, p. 606.

5. *Ibid.*, pp. 827, 817.

6. Quoted in Gaddis Smith, "Canadian External Affairs during World War I" in Hugh L. Keenleyside *et al.*, *The Growth of Canadian Policies in External Affairs* (Durham, N.C., 1960), p. 46.

7. H. M. Urquhart, *Arthur Currie: The Biography of a Great Canadian* (Toronto, 1950), pp. 274–81, 318–21.

8. Elizabeth Armstrong, *The Crisis of Quebec, 1914–18* (New York, 1937).

9. George F. G. Stanley, *Canada's Soldiers, 1604–1960: The Military History of an Unmilitary People* (Toronto, 1960), p. 347.

10. Canada, *House of Commons Debates*, April 4, 1922, p. 669.

11. Col. C. P. Stacey, *Six Years of War: The Army in Canada, Britain and the Pacific* (Ottawa, 1955), p. 9.

12. Quoted in *ibid.*, p. 8.

13. League of Nations, *Records of the Fifth Assembly* (1924), p. 222.

14. *Ibid.*, p. 221.

15. *Ibid.*, *Records of the Ninth Assembly* (1928), p. 61.

16. Stacey, *Six Years of War*, p. 30.

17. See, for evidence of such tension in the United States, Mark S. Watson, *Chief of Staff: Prewar Plans and Preparations* (Washington, D.C., 1950).

18. Samuel P. Huntington, *The Soldier and the State* (Cambridge, Mass., 1959), p. 315.

19. Stacey, *Six Years of War*, p. 321.

20. Canada, *H. of C. Debates*, Sept. 8, 1939, p. 36.

21. Quoted in Huntington, *The Soldier and the State*, p. 317.

22. Quoted in Stacey, *Six Years of War*, p. 47.

23. Quoted in J. W. Pickersgill, *The Mackenzie King Record*, I, *1939–1944* (Toronto, 1960), pp. 40–1.

24. Quoted in *ibid.*, p. 38.

25. Montreal *Star*, Nov. 20, 1939.

26. Marginal note on Norman Rogers' diary of his visit to the United Kingdom, entry for April 20, 1940, King Papers.

27. Quoted in Stacey, *Six Years of War*, p. 261.

28. Quoted in *ibid.*, p. 261.

29. Quoted in Pickersgill, *The Mackenzie King Record*, I, p. 156.

30. Quoted in Stacey, *Six Years of War*, p. 263.

31. Quoted in *ibid.*, p. 263.

32. Quoted in *ibid.*, p. 308.

33. *Ibid.*, p. 333.

34. *Ibid.*, p. 442.

35. Lt.-Col. G. W. L. Nicholson, *The Canadians in Italy, 1943–1945* (Ottawa, 1956), p. 24.

36. Quoted in *ibid.*, pp. 343–4.

37. Quoted in Pickersgill, *The Mackenzie King Record*, I, p. 545.

38. Stacey, *Six Years of War*, p. 497.

39. Quoted in Maurice Pope, unpublished manuscript.

40. Quoted in *ibid*.

41. *Ibid.*

42. Quoted in Stacey, *Six Years of War*, p. 498.

43. Pickersgill, *The Mackenzie King Record*, I, p. 515.

44. Quoted in *ibid.*, pp. 515–16.

45. Quoted in *ibid.*, p. 517.

46. Maurice Pope, unpublished manuscript.

47. Stacey, *Six Years of War*, p. 500.

48. Quoted in Col. C. P. Stacey, *The Victory Campaign: The Operations in North-West Europe, 1944–1945* (Ottawa, 1960), p. 42.

49. Quoted in *ibid.*, pp. 42–3.

50. Quoted in *ibid.*, pp. 648–9. The directive is printed in its entirety as App. "A," pp. 647–9.

51. Quoted in Pickersgill, *The Mackenzie King Record*, I, p. 75.

52. Stacey, *Six Years of War*, p. 81.

53. Quoted in *ibid.*, p. 81.

54. *Ibid.*, p. 82.

55. H. L. Keenleyside, "The Canada–United States Permanent Joint Board on Defence, 1940–1945," *International Journal*, vol. XVI, no. 1, Winter 1960–1, p. 55.

56. Stacey, *Six Years of War*, p. 215.

57. Quoted in *ibid.*, pp. 223–4.

58. Quoted in *ibid.*, p. 224.

59. Quoted in *ibid.*, pp. 224–5.

60. Quoted in *ibid.*, p. 225.

61. Quoted in Pickersgill, *The Mackenzie King Record*, I, p. 221.

62. Quoted in *ibid.*, pp. 303–4, 313.

63. R. MacGregor Dawson, "The Revolt of the Generals," *Weekend Magazine*, vol. X, no. 44, 1960.

64. *Ibid.*

65. Quoted in *ibid.*

66. Quoted in *ibid.*

67. Quoted in *ibid.*

68. Quoted in *ibid.*

69. Canada, *H. of C. Debates*, June 24, 1948, p. 5779.

70. *Ibid.*, p. 5810.

71. John W. Masland and Laurence I. Radway, *Soldiers and Scholars: Military Education and National Policy* (Princeton, 1957), p. 3.

72. Canada, *H. of C. Debates*, Aug. 31, 1950, p. 105.

73. *Ibid.*, May 8, 1951, p. 2801.

74. *Ibid.*, Feb. 2, 1953, p. 1532.

75. Speech at Depauw University, June 9, 1960.

76. Canada, *H. of C. Debates*, Feb. 2, 1953, p. 1527.

77. Lt.-Gen. G. G. Simonds, "Where We've Gone Wrong on Defense," *Maclean's Magazine*, June 23, 1956.

78. *Ibid.*

79. Quoted in Lady G. Cecil, *Life of Robert, Marquis of Salisbury*, II (London, 1921), p. 153.

80. Huntington, *The Soldier and the State*, p. 351.

81. Simonds, "Where We've Gone Wrong on Defense."

CHAPTER FOUR:

THE LEGISLATURE

1. R. MacGregor Dawson, *The Government of Canada* (Toronto, 1949), p. 434.

2. Quoted in R. MacGregor Dawson, *William Lyon Mackenzie King: A Political Biography*, I, *1874–1923* (Toronto, 1958), p. 411.

3. Mackenzie King to J. R. Boyle, Oct. 3, 1922. Quoted in *ibid.*, p. 413.

4. Canada, *House of Commons Debates*, Feb. 1, 1923, p. 33.
5. Quoted in Dawson, *Mackenzie King*, p. 465.
6. Canada, *H. of C. Debates*, June 21, 1926, p. 4762.
7. *Ibid.*
8. *Ibid.*, Feb. 25, 1929, pp. 422–3.
9. K. W. McNaught, "Canadian Foreign Policy and the Whig Interpretation, 1936–1939," *Report of the Canadian Historical Association*, 1957, pp. 51–3.
10. Eugene Forsey, "Mr. King and Parliamentary Government," *Canadian Journal of Economics and Political Science*, vol. XVII, no. 4, Nov. 1951, p. 458.
11. Canada, *H. of C. Debates*, March 15, 1926, p. 1561.
12. *Ibid.*, Nov. 18, 1932, p. 1368.
13. *Ibid.*, May 16, 1933, p. 5067.
14. *Ibid.*, March 23, 1936, p. 1332.
15. *Ibid.*
16. *Saturday Night*, Dec. 14, 1935; *Winnipeg Tribune*, May 14, 1936.
17. Canada, *H. of C. Debates*, June 18, 1936, p. 3862.
18. *Ibid.*, July 4, 1947, p. 5198.
19. Bruce Hutchison, *The Incredible Canadian* (Toronto, 1952), p. 267.
20. Forsey, "Mr. King and Parliamentary Government," p. 463.
21. Canada, *H. of C. Debates*, March 19, 1943.
22. C. G. Power, "Career Politicians: The Changing Role of the M.P.," *Queen's Quarterly*, vol. LXII, no. 4, Winter 1957, pp. 488–9.
23. Canada, H. of C. Standing Committee on External Affairs, *Minutes of Proceedings and Evidence*, no. 3, May 1, 1950, p. 77.
24. Quoted in Norman Ward, *The Canadian House of Commons: Representation* (Toronto, 1950), p. 10.
25. Canada, *H. of C. Debates*, June 15, 1923, p. 4001.
26. *Ibid.*, Nov. 12, 1940, p. 33.
27. Interview for the Canadian Broadcasting Corporation (hereafter cited as C.B.C. interview).
28. Quoted in H. A. Innis, *Great Britain, the United States and Canada* (Nottingham, 1948), p. 5.
29. Dawson, *The Government of Canada*, p. 452.
30. J. W. Pickersgill, *The Mackenzie King Record*, I, *1939–1944* (Toronto, 1960), p. 9.
31. C.B.C. interview.
32. Blair Fraser, "Backstage at Ottawa," *Maclean's Magazine*, March 12, 1960, p. 2.
33. C.B.C. interview.
34. Lee Beland, "Paul Martin: Architect with a Needle," *Toronto Star*, March 29, 1960.
35. See Donald Eldon, "Toward a Well Informed Parliament: The Uses of Research," *Queen's Quarterly*, vol. XLIII, no. 4, Winter 1957, p. 524.
36. J. A. Stevenson to J. W. Dafoe, Jan. 23, 1920, Dafoe Papers.
37. Canada, *H. of C. Debates*, May 10, 1946, p. 1395.
38. Canada, H. of C. Standing Committee on External Affairs, *Minutes of Proceedings and Evidence*, no. 1, May 21, 1946, p. 4.

39. *Ibid.*, no. 1, May 22, 1951, p. 8.

40. Canada, *H. of C. Debates*, Sept. 5, 1950, p. 296.

41. Canada, H. of C. Standing Committee on External Affairs, *Minutes of Proceedings and Evidence*, no. 5, May 20, 1947, p. 128.

42. *Ibid.*, p. 139.

43. *Ibid.*, no. 4, Nov. 24, 1949, p. 123.

44. *Ibid.*, no. 9, May 18, 1954, p. 249.

45. *Ibid.*, no. 4, Nov. 24, 1949, pp. 122, 125.

46. D. M. Fisher, "Parliamentary Committees in the 24th Parliament," *Waterloo Review*, vol. II, no. 1, 1960, p. 78.

47. Canada, *H. of C. Debates*, May 7, 1951, p. 2756.

48. Fisher, "Parliamentary Committees in the 24th Parliament," pp. 69–70.

49. Canada, *H. of C. Debates*, March 17, 1960, p. 2192.

50. *Ibid.*, p. 2178.

51. *Ibid.*, pp. 2189–90.

52. Canada, H. of C. Special Committee on Defence Expenditures, *Minutes of Proceedings and Evidence*, no. 8, June 1, 1960, p. 192.

CHAPTER FIVE:

INTELLIGENCE

1. Pope diary, June 22, 1899.

2. Joseph Pope to John Anderson, July 10, 1899, Pope Papers.

3. Pope to Anderson, Jan. 27, 1900, Pope Papers.

4. Anderson to Pope, Feb. 19, 1902, Pope Papers.

5. Joseph Pope to Clifford Sifton, July 8, 1903, Pope Papers.

6. Rodolphe Lemieux to Sir Louis Jetté, Dec. 4, 1907, Lemieux Papers.

7. Rodolphe Lemieux to Sir Edward Grey, Dec. 13, 1907; Grey to Lemieux, Feb. 11, 1908. Lemieux Papers.

8. Joseph Pope to Rodolphe Lemieux, Feb. 24, 1908, Lemieux Papers.

9. Lord Grey to Lord Elgin, Jan. 14, 1907, Grey Papers.

10. Sherman Kent, *Strategic Intelligence* (Princeton, 1949), p. 11.

11. "Memorandum for Consideration of the Civil Service Commissioners, May 25, 1907." Civil Service Commission 1908: Minutes of Evidence, I, pp. 48–50, *Sessional Papers of Canada*, vol. XLII, no. 15, 1907–8.

12. Kent, *Strategic Intelligence*, p. 39.

13. "Admiralty Memorandum on the General Naval Situation," Sept. 20, 1912, Borden Papers.

14. Henry Borden, ed., *Robert Laird Borden: His Memoirs* (2 vols., Toronto, 1938), II, p. 621 (hereafter cited as *Borden Memoirs*).

15. Bonar Law to Sir George Perley, Nov. 3, 1915. Quoted in *ibid.*, p. 621.

16. Sir Robert Borden to Sir George Perley, Jan. 4, 1916. Quoted in *ibid.*, p. 622.

17. *Ibid.*, p. 623.

18. Bonar Law to Sir Robert Borden, July 6, 1916, Borden Papers.

19. Secretary of State for the Colonies to the Governor General of Canada. Quoted in *Borden Memoirs*, II, p. 625.

20. Sir George Perley to Sir Robert Borden, May 31, 1918, Borden Papers.

21. *Borden Memoirs*, II, pp. 625–6.

22. Gaddis Smith, "Canadian External Relations during World War I" in H. L. Keenleyside *et al.*, *The Growth of Canadian Policies in External Affairs* (Durham, N.C., 1960), p. 47.

23. Loring Christie to George Wrong, Dec. 30, 1919, Wrong Papers.

24. *Report of the Canadian Economic Commission (Siberia)* (Ottawa, 1919).

25. "Notes of Meetings of Representatives of the United Kingdom, the Dominions, and India, held in London in June and July, 1921," King Papers.

26. "Memorandum for the Prime Minister," Dec. 16, 1922, King Papers.

27. *The Times*, Feb. 8, 1923.

28. Sir John Willison to Sir Campbell Stuart, Dec. 7, 1920, Willison Papers.

29. F. A. McGregor to Merchant Mahoney, Feb. 2, 1924, King Papers.

30. E.g., Herbert Marler to Mackenzie King, Dec. 28, 1931, King Papers.

31. Canada, *House of Commons Debates*, April 7, 1932, p. 1825.

32. See Thomas Jones, *A Diary with Letters* (London, 1954), pp. 179–81, 218; *The History of "The Times": The 150th Anniversary and Beyond, 1912–1948*, Part II, *1921–1948* (London, 1952), p. 938; John Evelyn Wrench, *Geoffrey Dawson and Our Times* (London, 1955), p. 369; Vincent Massey, *On Being Canadian* (Toronto, 1948), pp. 76–7.

33. W. S. Churchill, *The Second World War*, I, *The Gathering Storm* (London, 1949), p. 250.

34. Speech given over the national network of the Canadian Broadcasting Corporation, July 19, 1937.

35. Frank H. Underhill, "The Close of an Era: Twenty-Five Years of Mr. Mackenzie King," *Canadian Forum*, Sept. 1944.

36. Nicholas Mansergh, *Survey of British Commonwealth Affairs: Problems of Wartime Co-operation and Post-War Change, 1939–1952* (London, 1958), p. 402.

37. Speech of Lord Cranbourne, Feb. 19, 1945, quoted in *ibid.*, p. 401.

38. Quoted in *ibid.*, p. 46.

39. *Ibid.*, p. 41.

40. *Ibid.*, p. 42.

41. Maurice Pope, unpublished manuscript.

42. Quoted in J. H. Cranston, *Ink on My Fingers* (Toronto, 1951), p. 180.

43. King Diary, Aug. 21, 1943, quoted in J. W. Pickersgill, *The Mackenzie King Record*, I, *1939–1944* (Toronto, 1960), p. 553.

44. Canada, H. of C. Standing Committee on External Affairs, *Minutes of Proceedings and Evidence*, no. 1, Feb. 19, 1953, pp. 18–19.

45. E. L. Woodward, "The British Foreign Service" in J. E. McLean, ed., *The Public Service and University Education* (Princeton, 1949), p. 175.

46. J. D. B. Miller, in *Canadian Forum*, Aug. 1959.

47. Canada, H. of C. Standing Committee on External Affairs, *Minutes of Proceedings and Evidence*, no. 2, April 8, 1952, p. 35.

48. *Ibid.*

49. Canada, *H. of C. Debates*, March 28, 1960, p. 2508.

50. D. J. Goodspeed, *A History of the Defence Research Board of Canada* (Ottawa, 1959), p. 84.

51. Canada, *H. of C. Debates*, April 10, 1957, pp. 3358–9.

52. The Senate of Canada, *Proceedings of the Standing Committee on External Relations*, June 25, 1958, p. 23.

53. *The Report of the Royal Commission . . . to Investigate the Facts Relating to and the Circumstances Surrounding the Communication, by Public Officials and Other Persons in Positions of Trust of Secret and Confidential Information to Agents of a Foreign Power* (Ottawa, 1946), p. 83.

54. Canada, *H. of C. Debates*, July 9, 1959, p. 5741.

55. Canada, H. of C. Standing Committee on External Affairs, *Minutes of Proceedings and Evidence*, no. 4, June 4, 1946, p. 71.

56. "The Department of External Affairs," Reference Paper no. 69 of the Information Division of the Department of External Affairs (Ottawa, 1959, mimeo.), p. 9.

57. Col. C. P. Stacey, *Six Years of War: The Army in Canada, Britain and the Pacific* (Ottawa, 1955), p. 441.

58. "The Department of External Affairs," p. 7.

CHAPTER SIX:

PLANNING

1. Michael Oakeshott, *Political Education* (Cambridge, 1951), p. 22.

2. E. V. Tarlé, *Istoria Diplomatii*, III, pp. 763–4. Quoted in Max Beloff, *The Foreign Policy of Soviet Russia*, II, *1926–1941* (London, 1949), p. 394.

3. Quoted in W. W. Rostow, "The American National Style," *Daedalus: Proceedings of the American Academy of Arts and Sciences*, vol. LXXXVII, no. 2, 1958, p. 118.

4. *Ibid.*

5. W. A. Mackintosh, "Government Economic Policy: Scope and Principles," *Canadian Journal of Economics and Political Science*, vol. XVI, no. 3, Aug. 1950, p. 325.

6. Loring Christie, "Note on Munich," Nov. 1, 1938, Christie Papers.

7. Letter to the author, June 13, 1959.

8. Address by the Minister of National Health and Welfare, Mr. Paul Martin, Sept. 1, 1955. Dept. of External Affairs, *Statements and Speeches* (Ottawa, 1955, mimeo.), no. 29.

9. James A. Gibson, "Mr. Mackenzie King and Canadian Autonomy, 1921–1946" in Canadian Historical Association, *Annual Report*, 1951, p. 20.

10. Quoted in J. W. Pickersgill, *The Mackenzie King Record*, I, *1939–1944* (Toronto, 1960), p. 201.

11. Canada, *House of Commons Debates*, Feb. 10, 1960, p. 930.

12. George F. Kennan, "History and Diplomacy as Viewed by a Diplomatist" in Stephen D. Kertesz and M. A. Fitzsimmons, eds., *Diplomacy in a Changing World* (Notre Dame, 1959), pp. 107–8.

13. See J. E. Hodgetts, "The Civil Service and Policy Formation," *Canadian Journal of Economics and Political Science*, vol. XXIII, no. 4, Nov. 1957, p. 478.

CHAPTER SEVEN:

NEGOTIATION

1. Hugh Gibson, *The Road to Foreign Policy* (New York, 1944), p. 63.

2. George F. Kennan, *A History of Soviet-American Relations*, II, *The Decision to Intervene* (Princeton, 1958), p. 191.

3. Harold Nicolson, *Curzon: The Last Phase, 1919–1925* (New York, 1939), p. 54.

4. *Foreign Relations of the United States, 1941*, III, *The British Commonwealth, the Near East and Africa* (Washington, D.C., 1959), p. 27.

5. William H. Standley and Arthur A. Ageton, *Admiral Ambassador to Russia* (Chicago, 1955), pp. 195–6.

6. Quoted in Charles S. Campbell, Jr., *Anglo-American Understanding, 1898–1903* (Baltimore, 1957), p. 35.

7. Quoted in James Phinney Baxter III, "The British High Commissioners at Washington in 1871," *Proceedings of the Massachusetts Historical Society*, June 1934.

8. Sir Willoughby Maycock, *With Mr. Chamberlain in the United States and Canada, 1887–1888* (Toronto, 1914), p. 34.

9. Joseph Pope to Sir Wilfrid Laurier, Oct. 4, 1899, Laurier Papers.

10. George C. Gibbons to Sir Wilfrid Laurier, Dec. 16, 1907, Laurier Papers.

11. Gibbons to Laurier, Dec. 21, 1907, Laurier Papers.

12. Lord Grey to Lord Crewe, Jan. 11, 1909, Grey Papers.

13. Diary, entry for Feb. 20, 1912, Pope Papers.

14. "Canadian Representation in the United States," memorandum by W. S. Fielding, April 24, 1923, King Papers, Fielding Papers.

15. Mackenzie King to Charles McGrath, July 21, 1923, King Papers.

16. J. W. Pickersgill, *The Mackenzie King Record*, I, *1939–1944* (Toronto, 1960), p. 433.

17. "Some Recent Developments in Canada's External Relations," address by Mackenzie King before Toronto Board of Trade, Nov. 22, 1928.

18. Rodolphe Lemieux to Lord Grey, Dec. 13, 1907, Lemieux Papers.

19. Joseph Chamberlain to the Earl of Minto, May 31, 1900, Minto Papers.

20. G. W. M. Grigg to J. S. Willison, April 22, 1910, Willison Papers.

21. Rodolphe Lemieux to Sir Louis Jetté, Dec. 5, 1907, Lemieux Papers.

22. Lemieux to Jetté, Dec. 10, 1907, Lemieux Papers.

23. Lemieux to Sir Wilfrid Laurier, Dec. 10, 1907, Lemieux Papers.

24. Lemieux to W. T. R. Preston, Jan. 14, 1908, Lemieux Papers.

25. W. A. Riddell, *World Security by Conference* (Toronto, 1947), p. 124.

26. *Ibid.*, p. 130.

27. *Documents Relating to the Italo-Ethiopian Crisis* (Ottawa, 1935), p. 172.

28. Riddell, *World Security by Conference*, p. 129.

29. *St. John Telegraph Journal*, Sept. 4, 1935.

30. Canada, H. of C. Standing Committee on External Affairs, *Minutes of Proceedings and Evidence*, no. 3, March 12, 1959, pp. 48–9.

31. King Papers.

32. Canada, H. of C. Standing Committee on External Affairs, *Minutes of Proceedings and Evidence*, no. 12, April 6, 1960, pp. 302–3.

33. Gordon A. Craig, "The Professional Diplomat and His Problems, 1919–1939," *World Politics*, vol. IV, no. 2, Jan. 1952, pp. 147–8.

34. Quoted in Pickersgill, *The Mackenzie King Record*, I, p. 115.

35. Canada, *House of Commons Debates*, July 9, 1943, p. 4567.

36. Mackenzie King to O. F. Brothers, April 14, 1941, King Papers.

37. Canada, *H. of C. Debates*, Jan. 9, 1957, pp. 31–2.

38. See Lord Riddell, *An Intimate Diary of the Peace Conference and After* (London, 1933), p. 225.

39. Canada, *H. of C. Debates*, May 17, 1920, p. 2532.

40. Mackenzie King to A. F. Sladen, March 17, 1923, King Papers.

41. Sladen to Mackenzie King, April 12, 1923, King Papers.

42. Unpublished text, King Papers.

43. Mackenzie King to P. C. Larkin, Nov. 30, 1929, King Papers.

44. Quoted in Pickersgill, *The Mackenzie King Record*, I, p. 233.

45. Lester B. Pearson, *Democracy in World Politics* (Toronto, 1955), pp. 57, 62.

46. Lester B. Pearson, *Diplomacy in the Nuclear Age* (Toronto, 1959), pp. 35, 44.

CHAPTER EIGHT:

PROPAGANDA

1. Canada, House of Commons Standing Committee on External Affairs, *Minutes of Proceedings and Evidence*, no. 1, Feb. 19, 1953, p. 13.

2. Vincent Massey, *On Being Canadian* (Toronto, 1948), p. 159.

3. Canada, *House of Commons Journals*, 1900, App. I, p. 490.

4. Address by Mr. L. B. Pearson at Rollins College, Florida, Feb. 21, 1954, in Dept. of External Affairs, *Statements and Speeches* (Ottawa, 1954, mimeo.), no. 9.

5. Canada, *House of Commons Debates*, March 13, 1911, p. 5168.

6. Quoted in Beckles Willson, *The Life of Lord Strathcona & Mount Royal* (London, 1915), p. 496.

7. H. Gordon Skilling, *Canadian Representation Abroad: From Agency to Embassy* (Toronto, 1945), p. 18.

8. *Report of the Canadian Economic Commission (Siberia)* (Ottawa, 1919), p. 17.

9. Sir Robert Borden to Walter Long, April 12, 1917, Borden Papers.

10. Charles W. Gordon (Ralph Connor) to Sir George Foster, March 28, 1917, Borden Papers.

11. Sir Edmund Walker to Robert Donald, May 18, 1917, Walker Papers.

12. *Ottawa Citizen*, April 4, 1940.

13. *New York Times*, April 5, 1940.

14. Press statement by the Prime Minister, April 11, 1940.

15. Mackenzie King to Winston Churchill, May 24, 1940, King Papers.

16. Mackenzie King to Mrs. George de Grippenberg, Oct. 25, 1940, King Papers.

17. Canada, *H. of C. Debates*, July 13, 1943, pp. 4728–9.

18. Leighton McCarthy to Mackenzie King, May 7, 1941, King Papers.

19. Quoted in J. W. Pickersgill, *The Mackenzie King Record*, I, *1939–1944* (Toronto, 1960), p. 190.

20. Mackenzie King to Leighton McCarthy, Sept. 24, 1941, King Papers.

21. Leighton McCarthy to Mackenzie King, Sept. 27, 1941, King Papers.

22. Canada, *H. of C. Debates*, July 13, 1943, p. 4705.

23. Quoted in *ibid.*, p. 4709.

24. John Grierson to W. J. Turnbull, Nov. 2, 1939, King Papers.

25. John Grierson to A. D. P. Heeney, Nov. 2, 1939, King Papers.

26. Canada, *H. of C. Debates*, July 13, 1943, pp. 4709–11, 4713.

27. *Ibid.*, p. 4712.

28. Canada, H. of C. Standing Committee on External Affairs, *Minutes of Proceedings and Evidence*, no. 6, June 9, 1948, p. 146.

29. *Ibid.*, no. 7, May 27, 1947, p. 206.

30. *Ibid.*, no. 6, June 9, 1948, p. 147.

31. Memorandum for the Prime Minister, Sept. 18, 1941, King Papers.

32. Canada, H. of C. Standing Committee on External Affairs, *Minutes of Proceedings and Evidence*, no. 6, March 12, 1953, p. 142.

33. *Ibid.*, p. 142.

34. *Ibid.*, p. 142.

35. *Ibid.*, pp. 140–1.

36. *Ibid.*, p. 170.

37. *Ibid.*, no. 7, May 27, 1947, p. 209.

38. *Ibid.*, no. 1, May 17, 1951, p. 17.

39. *Ibid.*, no. 1, Feb. 19, p. 14.

40. *Ibid.*, p. 14.

41. *Ibid.*, no. 6, March 12, 1953, pp. 170–1.

42. *Ibid.*, p. 171.

43. *Ibid.*, no. 2, Feb. 26, 1953, p. 46.

44. *Ibid.*, p. 48.

45. In an interview with the author, Dec. 31, 1959.

46. Canada, H. of C. Standing Committee on External Affairs, *Minutes of Proceedings and Evidence*, no. 2, Feb. 26, 1953, p. 51.

47. *Ibid.*, no. 6, March 12, 1953, p. 138.

48. *Ibid.*, p. 170.

49. *Ibid.*, no. 2, Feb. 26, 1953, p. 53.

50. *Ibid.*, no. 12, June 10, 1954, pp. 400–1.

51. Peter Wiles, "Report on the Russian Service," *The Spectator* (London), Jan. 3, 1958. See also *ibid.*, correspondence columns from June 21, 1957, to Sept. 6, 1957, and in Dec. 1959.

52. *The Formulation and Administration of United States Foreign Policy* (Washington, D.C., 1960), p. 78.

53. Canada, H. of C. Special Committee on Broadcasting, *Minutes of Proceedings and Evidence*, no. 12, June 16, 1959, pp. 429–30, 434.

Index

ACTON, LORD, 104
Adak, 85
Admiralty, First Lord of (U.K.), 127
Afghanistan, 142
Africa south of the Sahara, 69; broadcasting to, 202
Afro-Asian nations: and planning, 152
Agriculture, Minister of, 17
Air Force Cambridge Research Center (U.S.), 146
Air Research and Development Command (U.S.), 146
Aitken, Sir Max, 128. *See also* Beaverbrook, Lord
Alaska Boundary, 163; documents, 124–5
Aleutian campaign: Canadian Army in, 82–5
Alexander, Field Marshal, Earl of Tunis: and W. L. Mackenzie King, 30
ambassadors: to North Atlantic Treaty Organization (NATO), 41; to Spain, 43; to China, 121; to United States, 141, 192; to Italy, 197
ambassadors, Germany: to United Kingdom, 183
ambassadors, United Kingdom: to United States, 5, 29, 162, 168, 185; as negotiators for Canada, 163–5, 168–70
Amery, L. S., 133n
Anderson, Major General T. V., 62
Andrew, Geoffrey C., 192
Anglo-Japanese alliance: proposed renewal, 8
apartheid, 145, 145n
appeasement, 11
Armistice (1918), 95
Army, British, 71
Army, Canadian, 72, 77, 81, 82, 86, 99n; in Siberia, 7, 130; official historian, 63, 73, 75, 149; Norwegian campaign, 77–8, 79; North Africa, 78–9; Dieppe Raid, 79–80; and government, 80–1; Italy, 80–2; Hong Kong, 80, 138, 138n; and post-war policy, 81; Aleutian cam-

paign, 82–5; Western Europe, 85–7, 90–5; and National Defence Headquarters (N.D.H.Q.), 89–91; and Canadian Military Headquarters (C.M.H.Q.), 89–91; manpower situation, 90–5; in First World War, 185
Army Council, 93
Ashton, Major General E. C., 61
Asquith, H. A., 129
Athlone, Earl of: and W. L. Mackenzie King, 30
Atlantic Charter, 138, 181
atomic attack, 15
attachés: diplomatists' dislike of, 56, 56n; agricultural, 57, 65; air, 62; commercial, 57–8; financial, 57, 65; labour, 57, 65; military, 56n, 57, 61–5; naval, 62; press, 57, 65; scientific, 57, 65; technical assistance, 57
Attlee, Clement, 25
Attu, 83
Augusta, Georgia, 176
Australia, 139, 142n, 192; Prime Minister of, 131, 138n, 186
Austria, 142
Axis powers, 194

BAGEHOT, WALTER, 30, 157
Balfour, A. J., 146n
Ballantyne, C. C., 7
Baltimore, Maryland, 146
Bandaranaike, S. W. R. D., 145
Bank of Canada, 33, 100; Deputy Governor of, 59n
Beaudry, Laurent, 68; and "Riddell incident," 172
Beaulne, Yvon, 197
Beaverbrook, Lord, 184, 184n; Minister of Information (U.K.), 129. *See also* Aitken, Sir Max
Behring Sea Seal Treaty, 5
Beirut, Lebanon, 143
Belgium, 64, 142, 142n. *See also* Low Countries